DATA BASE SYSTEMS

DATA BASE SYSTEMS

Design, Implementation, and Management

RONALD G. ROSS

a division of American Management Associations

The author is grateful for permission to use material from some of his earlier published works:

"Computerized Data Base Systems," *Computers and People,* January 1976; copyright © 1976 by and published by Berkeley Enterprises, Inc., 815 Washington Street, Newtonville, Mass. 02160.

The Nature of Computerized Data Base Systems, published by the Administrative Management Society of Willow Grove, Pennsylvania; copyright © 1976 by Ronald G. Ross. (Portions originally appeared in "Evaluating Data Base Systems," *Journal of Systems Management* (Cleveland, Ohio), January 1976.)

"Placing the DBA," *Journal of Systems Management,* May 1976.

"Data Base Management Systems: An Overview of Data Base Technology," *Government Data Systems,* December 1975/January 1976.

The author wishes to thank Robin Glatter for her professional contributions and literary assistance in the creation of this book.

Library of Congress Cataloging in Publication Data

Ross, Ronald G
Data base systems.

Bibliography: p.
Includes index.
1. Data base management. I. Title.
QA76.9.D3R67 001.6'442 78-550
ISBN 0-8144-5462-3

A division of American Management Associations, New York.

First Printing.

To my grandmother
Mrs. T. E. BLAIR
of Houston, Texas

FOREWORD

For many years the most important area of technical development in computing system software was that of programming languages. Many people felt that the need to make the computing system more easily and more immediately accessible to its programming users was of fundamental importance to data processing progress. This rather concentrated period of developmental activity culminated in the formal theory of mechanical languages. Languages developed during that time have become commonplace in systems today. It is more or less a closed chapter in data processing history.

In the late 1960s a growing interest in teleprocessing, data communications, and on-line systems gave birth to a new era of data processing system development. The idea of these technologies was to bring the end user and his data closer to the computing system and its resources, to a greater degree than was possible through programming languages alone. These areas in fact continue to be an important focus of development in system software, and the successes achieved in them to date have greatly increased the availability of the computer to an ever-widening community of end users.

In the 1970s a new and fundamentally important development area has arisen—that of data base management. A careful look at data base systems shows them to be powerful tools for describing and manipulating data and improving user control. It is another step toward bringing the user ever closer to the computing facility.

There is, however, a significant difference between the development life cycles of programming languages or data communications on the one hand and data base technology on the other. This difference, which deserves close examination, lies in the extent to which the end user is involved in the actual technology and its development.

In the case of programming languages, a homogeneous and pragmatically complete theory says essentially all there is to say about the language issue in commercial data processing. For practical purposes, it leaves the end user out of the picture entirely. Essentially the same is true of data communications. The theoretical and even technical issues in communication methodologies have been well established and have resulted in packages that nicely formulate the communications problem for specific environments. The challenge of that field lies as much in hardware development and coping with federal tariff structures as in software development. In either of these cases, the end user is really an outsider to the technology and its continuing evolution.

All this changes when we look at data base systems. That technology is unique, not only in the demands it makes on the user community, but in the very breadth of that community as well. Who exactly are the members of that community? On one hand we have the ultimate end users—those who actually create, manipulate, and interpret the data in the system; on the other, we have the people—designers, analysts, programmers, technical managers, and data base administrators—who create and maintain the actual data base system resource. Their task is ever more crucial as new ground within the organization is broken and as more of its minute-to-minute functions fall within the scope of the computer and its data base.

We find, then, that data base systems are becoming less and less the sole domain of a few technical types and increasingly more the concern of managers, administrators, and analysts, who must deal with them daily and therefore must understand something of their nature.

It is not by accident that this has occurred. Data base systems have a tenet: the organizationwide use and sharing of data—not data in the abstract but vital information about resources, clients, and dollars and cents. Given this basic orientation, it becomes clear that a successful data base system requires a broad interaction between many different people and departments within the organization. It is also clear that this community must be well informed about the concepts and, to some degree, the technology of data base systems.

Because data base technology is new, however, and because it evolves so rapidly, it is difficult to get a definite "fix" on it at any given point in time. This is further complicated by the wide diversity of approaches currently exhibited by that technology. Overall, data base technology is still in a state of rapid flux. Yet there is a constant element in this flux, and too little literature to date has made any serious attempt to distill these constants and interpret them in a fashion that translates into practical and technical wisdom. To my thinking, a work of this nature that captures the basics of data base technology in a moment of passage is both welcome and timely.

Since the advent of the computer itself, little in data processing has had so close a connection with end users or has created such a need for them to gain familiarity with the computer and its applications. In a broad sense, I find this aspect of data base systems a positive force, both for the technology and for the users themselves. But there is also a more immediate value in data base technology. Data—or rather, information—have been rightly identified as a resource. This in turn has created a near revolution in the way we use the computer and, perhaps more significantly, in the way we think about information problems. Data base technology, by emphasizing this view of data as a manageable resource, can be expected to maximize the benefits of this new philosophy.

In closing, I must sound a note of caution. There is no getting around the fact that understanding data base technology and data base management systems is something of a chore. The task requires perseverance and clear thinking. It also requires a presentation that not only is solidly based on competence in the technology but also understands the end user community and its need to know about the data base approach. This is exactly what I find this book to be all about.

Leo J. Cohen

CONTENTS

PART I

An Introduction to Data Base Management Systems

Chapter 1
COMPUTERIZED DATA BASE SYSTEMS

Data base philosophy in the data processing environment has a number of recurring themes. Here are some of them:

Independence of data between application programs and file storage.
Reduction of data redundancy.
Improvement of physical access to data.
Simplification of application programming.
Consolidation of update procedures.
Reduction of the need for program maintenance.
Standardization of data definition and documentation.

The present generation of data base management systems—the software packages that implement computerized data base systems—are achieving basic success in each of the above categories. This success has resulted directly in improved productivity for many installations.

This is not true, however, across the board. Some data base projects have proven ill-conceived at best and nightmarish at worst.

The term data base has several connotations.[1] Administrators and managers look upon the aggregate of data from which budgets and decisions are made and call it, nebulous as that term may be, the data base. Data processing people, especially those with little experience in the new technology, have tried to "capture" that "data base" all at once, without realizing the magnitude of the task.

Out of this situation have arisen some frightful structures that have surpassed the capabilities of the best data base management systems. Somewhat less ambitious systems, especially as starting points, are a prudent choice for most organizations.

To the technicians of data base systems, a data base is a collection of physical records that are similarly defined and serve a single general application purpose. Examples of physical data bases are customer files (lists of all customers with which an organization does business) and product files (files containing information about all products the organization has in its line).

The next level in data base design is the definition of the logical data base in which cross-references are generated between physical files so that individual data need not be duplicated. An example of such a logical data base is an order data base in which customer orders are cross-referenced against the two physical files mentioned above—customer and product data bases.

Data base management systems have no trouble in handling this type of organization, given appropriate design and support. When, however, additional levels of logical cross-referencing are defined, a pyramid-type structure results that greatly strains data base performance. At some point, the degradation in performance becomes intolerable.

Careful structuring of data bases is the key. Figures 1 through 3 give several guidelines for improving data base performance. As these guidelines suggest, data base management systems of this generation are not so generalized that application environments can be completely ignored. Nonetheless, many of their deficiencies are minor in comparison to the advances that they represent over systems available a few years ago.

A few of the areas in which truly significant advances in system technology have been achieved are the following:

- The size of application environment that can be supported and the number of files that can be joined.
- The ease with which the system may be interfaced with other useful systems, such as teleprocessing, report writers, and query languages.
- The ability of the system to preserve its own integrity through such features as checkpointing, restart, prevention of concurrent update, and so forth.
- The security features provided for the monitoring of data access and prevention of unauthorized transactions.
- The general accessibility of data—particularly for on-line processing—through primary and secondary data inversion[2] and through interfile linkage.

APPLICATION SYSTEMS

Data base management systems vary greatly in their approach to each of the above areas. There is much less difference, however,

Figure 1: Two versions of a data base supporting customer-order and inventory applications. In (a) a complex product master file, although relatively static in comparison with order and inventory activity, dominates data base access. In (b) the data base is restructured into a group of smaller files that accommodate this activity better and result in improved performance.

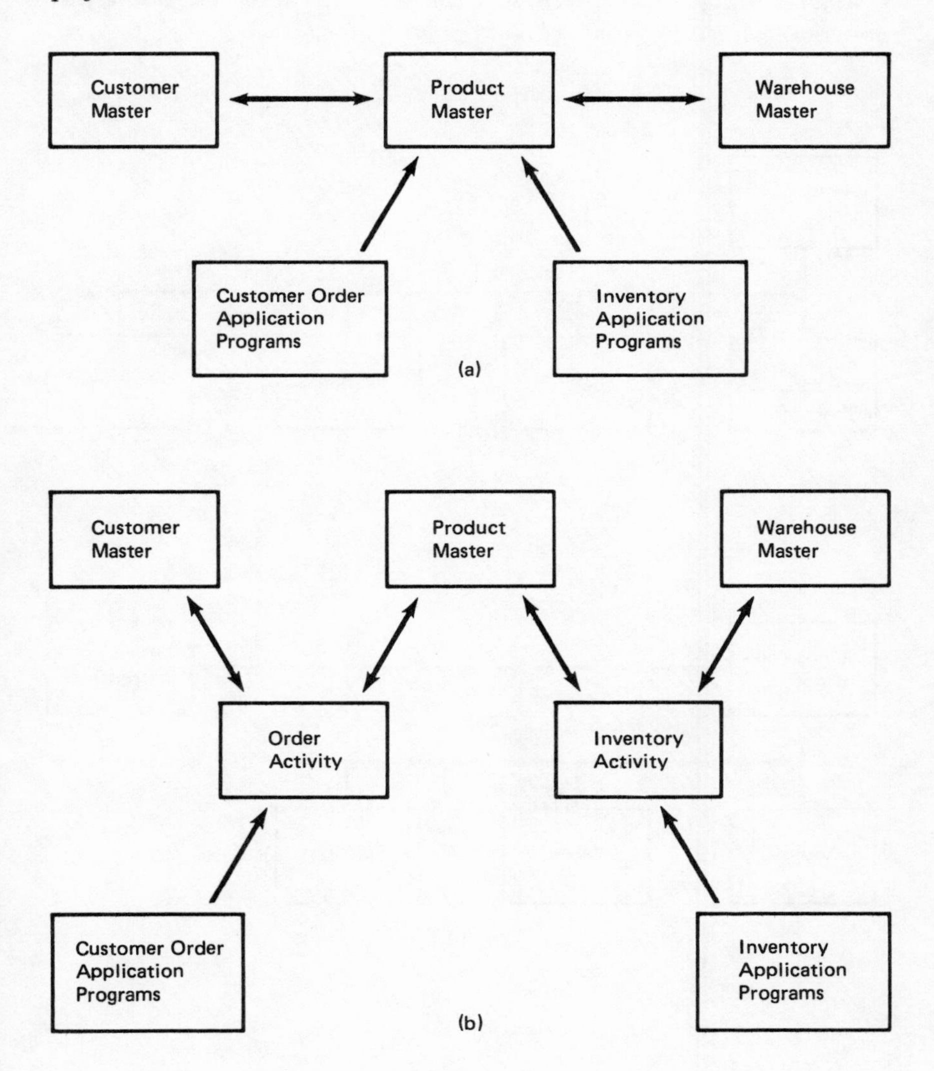

Figure 2: Two versions of record definition in a personnel data base. In the integrated design (a) a large but seldom accessed history segment greatly increases overall file size and unnecessarily burdens system performance. In (b) the history data are segregated into a separate file, improving access performance for most processing tasks.

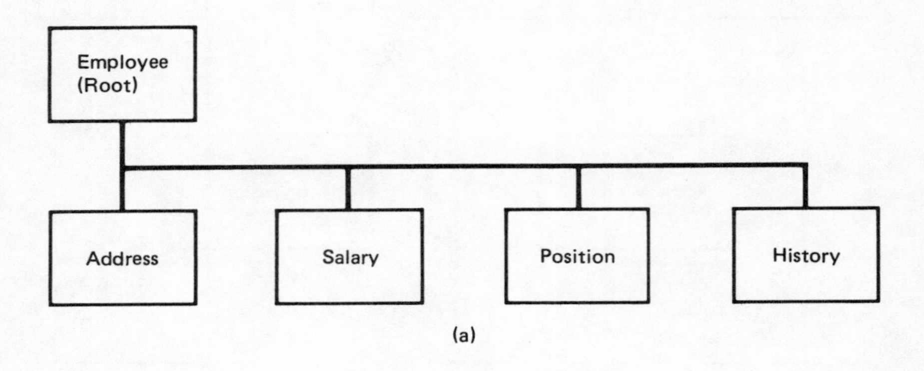

(a)

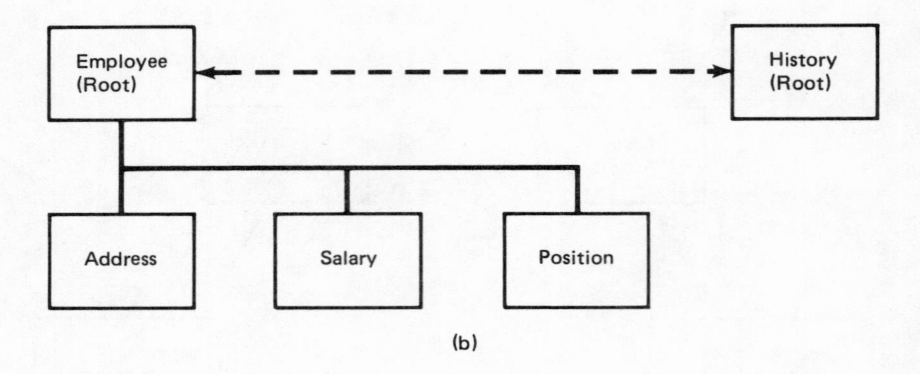

(b)

Figure 3: Access paths for two versions of a school data base. The structure in (a) supports some types of access well, such as documenting courses taken by a given student, but is unable to support documentation of students within a given course without performance-degrading searching or sorting. The restructured data base design in (b) addresses this problem in two ways: by providing linkage to the student file from within the course file and by providing an index within the student file itself.

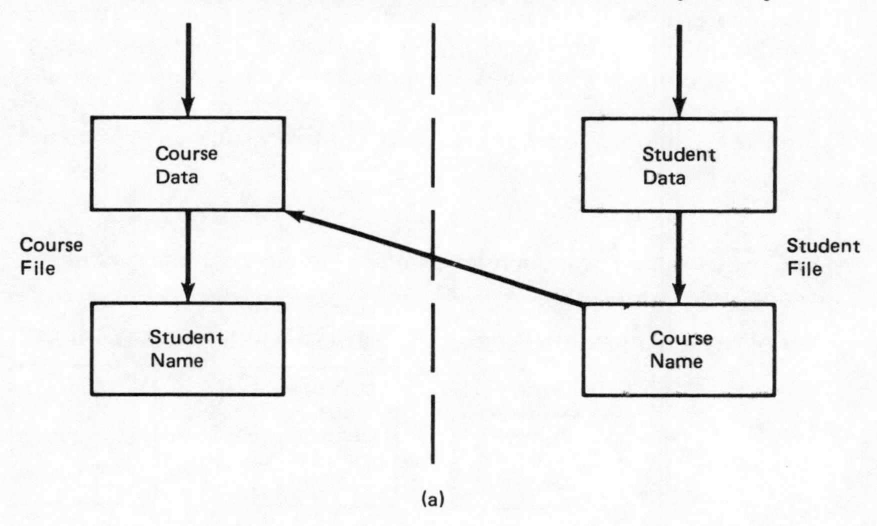

(a)

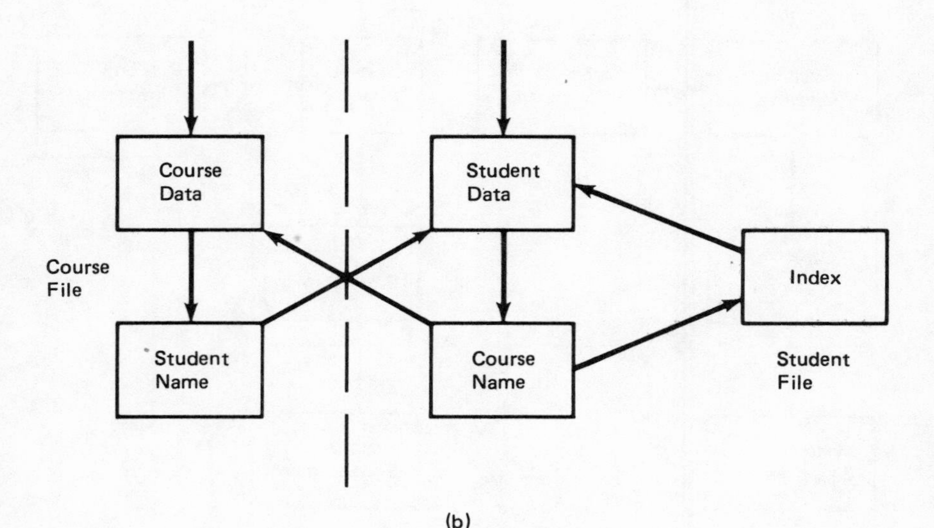

(b)

in the tasks involved in designing and implementing application systems under the various systems. It is not unreasonable, then, to take system design and implementation in the data base environment and compare them to corresponding activities in a traditional installation.

Figure 4 shows a comparative diagram of system design and implementation procedures in traditional and data base environments. These procedures envision the creation of a set of interrelated programs that process data for one moderately sized application purpose. Examples of such a system are payroll, student grade reporting, and inventory.

In the traditional third-generation data processing environment,

Figure 4: System design and implementation procedures in the traditional and data base environments.

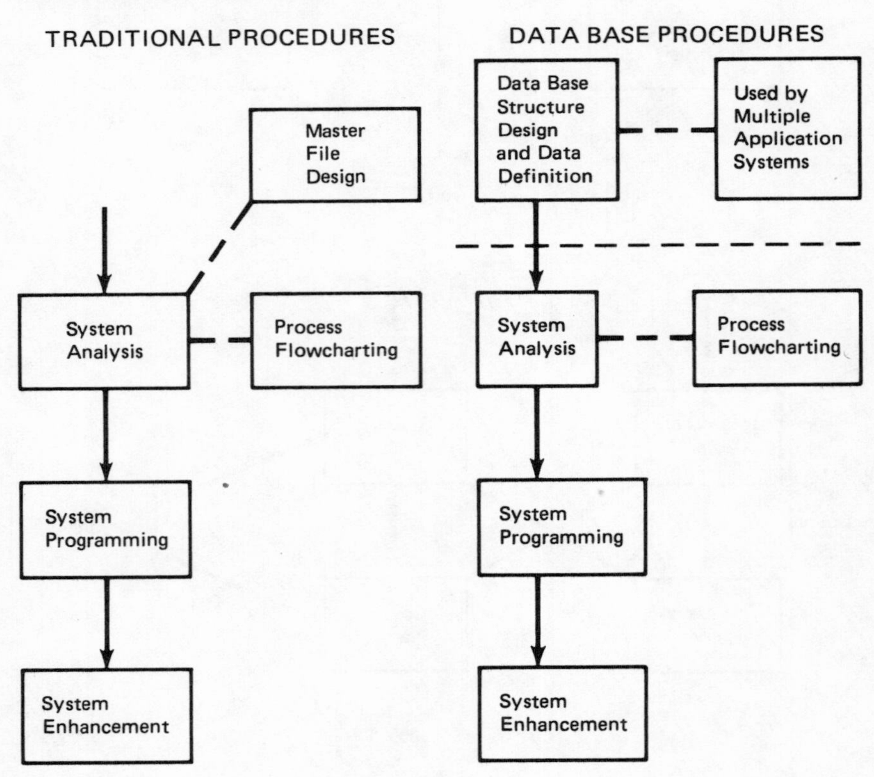

system analysis consists of two major tasks: file design and process flowcharting. A data base environment greatly simplifies system analysis by eliminating the master file design task. Preexisting data defined and retrieved under the data base management system are available for ready use in process flowcharting. This reduces the time and investment necessary for typical application system design.

A data base management system also has important advantages during the system programming stage, which may result in a significant reduction of the time required for coding and testing. For example, in the three areas of file definition, coding, and record formatting, the data base approach offers clear advantages over traditional systems, as the following comparison shows.

Function	*Traditional Systems*	*Data Base Systems*
File definition	Define access method, record size, block size, device type, input/output buffer, and core index.	Define input/output area and/or invoke an externally defined data area.
Coding	Open and close files, set up logic for searching through hierarchically structured files, read and write records, and set up logic for special file positioning.	Construct CALL parameter list or code specialized statement types; data base search and positioning is automatic.
Record formatting	Attribute field names.	Invoke standard field names in application programming.

Probably the most dramatic advantage associated with the data base environment becomes evident during system enhancement. Data independence, made possible by the intercession of the data base management system, allows a facility for system modification not available in the traditional environment. An example will illustrate this.

In a given application system that has been in production for several months, it is decided that a new data field must be added

Table 1: Operations required under a traditional and a data base approach.

	Change File Definition	Change Logic	Compile	Test
Programs using new data field				
Traditional	Yes	Yes	Yes	Yes
Data base	No	Yes	Yes	Yes
Programs not using new data field				
Traditional	Yes	No	Yes	No
Data base	No	No	No	No

to one of the system's files. Table 1 compares the operations necessary for this change under a traditional and a data base approach. A "yes" indicates that the operation is necessary; a "no," that it is not. Significant savings may be realized in the data base environment.

The overhead associated with system design in the data base environment is the task of data base structure design and data definition. This task, whose difficulty is not to be underestimated, precedes system analysis and may be performed by a separate team. The data base files in which the data base structure is realized are designed for use by multiple application systems, so the burden of investment in their creation is divided among many beneficiaries.

In contrast to the typical master file, however, data base structures render data much more available for ad hoc searching and access. Also, standardization of data definition and centralization of update procedures in data base systems offer a quality of system design that is harder to achieve in the traditional environment.

Notes

[1]Confusion has arisen between the disciplines of computer science and information science over the meaning of the term data base. In traditional information science, "data base" often refers to a consolidated file, often largely archival, containing bibliographic or similar types of information. A typical application might involve citations to biomedical literature (as is the case with the National Library of Medicine's MEDLINE service) or to legal data (as with the Department of Justice's JURIS). There is considerable activity in computerizing "data bases" of this type. As used in computer science, data base implies relatively less concern with informational content, instead emphasizing organizational methods for data of variable type and, in particular, the interrelation of files.

[2]For a discussion of data inversion, see Chapter 2.

Chapter 2

FEATURES OF DATA BASE MANAGEMENT SYSTEMS

A concept central to understanding the current generation of data base management systems (DBMS) is that data bases have *structures* by which data on storage are organized. These structures are as real in their own fashion as are architectural constructions, even though support for them (as is the case with the framework of a building) is largely invisible to the user. Perhaps the single most important characteristic of data base management systems is that they provide data description languages (DDL) for implementing structures *apart* from actual programs.

DATA BASE STRUCTURES

Understanding data base structures is basic not only to understanding DBMS themselves but also for assessing the differences between contemporary systems. In Chapter 3, DBMS are classified into groups, in which membership is largely defined on the basis of structural support.

For the present discussion, data structuring may be defined as the computerized representation of the relationship between distinct data items or groups. This is illustrated as follows. For a given school there are two basic sets of information: student data and course data (see Figure 5). For the purpose of computer storage, data about each student or each course become a record; like records are grouped into files.[1] Each of these two files is in fact a primitive data base.

Certain facts are known about the information contained in these files. Students, for example, have been scheduled into classes, as indicated in Figure 6. The arrows in this representation (signifying storage addresses in the computer's memory) are shown pointing in both directions, which indicates that students *take* classes, but that classes *have* students as well. This dual relationship reflects the

Figure 5: A school data base.

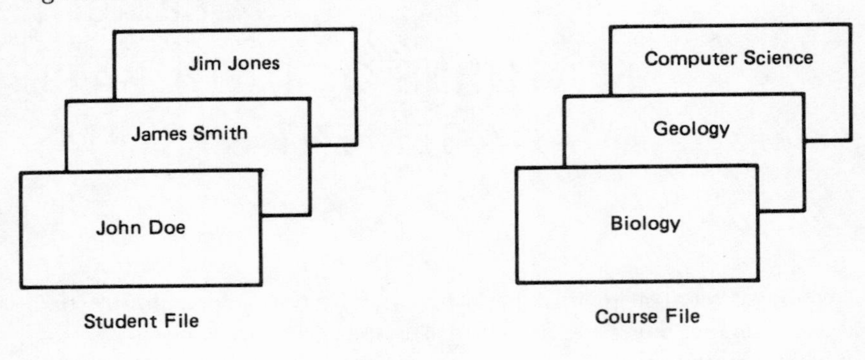

Figure 6: Students scheduled for classes.

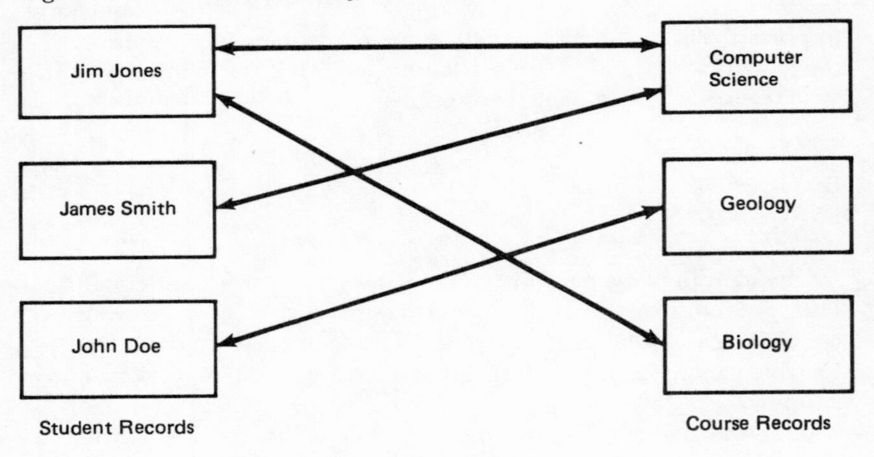

processing requirements of the school: student schedules (courses taken) must be generated in addition to class rolls (students enrolled).

The school data base becomes more complex as additional record types are added. For example, a teacher data base (another primitive data base like the original student and course files) might be interconnected with the course file in order to produce teacher schedules. Other types of information might be maintained as well.

It should be clear from this example that the process of structuring a data base is a means of mirroring or *modeling* the information perceived as arising from various data; in particular, it is a way of modeling the *intersection* of different data types. In the school data base, for example, a student record intersects with a course record in the sense of *course-taken* (or *student-enrolled*). In a given case it is possible that there exists information specifically related to this intersection. In Figure 6, for example, Jim Jones may have taken biology during fifth period and got a C in the course.

The data description language (DDL) supported by the DBMS provides the means for abstracting or generalizing these types of information. Figure 7 illustrates the school data base as it might appear in a DDL. Although the structure itself is powerful, the amount of specification required by the DDL is often minimal. In general, a DDL presents the user with a set of symbolic parameters from which virtually unlimited structures can be defined. These structures are then supported *automatically* by the DBMS.

The vocabularies of various DBMS differ, of course, in the way they model identical information. This is illustrated for the school data base in Figure 8. The differences between the DDL of the various DBMS are also evident in the structures actually implemented, although there are often numerous similarities.

Regardless of the differences that may exist, the key to performance in data base processing is the "appropriateness" of the structures defined—that is, a careful data base design. The activities essential for this step are listed below (see also Chapter 1 for a discussion of some of these guidelines).

- Appropriate distribution of the data base structure across actual data files.
- An activity-oriented positioning of data types within the data base structure.

Figure 7: The DDL representation of the school data base.

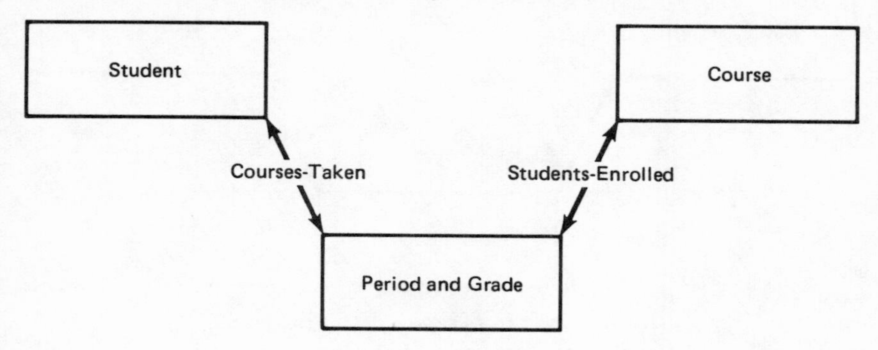

Figure 8: Graphic representation of the DDL for three DBMS, using the school data base structure.[2]

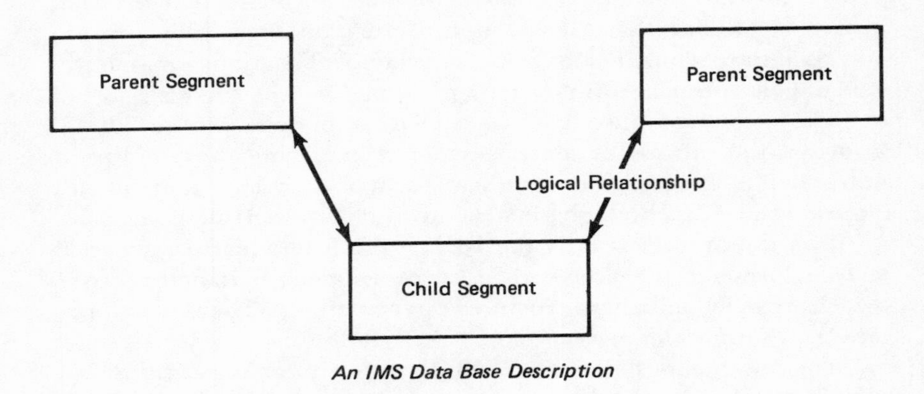

An IMS Data Base Description

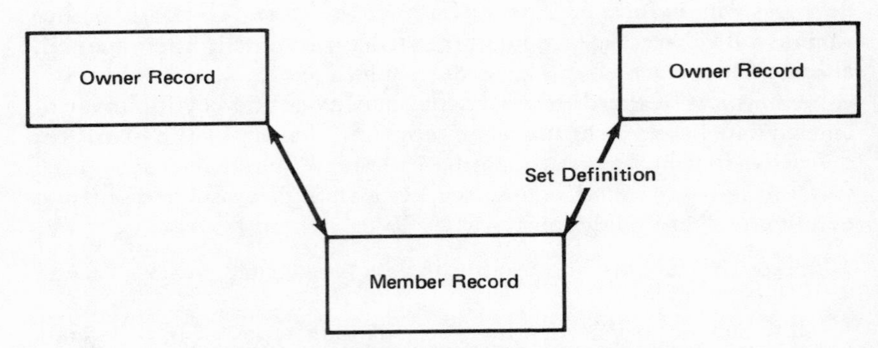

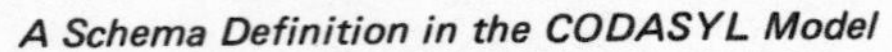

A Schema Definition in the CODASYL Model

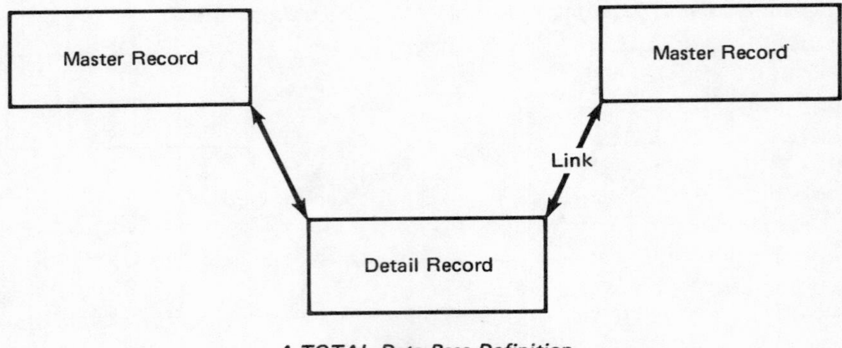

A TOTAL Data Base Definition

- ◦ Specification of interrecord linkage tuned to processing requirements.
- ◦ Creation of indexes to enhance access to data base records on the basis of given keys.
- ◦ Selection of pointer and linkage types.
- ◦ Selection of access methods.

It is significant that each item in this list involves a choice between alternatives. These choices must be based on a careful analysis of the applications for which the structure is intended.

The discussion thus far in this chapter has dealt implicitly with physical linkage between records as a means of modeling the relationships between data groups. This implies that record addresses are stored within the data groups themselves so that access may be effected to related records. This is not the only fashion in which these relationships may be implemented.

A second major method of modeling data relationships is the creation of index files that contain pointers to all similarly valued records. The process of creating these index files is called inversion. An example of a data base structure created by "inverting" record fields is given in Figure 9. This structure is essentially a reimplementation of the school data model presented in Figure 6.

Although the inverted structure appears to be more complex than its physically linked counterpart, the actual implementation tends to be less so. In particular, the DDL for an inverted structure tends to be relatively simple; for the most part it is only necessary to indicate whether or not a particular field is to be inverted. (In Figure 9, two fields were chosen: the *courses-taken* field within the student record and the *students-enrolled* field within the course record.) The DBMS performs the inversion automatically.

An additional capability is offered by the inversion technique when the *same* data item is inverted in separate files. This is illustrated in Figure 10, in which the course data item has been inverted within both student and course records. By this means a natural equivalence has been established between the two sets of records, on the basis of which *automatic* concatenation of records from the two files is possible.

For example, a single request might be sufficient for retrieving information on the student John Doe and the class he takes, geology. Or conversely, a request could access geology and a student enrolled, John Doe. The DBMS performs this service, though the match-up between the indexes need not necessarily be established until the

Figure 9: An inverted structure for the school data base.

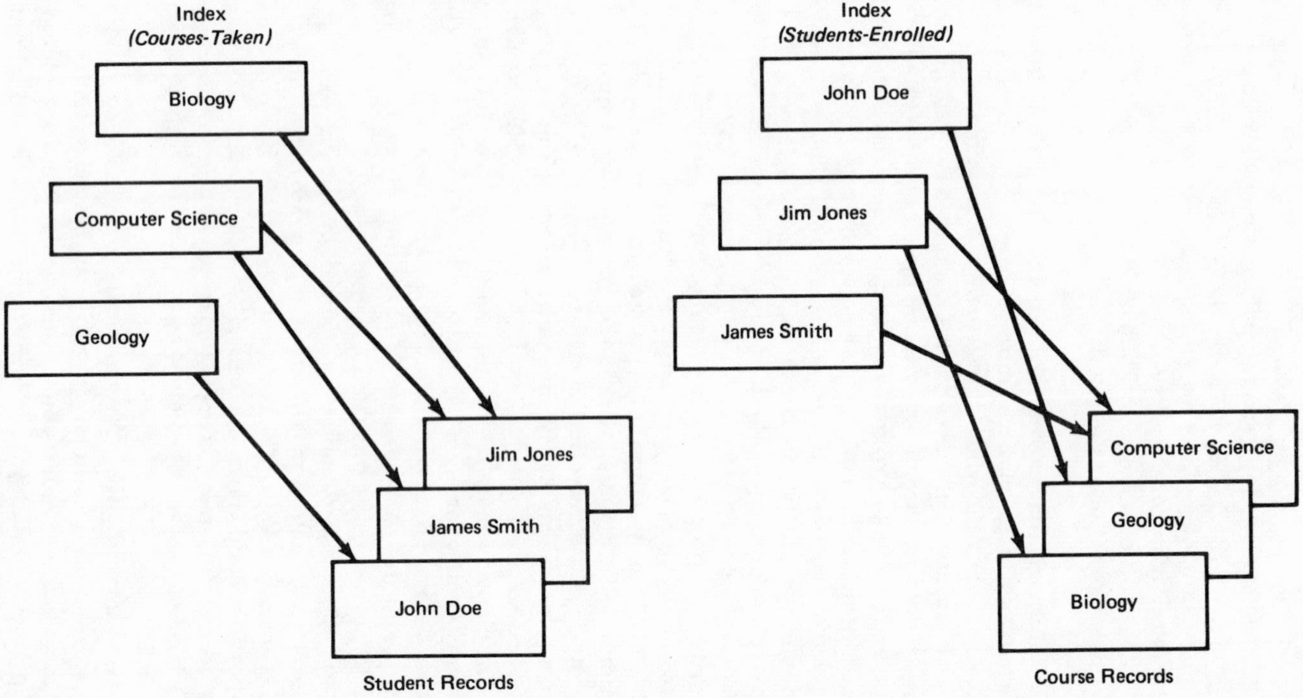

Figure 10: Inversion of the same data item within distinct records.

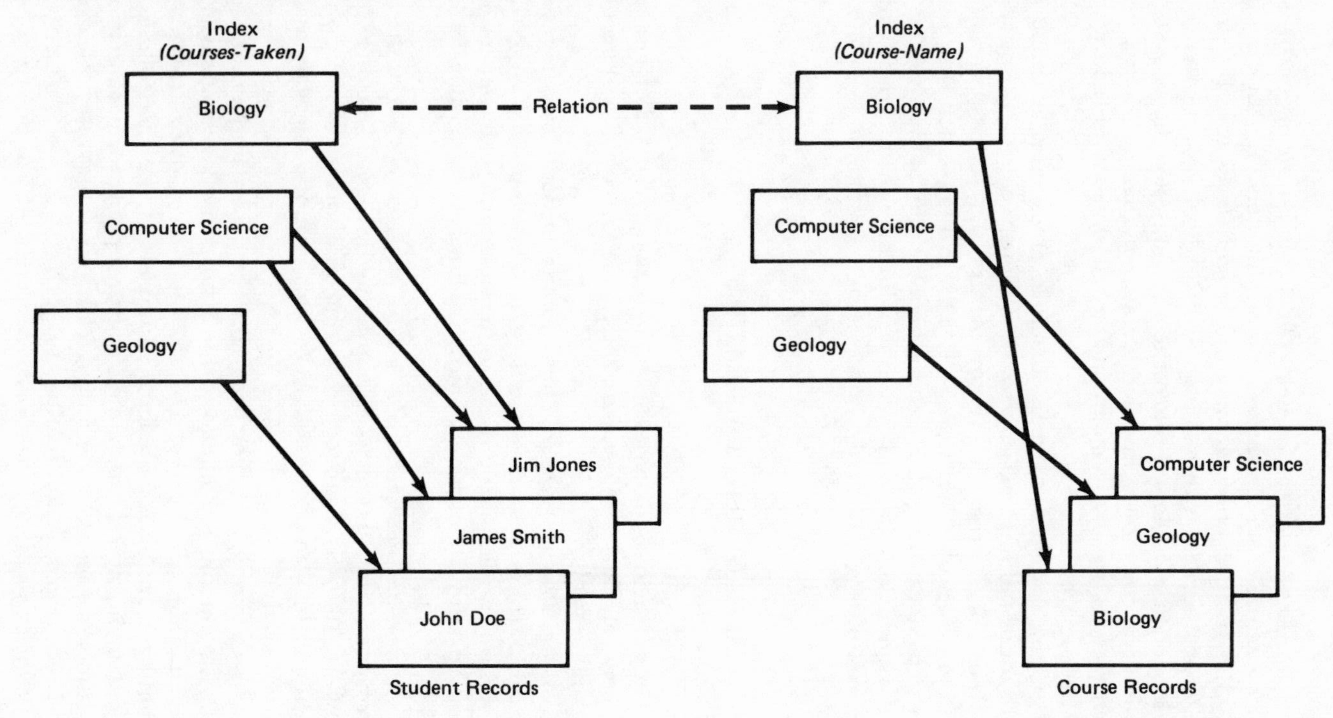

actual processing of the request. (This match-up can also be effected before actual request processing. See Chapter 3 for an example.)

One further observation is in order. In Figure 10, the index on *students-enrolled* within the course record (which appeared in Figure 9) has been eliminated. Since the files may now be related on the basis of a commonly inverted data item (namely, *course name*), it is in fact *unnecessary* to maintain the *students-enrolled* field within the course record.

In the "integrated" data structure envisioned, a single update procedure (adding *courses-taken* to student records) is thus sufficient for meeting all processing requirements—that is, for generating both student schedules and class rolls. DBMS that depend on inversion for data structuring thus exhibit benefits similar to those associated with systems that depend on physical linkage: the means for eliminating redundant data and, thereby, for consolidating update procedures.

DATA MANAGEMENT CAPABILITIES OF DBMS

Beyond providing data description languages, DBMS offer a number of general data management capabilities. A brief outline of these capabilities follows.

Storage structure support. The mapping of data structures (defined by the DDL) onto storage media generally involves physical linkage, inversion, randomization, and other techniques. Lower-level access methods and file management capabilities are often borrowed from the operating system.

Support for multiple access to data bases. A DBMS addresses the problem of concurrent record updating by record "locking" or other devices. An interface to teleprocessing monitors is generally provided, although in some cases teleprocessing support is largely integrated with the DBMS.

User access support. The provision of a data manipulation language (DML), which is embedded within a host language such as COBOL, is fundamental to most DBMS. High-level, user-oriented query languages are also sometimes supported. Other capabilities aimed at enhancing access capabilities include support for parametric search arguments, special user-oriented DDL extensions, interindex relation, and report generation features.

Support for data base security. Most DBMS support a subschema capability, which provides a means for restricting a given user to selected portions of the data structure and to selected operations on the available portion. Password protection, procedural exits, and encoding of data are often also supported.

Support for data base integrity. Through transaction logging, checkpointing, and restart capabilities, a DBMS ensures that the data base is not lost by the abnormal termination of an application program or by a crash of the system itself.

Support for operational utilities. DBMS support utilities for a number of functions: initial load, reorganization, data compression, statistical reporting, and so forth. Additional capabilities—for example, a data dictionary—are sometimes supported.

From this outline and the preceding discussion on data structuring, DBMS emerge as comprehensive data management facilities in which streamlined and centralized control of data is possible.

Commonly cited among the benefits of DBMS is their capacity for reducing data redundancy. Although this capacity is often equated with savings in disk storage space (which are not a necessary result[3]), a more significant aspect is the consolidation of application update procedures. This consolidation, which was suggested in our discussion of Figure 10, is an evident advantage over traditional systems.

In the data base environment, an update generally renders new data available immediately to all relevant applications. In the traditional environment, on the other hand, an update must generally cascade between two or more master files, often after noticeable delay. At best, special programs must be scheduled to effect the cross-updating; at worst, partially redundant files will remain unnotified of the changes. In either case, a period of data inconsistency results, although in the former it is under more apparent "control."

A data base system eliminates the need for this altogether. The reduction of data redundancy thus implies the merging or integration of partially redundant master files[4] and, thereby, the elimination of certain update ills.

A somewhat less obvious advantage of data management under a DBMS is the significant reduction in data sorting. Physical linkage between files, for example, often serves this purpose.

This may be illustrated by examining the school data base as it might be implemented in the traditional environment. Two master files are required—one for students and one for courses; *courses-taken* information is added to student records. In contrast to the configuration under a DBMS (Figure 7 for physical linkage; Figure 10 for inversion), there is no means of knowing within a course record what students have enrolled. Under this circumstance, the only means to produce class rolls is by *sorting* the student file on the basis of *courses-taken,* then merging the sorted file with the course file.[5] This process is illustrated in Figure 11.

A more direct means of eliminating sorting in the data base environment is the use of indexes, which in essence reorder data base records on the basis of nonprimary keys. For example, student records are often keyed by student number rather than by student name since names tend to be nonunique. Even so, by inverting the name field, an alphabetical list of students can be produced *without* sorting the entire file. Similar results could be achieved by inverting homeroom teacher, bus route, and so forth.

In general, the elimination of sorting overhead in DBMS, whether by physical linkage or by inversion, is especially relevant to time-critical environments. This is characteristic, of course, of on-line applications.

DATA INDEPENDENCE

Data independence in the data base environment is most commonly identified with the existence of data description languages (DDL), which stand apart from individual application programs. The DDL assumes responsibility for structuring all data base files, given the formulation of the data model set forth by the user. A corresponding capability without a DDL (and DBMS) requires complex programmatic involvement with the physical organization of the data in at least one, and possibly all, user programs.

From the perspective of application programming, the advantage of this arrangement is straightforward: access requirements are stated in terms of actual data rather than in terms of physical parameters. For example, a typical access request might be stated as follows: get the grade of Jim Jones for the class he took, computer science. The simplicity of this request is significant in an additional sense: to achieve equivalent results under a traditional file organization often involves reiterative searching of records, something not usually required under a DBMS. Although application programming under a DBMS is not trivial, it is at least freed from two types of activity: storage support and many types of record searching.

From more or less the opposite point of view, data independence applies to the data base itself, which under a DBMS is not bound up in the continued welfare of any one (or several) application

Figure 11: Class roll production in the traditional environment.

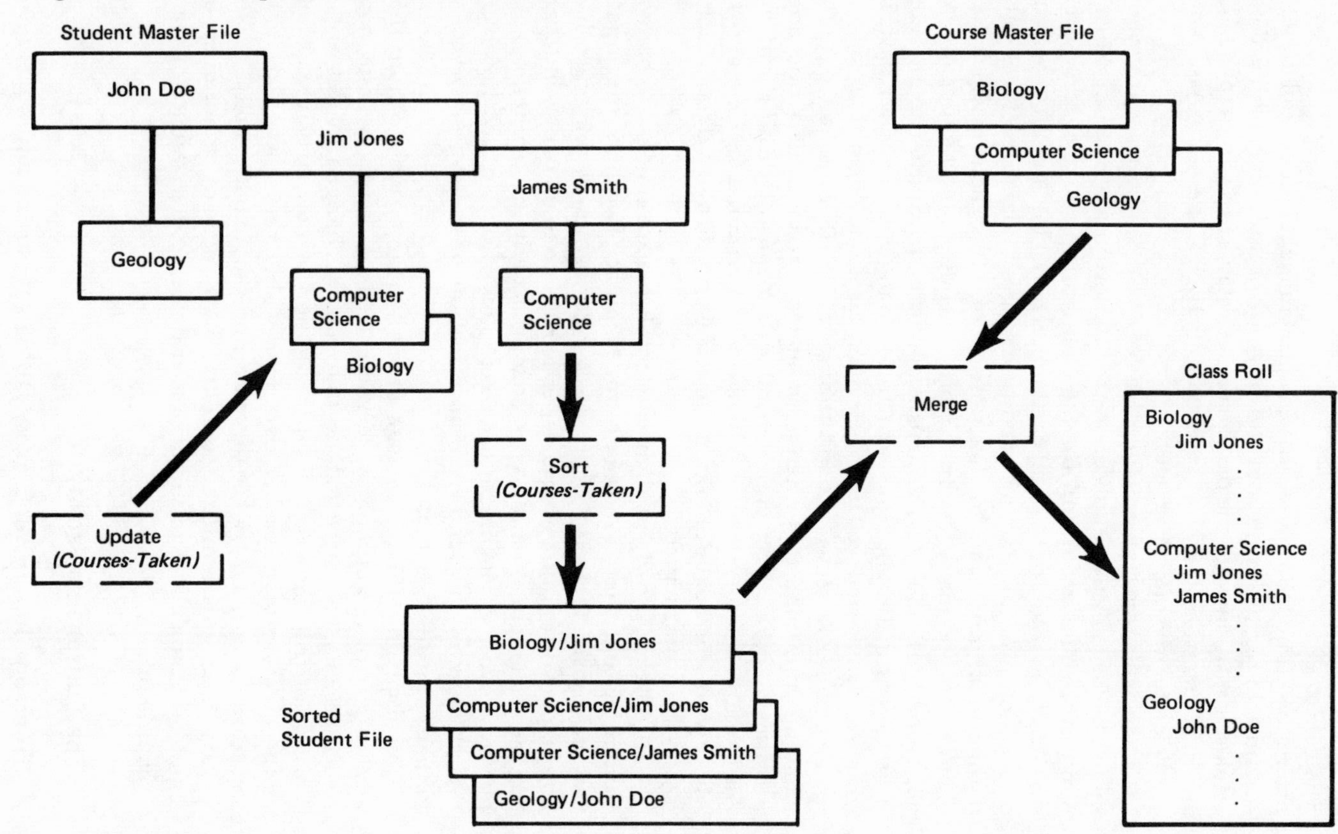

program(s). The DBMS itself is the central manager and is unilaterally responsible for ensuring that the physical organization of the data remains consistent with the data structure established within the DDL. By this means a layer of insulation between the data base and application programs is created.

This insulation between the data base and application programming also has positive implications for the evolution of an organization's processing needs and for the changes in basic data structures that may be required to meet these needs. In general, existing application programs are affected by changes in data structures only if they make reference to that portion of the structure which has changed. Since many programs often require no modification at all, an organization's investment in application programs is thereby protected. In addition, the structural change to the data base is easier to make since DDL rather than program logic is involved.

In general, it is true that although a DBMS does not entirely eliminate the impact of change, it at least reduces its scope and provides a more direct (and centralized) means of dealing with it. An example of one type of change was presented in Chapter 1, where we discussed the operations necessary to add a new data element to an existing structure.

DBMS vary greatly in their capacity for managing such change. In some systems there would be minimal impact; in others, the impact may be considerable. In many cases, adding new *record* types has little impact on existing programs, as does the creation of new indexes. Similarly, changing pointer types, so long as paths are neither created nor destroyed, often has little effect. This is not to say, however, that changes of this kind have no effect on processing *performance;* in many cases they can and do.

In discussing change to data bases it is important to note that application programming is very much dependent on basic data structures, so that there is little that can be changed in this area.[6] This is not true, however, for the addition of new structures, such as the creation of a teacher data base within the school data base structure. In summary, while there are limits to "expandability" within a data base environment, current DBMS provide a number of significant capabilities in this area that decrease dependence on data organization.

The Subschema Facility

To go one step further, many DBMS support an additional level of insulation between application programs and the data base through a facility called a subschema.[7] This facility may be viewed as a means to tailor the structure of the data base in a fashion most appropriate to the application program.

This tailoring has two aspects. First, the subschema serves to *protect* the data base from the application program. For example, a subschema may allow a given program to read a certain record but not to change it, or it might deny the program access to the record altogether. In similar fashion, the subschema may omit certain relationships within the data that were established by the DDL.

Second, the subschema facility extends the basic data structuring provided by the DDL. In particular, in a given DBMS it may support some, although usually not all, of the following activities:

- The elimination of unnecessary record types from the data structure.
- The elimination of unnecessary data elements from given records.
- The redefinition and/or reordering of data elements within records.
- The creation of new data elements (for example, a calculated value) from existing items.
- The concatenation of data elements or records from distinct locations in the data structure.
- The reorganization of the data structure (in concept) by use of indexes or specified linkage paths.
- The provision of exits to user-written routines.

The need arises for a subschema capability in the data base environment because many applications share a central data base, although prerogatives among the applications differ from one to the next. The subschema capability, an important extension of the basic concept of data independence, provides a relatively streamlined and centralized method of implementing these prerogatives.

Other Features Relating to Data Independence

The concept of data independence, which provided a focal point for much of the evolutionary progress in data base systems, has been developed toward maturity in additional areas. Four of these areas are discussed below. Beyond these, data independence becomes intimately involved with the future of DBMS, an area in which there is considerable debate. Two additional topics, often voiced in this debate, are presented in the next section.

1. *Element-level independence.* Many DBMS are able to support

access requirements to the level of individual data fields rather than pass groups of fields (that is, records or segments) to the application program as stored in the data base. This may be viewed as an additional capability of tailoring data into the format required by the application and of insulating the application program from changes in record or segment definitions. As suggested in our list of subschema capabilities in the preceding section, one means of achieving element-level independence is by subschema support; another is by passing lists of data elements to the DBMS from within the data manipulation language (DML) of the application program. (The data manipulation language of many DBMS consists of CALL statements, in which data element names can be passed as arguments.) Item omission, reordering, and redefinition can be achieved by either of these means.

2. *Machine independence.* A data base system should not be dependent on the hardware of any one manufacturer but should instead be supported under distinct hardware lines. This requires, of course, that the same DBMS (including DDL, DML, and all other facilities) be programmed to run on each machine so that applications written in standardized language (for example, COBOL) can be shifted without significant change. Some DBMS have, in fact, been implemented across mainframe boundaries; examples are TOTAL by Cincom Systems, Inc., and SYSTEM 2000 by MRI Systems Corp.

The most pervasive type of machine independence could be achieved if all DBMS were identical at the language level (DDL and DML), meaning in effect the *standardization* of the language in a fashion similar to ANSI COBOL. The CODASYL model is the most vigorous step in that direction to date. CODASYL-like DBMS have been released by Honeywell Information Systems, UNIVAC, and Digital Equipment, and by the Cullinane Corporation for IBM hardware.

3. *Device independence.* A data base system should not be dependent on particular types of storage media, and the varying support requirements of different media (including space allocation) should be largely invisible to the user. Support for device independence often falls to the operating system rather than the DBMS itself; still, it is an important element in overall data independence.

4. *Concurrent usage of the data base.* A data base system should support simultaneous updating by multiple users (either on-line or batch) and have the means to resolve access conflicts.[8] DBMS vary greatly in their ability to support updates by concurrently executed tasks; common to many, however, is the concept of "lock-out," by which all applications except one are prevented from accessing a

record (or block) for update. In some systems, lock-out effectively occurs at the *file* level, which results in significant delay for other applications seeking to process that same file. In this circumstance there is a high level of dependence on other tasks being executed in the machine, and consequently there is a lack of independence for multiple data base use.

Two Issues in the Debate on Data Independence

Two additional topics often voiced in the debate on data independence and the future of DBMS are language independence and path independence.

Language independence. DBMS should not require a "host" language in which the DML is embedded but rather should support a high-level, user-oriented language that stands alone in support of data base access. In particular, this represents a reaction against COBOL as a language and against the increasingly complex COBOL systems normally required for data base processing.

This reaction reflects unfavorably on the CODASYL model (as well as most current DBMS), because of its alleged dependence on COBOL. There are several alternatives to host language systems, including query languages and similar facilities. Another is implementation of the relational model (see Chapter 6), which takes language development of this sort as a major point of departure from current systems.

Path independence. DBMS files should be structured as simply as possible and be free of internally supported linkage paths. There are several reasons why these paths limit independence. For one thing, "supported" paths are highly favored over "unsupported" paths, a fact that restricts the responsiveness of the data base to certain types of unanticipated processing tasks. By the same token, the navigational access required to traverse these paths is undesirably difficult, requiring undue structural knowledge on the part of the programmer.[9] In addition, since data base files are "hard-wired" together, reorganization of the data base becomes a difficult and extensive operation.

In summary, the argument in favor of path independence is against complex file structuring, substituting instead powerful language operations to accomplish file relation. Some observers see the relation capability within inverted systems as a step in that direction; as mentioned previously, the relational model heavily favors powerful language operations.

Notes

[1]Data management at the file level, though not always as simple as this example suggests, is almost always supported by the operating system of the machine rather than by the DBMS itself. The content of a given record in the data base environment is often less comprehensive than its counterpart in the traditional environment, but there tend to be more records. Terminology in this area varies greatly from system to system. In IBM's IMS, for example, records as used here are actually equivalent to segments, which themselves are grouped into collections called data base records.

[2]IMS and TOTAL are proprietary software products of the IBM Corporation and Cincom Systems, Inc., respectively. The CODASYL model is a set of language specifications created by the Conference on Data Systems Languages, perhaps best known for its work on COBOL. A number of manufacturers and at least one independent software company have released CODASYL-like data base management systems.

[3]Analysis of disk space usage under a DBMS is not trivial. Space requirements vary greatly depending on the DBMS implemented and the type of applications supported. In addition, data base systems often imply radical departures from traditional systems, coincidental with the expansion of processing services. Both of these factors make direct comparison inappropriate in many cases. Savings of disk storage space are common, however, in the following limited sense: by providing linkage between files, a DBMS eliminates the need for storing data "redundantly" within given records. For example, so long as linkage is provided to course information from student records, that information need not be stored within the student record. This represents space "saved."

[4]The theme of integration is as old as data base technology itself. In fact, the prototype for many of today's systems (including the CODASYL model) was named Integrated Data Store (I-D-S). A descendant of this system, which dates to 1961, is Honeywell Information System's I-D-S/II. A name more familiar to IBM users is Cullinane Corporation's IDMS, "Integrated Database Management System." Another term that sometimes appears in descriptions of integrated data structuring is "corporate" data base.

[5]The alternative to this file organization is to create a program which posts transactions to the course file (that is, which adds *students-enrolled*) whenever *courses-taken* updates are processed for the student file. This, however, introduces the type of data redundancy just discussed.

[6]This tends to apply less to inversion-type DBMS, which have less "structure" to change. Even among physically linked DBMS there is noticeable variance among capabilities in this area. Given this fact, the capacity for change becomes an important topic in the selection of a DBMS—and, *after* selection, in data base administration.

[7]Subschema is a term proposed by CODASYL to refer to a subdivision

or subdefinition of the overall data base, known as a schema. The subschema is usually supported by a stand-alone language, in a fashion similar to the DDL. In IBM's IMS, an equivalent function is performed in part by the PSB (program specification block) and in part by the logical data base description (DBD) capability. Other DBMS exhibit similar capabilities, although in some the capability is implicit rather than explicit.

[8]In particular, access conflicts involve the problem of "deadlock," in which two (or more) programs have "locked" records needed by the other(s) to complete their update task.

[9]Structural knowledge is not to be confused with knowledge of physical access methods; the latter is basic to the traditional concept of data independence. Navigational access is examined in greater detail in Chapter 3.

Chapter 3

CLASSIFICATION OF DATA MANAGEMENT SOFTWARE

Mainframe data management software can be classified into four groups representing qualitatively different approaches to the data management problem:

1. Physically linked DBMS (hierarchical and network data structures).
2. Inverted DBMS (with support for interfile relation).
3. Inverted DMS (without support for interfile relation).
4. File-pass DMS (sophisticated report generation).

The boundary between inverted DBMS and inverted DMS is somewhat ill-defined since upgrading from the latter to the former is relatively simple. Other factors are involved, however, such as the size of applications that may be supported, on-line access support, support for concurrent access, and the integration of multiple record types. In addition, there are programmatic means for circumventing the file relation problem, although in order to do so, the user must ply the data structure.

File-pass DMS, by comparison, are a relatively fixed class and are largely restricted from evolving into full-scale DBMS. DMS of this class often support interfaces with physically linked DBMS, thereby providing significant user-oriented enhancements to those systems. File-pass DMS tend to be predominantly batch-oriented.

Two of these groups—physically linked DBMS and inverted DBMS—are already familiar; the other two, which together comprise data management systems (DMS), will be examined later in this chapter.

Commercially available mainframe software is listed below in three categories loosely corresponding to these four groups. (Inverted DMS have not been segregated into a distinct class.) A number of the systems listed actually represent *families* of systems, the members of which cut across software and hardware versions.

PHYSICALLY LINKED DBMS

System	*Vendor*	*Type*
IMS/VS	IBM	hierarchical
TOTAL	Cincom Systems, Inc.	network
DMS-II	Burroughs	mixed
I-D-S/II	H.I.S. (Honeywell)	CODASYL
IDMS	Cullinane Corp.	CODASYL
DMS 1100	UNIVAC	CODASYL
DMS/90	UNIVAC	CODASYL
DBMS-10	Digital Equipment (DEC)	CODASYL
EDMS	H.I.S. (formerly Xerox)	CODASYL

INVERTED DBMS

System	*Vendor*
SYSTEM 2000	MRI Systems Corp.
ADABAS	Software AG
Model 204	Computer Corporation of America
DATACOM/DB	Insyte Corp. (formerly C.I.M.)
DMS-170	Control Data Corp. (CDC)
INQUIRE	Infodata Systems, Inc.

FILE-PASS DMS

System	*Vendor*	*DBMS Interface*
MARK IV	Informatics, Inc.	TOTAL, IMS
Easytrieve	Pansophic Systems, Inc.	TOTAL, IMS, ADABAS
ASI-ST	Applications Software, Inc.	TOTAL, IMS
Data Analyzer	Program Products, Inc.	TOTAL, IMS, ADABAS
CULPRIT	Cullinane Corp.	TOTAL, IMS, IDMS, DATACOM/DB

OTHER SYSTEMS

System	*Vendor*
MAGNUM	Tymshare, Inc.
NOMAD	National CSS, Inc.
RAMIS	Mathematica, Inc.

There are many file-pass DMS, and only the most widely implemented are listed above. (Data management software for mini-computers is presented in Chapter 6.)

PHYSICALLY LINKED DBMS

Within the classification presented here, two types of DBMS have been grouped into the category of physically linked DBMS: hierarchical and network systems. Although these two types of systems are often contrasted, in comparison to other types of data management software, they actually exhibit more similarity than difference. The dependence on physical linkage for data structuring is, of course, the major feature of that similarity.

Reviewing briefly, physical linkage implies that addresses of related records are stored within records themselves so that linkage "paths" exist within and among physical files. The DBMS follows these paths in order to access data. By way of contrast, inverted DBMS depend on the segregation of data values for given record fields and on their organization into index files, with pointers back to the original data. To effect data access, the inverted DBMS mostly operates on the indexes themselves, prior to actual record access.

Within the physically linked class, hierarchical and network systems are basically distinguished by the way they conceptualize the relationships between segments or records—that is, by the way they structure the data model. For IBM's IMS/VS—the major representative of the hierarchical family—data are structured into trees, which may be "logically related" (by physical linkage in most cases) into a network-like arrangement. "Logical views" of data related in this fashion are remodeled in order to appear hierarchical to the user.[1] In network systems, which include the CODASYL systems and Cincom's TOTAL, the emphasis is placed on *sets* of records, which are normally linked by physical means. A given record may be involved in many sets, as defined within the DDL.

Figures 12 and 13 illustrate the varying conceptualizations of the school data base in a hierarchical and in a network system. As the figures demonstrate, differences arise in the structuring of an identical data model.

For example, the hierarchical approach sometimes requires an extra record type to effect linkage between files, particularly in the case of one-to-many set relationship. This is the relationship that holds between the teacher file and the course file in Figure 12; unlike the network structure, the hierarchical structure requires a record type that specifies the *courses-taught* logical relationship.

When the relationship between records becomes many-to-many—for example, if a course is to be taught by more than one teacher—then an extra record type is required by either structure. This is the type of relationship that holds between students and course records in the school data model.[2]

Theorists contend that the hierarchical view is in fact a special case of the network model and that the set terminology of the latter is more precise. From the perspective of traditional methods in data processing, however, the hierarchical view represents less of a departure; for example, the typical COBOL record description may be easily represented by a tree structure (each OCCURS becomes a repeating segment type).

In spite of the differences between the hierarchical and network models, the dependence on physical linkage for DBMS of this class results in several concerns that are largely identical for any member DBMS. The first of these concerns is navigational access,[3] which characterizes programming in physically linked systems. Navigational access means that "position" in the data base is established on the basis of the currently accessed record. The programmer must then supply information so that the DBMS can "choose" between paths to get the next record.

It is important to note that for the programmer, paths exist within the data structure; in all cases, the DBMS is responsible for access at the storage structure level. Path selection is typically a matter of specifying function, record (or set) type, and key value(s) where appropriate. After each access, status checking is required to ensure that the operation succeeded as intended.

A second concern in physically linked DBMS, related to data base design rather than programming, is the definition of paths that match navigational requirements in direction, volume, and type. This definition requires, on the one hand, adequate analysis of the data model and its use, and on the other, appropriate selection of

Figure 12: Sample conceptualization of the school data base by a hierarchical DBMS.

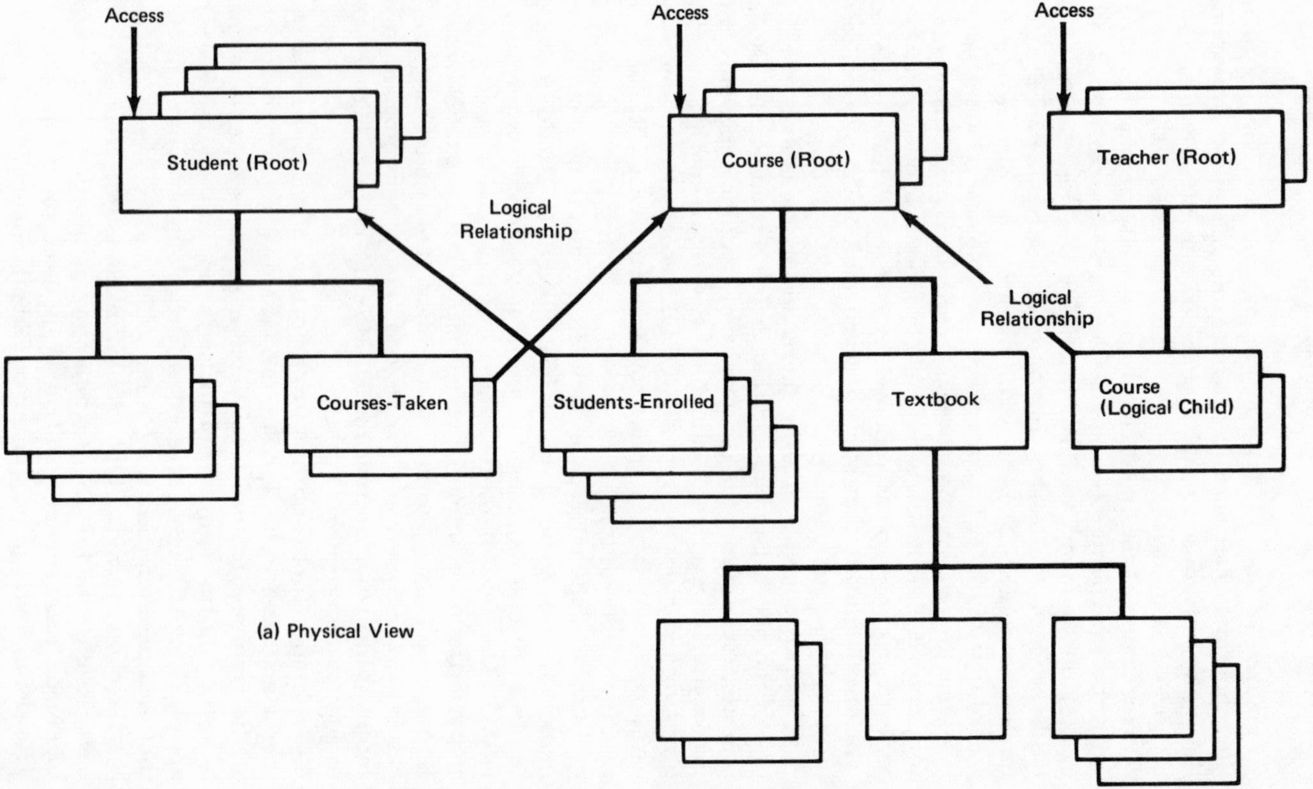

Access
Student (Root)
Courses-Taken
Logical Relationship
Access
Course (Root)
Students-Enrolled
Textbook
Logical Relationship
Access
Teacher (Root)
Course (Logical Child)

(a) Physical View

(b) Logical Views

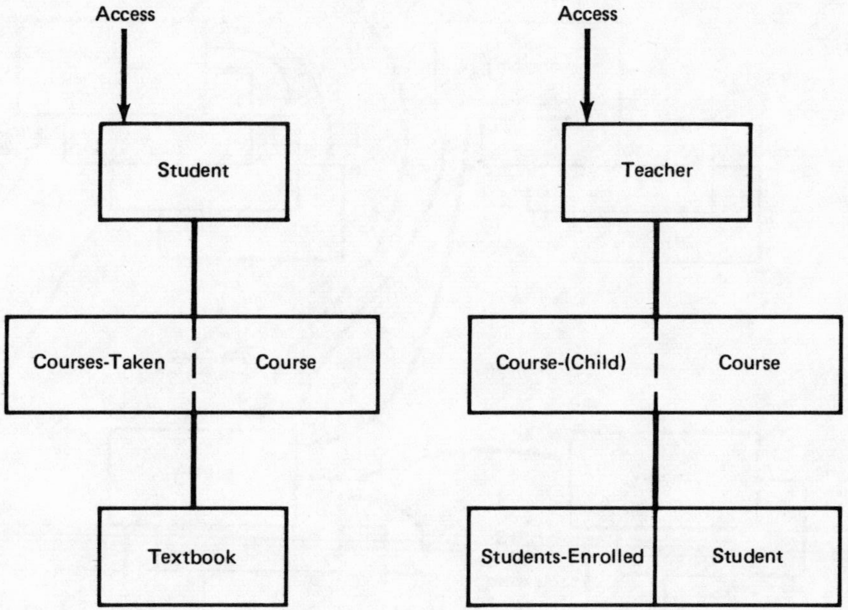

Access

Student

Courses-Taken

Course

Textbook

Access

Teacher

Course-(Child)

Course

Students-Enrolled

Student

Figure 13: Sample conceptualization (schema) of the school data base by a network DBMS.

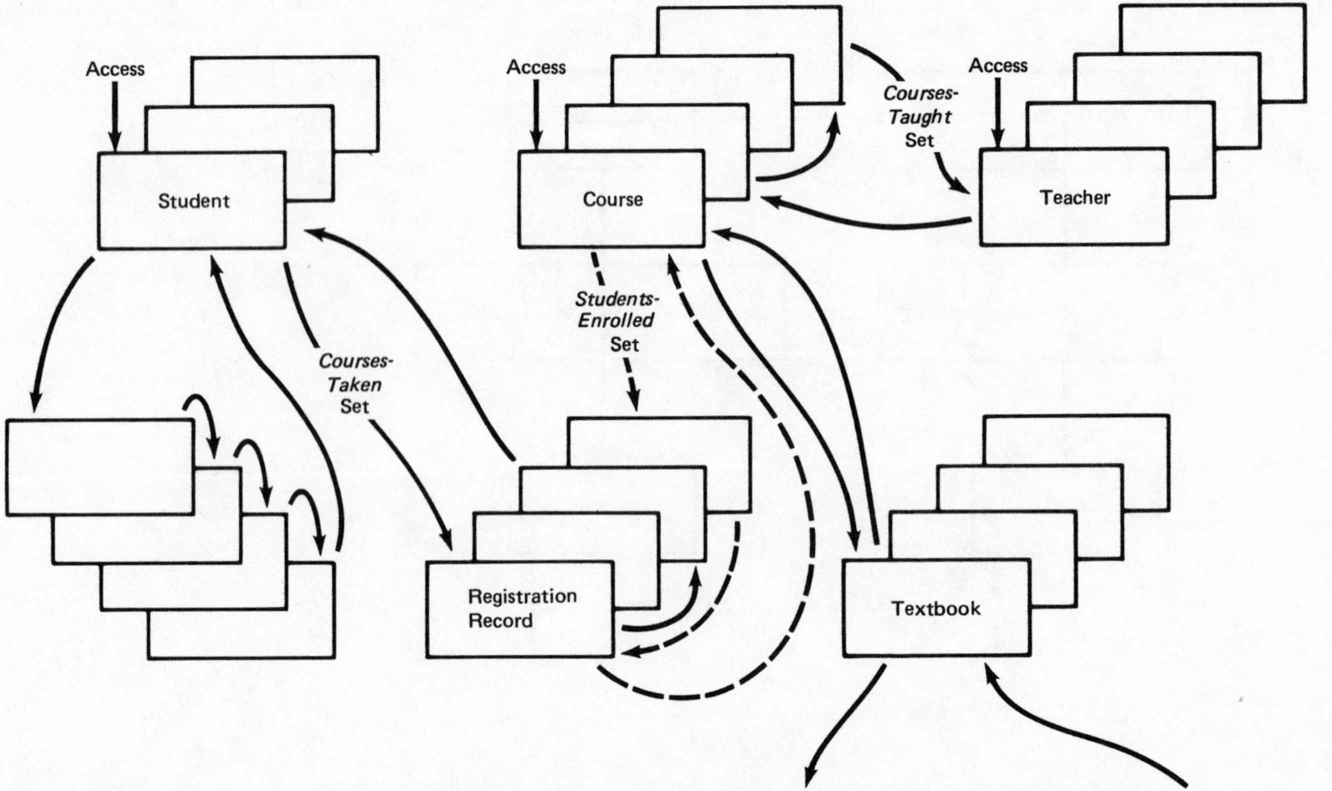

pointer types within the DDL for the data structure; in other words, it is a question of both "where" and "how." The following list presents various options in the definition of pointer types, along with typical functions in navigational access.[4]

Pointer types

IMS/VS

SNGL A pointer to the first occurrence of a subordinate segment is placed in the parent.

DBLE Pointers to the first and last occurrences of a subordinate segment are placed in the parent.

HIER A pointer to the next segment occurrence is placed in each occurrence of given segment types.

HIERBW Pointers to the next and previous segment occurrences are placed in each occurrence of given segment types.

TWIN A pointer to the next segment occurrence is placed in each occurrence of a given segment type.

TWINBWD Pointers to the next and previous segment occurrences are placed in each occurrence of a given segment type.

LPARNT A pointer to a segment occurrence in another data base is placed in a given segment occurrence.

CODASYL

SET: MODE IS CHAIN [LINKED TO PRIOR]

- If LINKED TO PRIOR clause is included, pointers to the next and previous record occurrences are placed in each record occurrence of a set.
- If LINKED TO PRIOR clause is omitted, a pointer to the next record occurrence is placed in each record occurrence of a set.

MEMBER: [LINKED TO OWNER]

- If LINKED TO OWNER clause is included, a pointer to the owner record occurrence is placed in each record occurrence of the given type.
- If LINKED TO OWNER clause is omitted, no pointer is stored.

Access functions

IMS/VS

GET UNIQUE Access a segment occurrence on the basis of supplied keys.

GET NEXT Access the next segment occurrence within the tree structure on the basis of current position and supplied information.
GET NEXT WITHIN PARENT Access the next segment occurrence under a given segment on which position was previously established.

CODASYL

FIND . . . USING Access a record occurrence of a set on the basis of item values.
FIND NEXT . . . Access the next record occurrence within the data base on the basis of current position and supplied information.
FIND CURRENT . . . Access the record occurrence on which position is established, supplying set and record information.
FIND OWNER . . . Access the owner record occurrence of a given set.

The similarity ot the concerns in physically linked DBMS, whether under IMS/VS or a CODASYL system, demonstrates a correspondence of function between these systems. This correspondence has recently been matched by a convergence of operational capabilities. UNIVAC's DMS 1100, for example, supports an indexed-sequential RECORD LOCATION MODE (entry-point access), indexing, and variable length records—all also offered by IMS/VS under the VSAM access method (enhanced ISAM). These similarities are often obscured by the more noticeable, yet less significant, differences in data structuring.

MORE ON DATA STRUCTURING

Before proceeding to a discussion of inverted DBMS, it is worth noting that the data structuring involved in the hierarchical and network models may be implemented by inversion as well as by physical linkage. SYSTEM 2000, for example—an inverted DBMS—follows the hierarchical model. The CODASYL specifications allow for implementation by inversion, although DBMS of that group up until recently tended not to support it.

From this, it is clear that the distinction between physically linked DBMS and inverted DBMS is basically defined by characteristics at the storage structure level (that is, by access methods), whereas the distinction between hierarchical DBMS and network DBMS is more closely associated with differences in the conceptualization of data models—that is, by the data structures supported within the DDL. These several dimensions make possible the classification presented in Table 2.

There are, however, several limitations to this classification. For one thing, physically linked DBMS sometimes offer supplemental indexing capabilities. Examples of such capabilities may be found within IMS/VS and DMS 1100. A more significant problem is that there are a number of systems, particularly among inverted DBMS, which simply do not fall neatly within the strict hierarchical versus network groupings. Such systems include Software AG's ADABAS and Control Data Corporation's DMS-170, which might be placed within the network class, although this does not entirely characterize their approach to data structuring.[5] Finally, there is inevitably some overlap between data structuring and access methods since the DDL is often involved in defining both. In spite of these limitations, the classification in Table 2 is useful as far as it goes.

Table 2: A classification of DBMS by data structuring and principal access method.

DATA STRUCTURING	PRINCIPAL ACCESS METHOD: *Physical Linkage*	PRINCIPAL ACCESS METHOD: *Inversion*
Hierarchical	IMS/VS	SYSTEM 2000
Network	TOTAL CODASYL Systems*	(possible)

*Support is provided within the CODASYL DDL specifications for the indexing of sets.

CONSIDERATIONS IN DATA INVERSION

There are several issues in data inversion at the storage structure level that must be clarified in order to reach a full understanding of inverted DBMS. The first of these is the distinction between indexed access and inverted access, both of which exemplify the general access method of inversion. In both cases, indexes are established apart from actual data and organized on the basis of given keys.

The indexed access method is perhaps more familiar than inverted access because ISAM (a member of the class) has had wide application. Indexed access becomes complicated beyond ISAM, however, when allowance is made for duplicate keys or when the order of the indexed file is not that of the index itself. This latter case occurs when the indexed field is *not* the primary key of the target file, and is properly known as indexed-random.[6]

The distinctive feature of indexed access as used in DBMS (whether indexed-sequential or indexed-random) is that an index record is stored for every indexed record, regardless of whether other records have an identical value for the indexed field. This is not the case for the inverted access method. Under this method, a key value is generally stored once and only once within the index, and associated with it are the addresses of all like-valued records. This distinction is illustrated in Figure 14.

The result of the inverted access technique is a more streamlined and compact index, in particular where the percentage of like-valued records is relatively high. Because inverted DBMS depend heavily on the efficiency of indexes (conservation of storage space is one relevant consideration), they tend to use this method rather than the indexed alternative.

In the process, however, the advantage of using the index as a data base in its own right (often possible under the indexed access method) is lost. In addition, indexes under the inverted access method

Figure 14: Index storage structures under (a) the indexed access method and (b) the inverted access method, for the student record file in Figures 9 and 10 in Chapter 2.

Biology	(Jim Jones)
Computer Science	(Jim Jones)
Computer Science	(James Smith)
Geology	(John Doe)

(a)

Biology	(Jim Jones)
Computer Science	(Jim Jones, James Smith)
Geology	(John Doe)

(b)

tend to be relatively difficult to manage because the pointer arrays associated with each index value are of variable length. Much of the attention in inverted DBMS therefore centers on the construction of indexes.

A second issue essential to understanding inverted DBMS is the distinction between partial and full inversion. Partial inversion, as the name suggests, means that only a small proportion of fields within a data base record are inverted. In a typical application, this might be 10 to 25 percent of all data elements, corresponding to those items most frequently used in queries or straightforward access. A basic consideration in data base design under systems of this type is thus the frequency of item usage. In addition, it must be determined whether given items yield discriminating indexes; for example, a sex data item yields a poor index since only two data values are possible.

By way of contrast, full inversion means that *every* data element in a data base record is inverted. This makes possible a significant innovation at the storage structure level: since the data value of every data element in a record resides somewhere else in the data base (namely, in an index), the record itself *need not be stored.* In its place, a pointer array surrogate is stored so that the record can be reconstituted if its retrieval is required.

Under this strategy, it is to be expected that the overhead of reconstituting records from surrogates will become prohibitive as the number of retrieved records increases. Since many applications focus on producing sequential reports of various types, the full inversion approach is less prevalent than partial inversion among the major systems of the inverted class.

INVERTED DBMS

Inverted DBMS have several advantages as well as disadvantages relative to physically linked DBMS. These are summarized below.

Advantages

- The DDL is simple (structural specifications are limited basically to the designation of fields for inversion).
- Changes in data structures have less impact on application programming; also, there are fewer rules to follow in changing structures.

- Support for new linkage (relation) between existing files is easier to establish.
- Data storage is "purer" since physical support for the data structure is not contained within the data themselves.
- Reorganization of data base files is less complex since files are not physically interrelated; unloading and reloading is not as often required for making structural changes.
- Ad hoc searching is strongly supported since indexes rather than data base records themselves may be examined by the DBMS.
- Programming in inverted DBMS is less involved since navigational access is not so much a factor (query languages in inverted DBMS are strong largely for this reason).

Disadvantages

- The indexes required in inverted DBMS represent significant overhead, especially where many fields are inverted.
- The overhead for update activity tends to be higher since changes to appropriate indexes are required for each update action.
- The overhead for known repetitive reporting tasks tends to be higher in inverted DBMS; in physically linked DBMS such tasks are typically supported by direct pointers, particularly where interfile relation is involved.
- Indexes in inverted DBMS are in a sense "redundant" since data values are identical to those stored in data base records; significant storage space is required for indexes.

Although these points appear to be clear-cut, it is nonetheless difficult, if not impossible, to determine which of the systems—physically linked or inverted DBMS—is better for given tasks, because this is largely system- and application-dependent. It is, however, accurate to characterize inverted DBMS as especially strong for ad hoc retrieval, in particular by query language facilities. For this reason, systems of this type have been used more commonly in information storage and retrieval applications than physically linked DBMS, which have traditionally been associated more with production-type data and their application.

By the same token, it has traditionally been contended that physically linked DBMS are more proficient in applications where the ratio of update processing to retrieval processing is high. (The presence of chains within the data themselves eliminates the need to update segregated indexes.) However, the issue is more complex than this would indicate, and the point is not at all conceded by vendors of inverted DBMS. These vendors (which include independents on IBM hardware) tend to be aggressive about performance and have successfully encroached upon the traditional territory of physically linked DBMS with numerous implementations. Thus traditional lines, whether fact or fancy, have blurred in recent times.

A dimension important to the success of inverted DBMS is the evolution of interfile relation capabilities within a number of systems.[7] There are several ways in which such a relation can be established. One way is by user request at run time, which requires simply the specification of the data base files to be related and of the field on which the relation is to occur. The DBMS can then present the user with concatenated records by matching corresponding indexes.

A similar method, but one that removes the relational specification from the user, is to designate the relation of data base files within the user's subschema. The user then requests a given record type and receives, in fact, a record concatenated from several other record occurrences.

These two methods for relating files rely on the run-time matching of indexes. It is possible, however, to match up indexes *before* the request is issued in order to reduce the number of operations necessary at execution time and thus improve performance for retrieval. In Software AG's ADABAS, for example, two matched lists are kept, in addition to the regular indexes, for each related field. One of the matched lists "belongs" to each of the two data base files so that the other file may be directly accessed on the basis of matched values.

This strategy, which is illustrated in Figure 15, is especially effective for improving performance when the related field is not one for which values have previously been entered by the user in his query specification. Consistent with the keynote in inverted DBMS, the effect of this strategy is to avoid access to the data itself in order to satisfy selection criteria.

It is interesting to note that interfile relation established by this strategy approaches physical linkage between the files, even though the relation remains external to the files themselves. Actual retrieval of records, however, is still basically effected by inversion, which remains the distinguishing characteristic of the system.

DATA MANAGEMENT SYSTEMS (DMS)

Data management systems—sometimes labeled report writers, although they surpass the capability suggested by that name—represent

Figure 15: Interfile relation (coupling) in Software AG's ADABAS. The two matched lists shown result from the merging of the indexes for the school data base presented in Figure 10 in Chapter 2. The two files are related on the basis of the course data element.

	Student File Index Values*		Matched Course File Index Values*	
List 1 (Student File)	Biology	(Jim Jones)	Biology	(Biology)
	Computer Science	(Jim Jones)	Computer Science	(Computer Science)
	Computer Science	(James Smith)	Computer Science	(Computer Science)
	Geology	(John Doe)	Geology	(Geology)

	Course File Index Values*		Matched Student File Index Values*	
List 2 (Course File)	Biology	(Biology)	Biology	(Jim Jones)
	Computer Science	(Computer Science)	Computer Science	(Jim Jones, James Smith)
	Geology	(Geology)	Geology	(John Doe)

*The values for the course data element are not stored in practice.

a significant counterpart to DBMS software. The total number of DMS users is comparable, in fact, to that of DBMS users.

An interesting development within the past several years was the creation of interfaces of the major DMS packages with DBMS systems, with the implication that DMS and DBMS can coexist within the same application environment. From this it can be concluded that DMS serve to enhance the retrieval capability from DBMS-managed files.

In our earlier review of inversion-type systems, we noted that the differentiation between inverted DBMS and inverted DMS is rather ill-defined. This is not true for the distinction between physically linked DBMS and file-pass DMS.

The common denominator among file-pass DMS is the ability to create multiple reports (in different sequences) from a single pass of an input master file. This normally requires, of course, a sort for each sequence, although in a typical implementation, record surrogates (that is, temporary indexes) are sorted rather than the records themselves. By contrast, a DBMS (whether physically linked or inverted) establishes a means of achieving a given report sequence *directly*—that is, by means of an ordered set or index maintained during data *storage*.

In essence, a DMS automates a more traditional method of processing; it is possible, for example, to visualize a DMS following much the same pattern for producing class roles as was illustrated in Figure 11 of Chapter 2. There are, however, significant potentials offered by the DMS. For instance, during the single pass of the file, other reports—bus schedules, homeroom lists, and so forth—might be generated.

The distinction between physically linked (or inverted) DBMS and file-pass DMS is significant, in that the requirements of the latter for file-pass and record sorting generally render them much less effective than DBMS in on-line and multiple update tasks. In one sense, record sorting in a file-pass DMS is made necessary by a lack of data structuring and amounts to the introduction (if temporary) of data redundancy into the system. In general, DMS allow the continuation of traditional master file schemes, with their tendency toward data redundancy and inconsistency. Since the DMS environment is largely nonintegrated, DMS are often correctly designated file management systems.

Both file-pass and inverted DMS do, however, exhibit significant degrees of data independence. Like DBMS, DMS often support an independent DDL (that is, a DDL apart from application programming), frequently in conjunction with data dictionary facilities. This DDL tends to be restrictive, of course; file-pass DMS usually support only sequential and index-sequential files.

Perhaps the most noteworthy feature of DMS, one particularly conducive to improving application productivity, is the provision of high-level user interface languages, which in many cases eliminates the need for cumbersome COBOL programming. An immediate result of this is a greater responsiveness to ad hoc requirements—an area in which DBMS are often significantly wanting.

DMS of the file-pass sort exhibit an additional capability; the ability to relate multiple files. Again, however, this capability is restricted in comparison with DBMS. For DMS, a related file is often labeled "coordinate"[8] and is normally indexed-sequential in organization. A key from the master file (or from another appropriate source) serves as a means of entry into the coordinate file *at run time* via its primary index. Many files may be "related" in this manner.

In summary, it may be said that DMS automate and enhance the activity normally associated with master file processing, although they do not achieve the integration of data and associated benefits available in DBMS. Nonetheless, they are viable alternatives in many environments and may in fact not be as distant from the mainstream of data base evolution as is often thought.

Notes

[1]This requires the generation of pseudo data base descriptions, called logical DBD, using a simple subset of the regular DDL. Logical DBD follow paths established in the physical DBD.

[2]In the hierarchical data structure in Figure 12, two record types are shown effecting linkage between student and course records. In practice, one or the other of these can be "virtual," that is, not actually stored. It should be noted that the *courses-taught* set in Figure 13 cannot be directly implemented in TOTAL, even though that DBMS is classified as a network system. Distinctions like the one between hierarchical and network data structures are often subtle but nonetheless significant in implementing data models. The major feature distinguishing network from hierarchical data structures is the view that the programmer "sees." Hierarchical views are supposedly easier for the programmer to use, although under existing DBMS the point is debatable.

[3]Navigational access is a term suggested by Charles W. Bachman, winner of the 1973 ACM Turing award and principal architect of I-D-S, prototype for the CODASYL model. Navigational access in the hierarchical model is referred to as "tree traversal access."

[4]The pointer types shown for IMS/VS may be mutually exclusive in some cases. Not all options are given. The CODASYL pointer options are taken from the 1971 *CODASYL Data Base Task Group Report,* on which most current CODASYL DBMS are based. The access functions for the CODASYL model are taken from the 1976 *CODASYL COBOL JOD* and do not include all possible variations.

[5]These systems are sometimes characterized as relational, although they do not implement the relational model in full. The relational model itself is an additional problem for the classification in Table 2.

[6]Secondary indexing in IMS/VS is of this type. As mentioned previously, file level support in a DBMS is often provided by the operating system.

This means, for example, that an index file in IMS/VS may itself be managed by ISAM or VSAM, with the implication that the index is itself indexed. The result is a pyramiding access structure that improves overall performance. In this discussion, "index" refers to the data base index rather than to any lower-level index.

[7]Such capabilities include "coupling" in ADABAS, "connection" in INQUIRE, "link" in SYSTEM 2000, and "join" in DMS-170. A good deal of variation exists in the nature of these various implementations, as well as in their complexity. Interfile relation is an important, but not the sole, ingredient in distinguishing between inverted DBMS and inverted DMS.

[8]This corresponds to "indexed-coordinate" files in Informatic's MARK IV. The operation establishing the relation, though restricted to the primary key of the coordinate file, is somewhat similar to file relation in inverted DBMS.

Chapter 4
SELECTION OF DATA MANAGEMENT SOFTWARE

Two distinct questions arise in the evaluation of commercial DBMS, neither of which lends itself to easy answers. The first question has to do with what should be considered in selecting a DBMS. A fully justified answer to this question presupposes a comprehensive determination of needs, a consideration of the alternatives, and an investigation of the impact of DBMS on the organization.

Only after these topics have been explored should the second question be addressed—but only if DBMS are still perceived to be a viable alternative in solving organizational needs. This second question asks how the DBMS on the market today are to be properly evaluated.

Answering this second question will of course involve establishing contact with DBMS vendors, who will supply additional data base information. This information is naturally slanted to their own product. Too many organizations have allowed vendors to answer question *one* as well as question two. An organization is well advised to remain within the framework of a two-stage evaluation, in which vendors address question two. In surveying the DBMS on the market, there is no definitive answer to the question of which system is best. All have their merits, and all have shortcomings. Which is best really depends on the specific needs of a given organization.

CONSIDERATIONS IN SELECTING A DBMS

There are two alternatives to DBMS, given the need to upgrade data services. The first is enhancement of existing in-house software; the second is purchase of a data management system, a less complex version of DBMS. Opting for either of these alternatives over DBMS indicates that organizational data needs, including needs projected for the future, do not require the data structuring and management services offered by DBMS.

How are these data needs to be determined? There are general guidelines that can be followed; these aim at pinpointing significant deficiencies in current data management.

The problem most often cited is the extensive duplication of identical data within two or more existing master files. DBMS have facilities for reducing these redundant data, consequently streamlining data access and improving update procedures. A second common problem in data management is the need for extensive record sorting to produce high-volume reports. Again, DBMS have facilities that provide more direct access to individual data.

Another guideline, less tangible perhaps than the first two, is difficulty in implementing changes to record descriptions because of the need for extensive program modification and recompilation. A case study that illustrates this problem is presented in the following. Data independence, sometimes overplayed as a DBMS virtue, does in fact mean significant savings in this type of program maintenance.

A Case Study

A large public organization employs approximately 25,000 people in various capacities. The data processing department is responsible for maintaining the payroll-personnel system, which has been automated for some time.

The personnel master file is created and maintained using COBOL file descriptions. Approximately 80 active programs (about 40 percent of the total for the entire system) process this file.

In July 1977, at the end of the fiscal year, it was decided that a new data element was needed in this file, although the same element already existed in the payroll master file. The new data element added 35 bytes to the length of the personnel file.

Each of the 80 programs processing this file had to be recompiled to accommodate the new data element, even though only 10 of these programs actually used it in their respective processing tasks. Logic changes in these 10 programs were relatively straightforward, but some retesting was required.

An especially troublesome matter was updating the new data element. Established procedures existed to update the data element in the payroll file, but these could not be applied directly to the personnel master file. It was decided that a special program was to be written that copied over update transactions from the payroll system to the personnel system. After some minor editing, these transactions could be applied to the personnel master file.

This new program was to be run periodically, depending on the processing load in the payroll-personnel system. The actual time lag in updating the personnel master file turned out to be a week or, in some cases, even more. On several occasions users complained that they could not use the reports they were receiving because of discrepancies in control totals and other information. This problem was partially resolved by running the program nightly.

A post-project study showed that approximately three man-months' effort had been required to effect the changeover. This manpower investment came at a critical time because of year-end processing in several departments in the organization, including in the budget area. During this period there was noticeable strain on computer resources, which revealed itself most clearly in prolonged turnaround. A number of people felt that the change had not been worth its cost in implementation.

Figure 16 outlines the manpower savings that would have accrued had the payroll-personnel system been implemented under a data base management system. This analysis reveals a saving of approximately 50 percent to effect the changeover in a data base environment.

Other benefits would have resulted in the following areas:

1. Reduction in storage: approximately (35 bytes − 4 bytes for pointers) × (25,000 records) = 775,000 bytes.
2. Savings in compile time for programs not using the new data elements (see Figure 16).
3. Uniformity in update: a payroll update renders the data element immediately current to the personnel system.

There are other guidelines, too numerous to discuss individually, for determining data needs and the advisability of selecting a DBMS. A useful exercise at this point is to consider the advantages of DBMS (see Table 3) in an examination of current conditions in the organization. This exercise may or may not reveal facts of considerable interest; in either case its purpose is served. Investment of several man-months and careful documentation of the results are recommended.

The alternatives to DBMS, as mentioned, are enhancement of in-house software and acquisition of a data management system.

It is generally accepted that it is unwise to attempt development of in-house software that matches the capabilities of DBMS. This consensus is based on the extent of costs for both initial investment

*Figure 16: Man-months for changeover under traditional and DBMS approach.**

	Change File Descr.	Change Logic	Compile	Test	Man-Months
Programs using new data elements:					
Traditional:	Yes	Yes	Yes	Yes	1.00
Data Base:	No	Yes	Yes	Yes	.95
Programs not using new data elements:					
Traditional:	Yes	No	Yes	No	1.25
Data Base:	No	No	No	No	0.00
Other modifications:					
Traditional: write update program, test and document.					.75
Data Base: change data base description; reload data base; document.					.50
Total man-months:					
Traditional: 3.00					
Data Base: 1.45					

*This illustration assumes a DBMS with data element level independence. Without this, the data base programs not using the new data element would probably have to be recompiled in order to accommodate a new record description. This would not be the case if the new data element were placed in a record by itself or in one that was not used.

and continuing support; it is no small item that the vendor is responsible for maintaining DBMS software. Although in-house I-O modules and data managers are by no means a thing of the past, there is some feeling, well justified by experience, that these types of projects are not for any but the best (and best funded) data processing department.

Projects of less than DBMS scope must of course be judged on individual merit. An additional consideration, however, is the delay in implementation time of in-house projects; DBMS (and DMS) packages are "up" rather quickly, *and at a relatively fixed cost.*

Data management systems may be an attractive alternative for some organizations, especially where organizational needs fall somewhat below the capabilities provided by DBMS. Generally, DMS do provide a degree of data independence, again with the advantage

Table 3: The benefits associated with data base organization, as compared with traditional organization.

Traditional Organization	Data Base Organization	Benefits
Each application typically has its own master file, which contains data duplicated in files of related systems.	The DBMS creates and maintains interfile access paths automatically so that the same data may be used by multiple applications.	Reduce general data redundancy across application files.
Each physical file containing the data to be updated must be processed separately. This is usually done at different times, causing discrepancies in various reports.	A program updates data in a single shared data base. The new data are immediately available for all applications.	Reduce the programming effort required for file updating.
Changes in record definition or expansion of record sizes must be reflected in every program accessing the data.	Data description is segregated from application programs. Only those programs actually referring to the changed data type need be modified.	Reduce the program modification brought about by changes in data definition.
Most traditional file systems support a single access path so that additional retrieval requirements must be satisfied by search and sort procedures.	DBMS provide automatic generation and maintenance of interfile linkage and indexes, which allows tailoring of access to meet the requirements of application systems.	Increase the accessibility of data by providing multiple access paths and retrieval sequences.
Application programmers often supply their own data names.	For many access operations, the applications programmer must use names known to the DBMS. Central data definitions are often maintained in a data dictionary system.	Encourage the use of standardized data-naming conventions.
Coding of security systems is an independent task. Such systems are difficult to implement, especially in COBOL.	Control blocks are generated that specify which data elements an individual application program can access. Control information and undesignated data are not available to the program.	Provide data security.
No automatic facility is provided; therefore, each application system must program its own recovery procedures. Standardized recovery procedures are difficult to define and implement.	Recoverability is an automatic feature of DBMS. Once processing errors are detected, the system can restore the data base files to the last intact file copy. All transactions against the data base are logged on tape, from which quick file restoration is possible.	Provide recoverability.
Tape handling is a major activity in production runs.	Data base files reside on disk.	Reduce operator intervention and associated production errors.
Application systems and data communications are sometimes difficult to integrate within acceptable standards of performance.	Most DBMS have integrated or interfaced teleprocessing monitors.	Promote data communications services.

of vendor-supported software, but do not attempt to lessen data redundancy or streamline data access on a large scale.

As a rule, DMS concentrate on improved data access from a single file for a single, although not necessarily small, application. Improved data access is especially defined as optimization of report generation. DBMS, on the other hand, are oriented toward support of more than one application by the interrelation of multiple files. Improved data access is defined more broadly, especially as it refers to telecommunications. Both types of system—DMS and DBMS—generally support high-level search capabilities, which are somewhat more restricted in DMS because of the limitations in file structuring.

DMS vendors claim that their systems can significantly reduce the implementation time of application systems. This claim has substantial justification in fact. Some DMS packages—for example, MARK IV from Informatics, Inc., and RAMIS from Mathematica—are very popular and may indeed be a viable alternative for some organizations. In investigating these systems it is important to keep in mind the distinctions between DMS and DBMS, which tend to be obscured by vendor terminology.

If either of the alternatives to DBMS—DMS or software enhancement—proves to be entirely sufficient to meet organizational needs, there is no need to continue with the selection analysis. If not, important considerations remain before the actual selection of a DBMS. Experience with data base systems shows that these considerations are often underrated or neglected, *at great future cost.*

The impact of a DBMS on an organization is disruptive. The technology of DBMS is new and difficult and requires substantial investment in training. More than this, the data base approach cuts across traditional installation management and requires staff reorganization and hiring. The transition to a data base system is highly visible, in particular because users outside the data processing department are inevitably involved in the reshaping of data needs and goals.

In fact, although the majority of nightmare tales about DBMS are not actually true, there are a number of areas in DBMS design and application that present problems too significant to overlook. A list of these problem areas is presented here.

Operations

1. Data base management systems often require a great deal of overhead in hardware and software resources, not only during implementation but on a continuing basis.

2. Production is often disrupted during conversion to the data base system.
3. DBMS operation costs, especially the costs associated with periodic reorganization of data base files, can be deceptive and thus reduce efficient resource allocation.
4. Some DBMS have inadequate or difficult restart capabilities and system crash protection.
5. Most DBMS do not report adequate statistics on internal data structuring status.

Programming

1. Installation and maintenance of the data base system requires a continuing investment of professional resources that may retard other project development.
2. DBMS require conversion programs for transferring data from existing files to data base format.
3. Increased dependence on an externally supplied DBMS package may decrease the organization's ability to rely on in-house personnel for system support.
4. Some DBMS have undesirable restrictions in data handling and cumbersome interface standards.
5. Some DBMS lack an effective query language and/or generalized report feature.

Personnel

1. Sufficient education of personnel in data base use is expensive and time-consuming.
2. It may prove difficult to acquire and keep qualified personnel, especially people knowledgeable of a particular system.
3. The implementation of data base systems disrupts established organizational patterns and precipitates a degree of organizational stress.

Service

1. Some DBMS have inadequate capabilities for preventing unauthorized access to data. This problem is made more significant by the centralization of data base files.
2. Because of this centralization, loss of data base files may have even worse implications for service than a corresponding loss in traditional application files.
3. Unless they are properly structured and maintained, the data collected in the data base may appear inertial to users and programmers alike.

4. System reorganization requires periodic downtime.

Future Development

1. DBMS tend to cause lock-in to a particular format and system, which may restrict choices among new software and/or hardware.
2. The inappropriate application of DBMS capabilities may cause performance degradation over a period extending well into the future.

The impact of most of these problems can be minimized by careful implementation of the data base system. This implementation requires a significant investment of time and money, but considerable payoff can be expected in the long run.

There is, of course, substantial opportunity for improved data service in changing to a DBMS, provided the change is properly managed. Even so, full analysis of projected changes beforehand is wise. This analysis involves planning for evaluation of conversion paths, including the need for file conversion and program modification. A data base administrator position should be carefully analyzed and its impact estimated. Hardware configurations should be studied carefully in order to determine what upgrading will be required.

In summary, a DBMS package selected and purchased is not a data base system up and running. The commitment required to reach this goal is so substantial that it alone should deter those who have not already decided that a DBMS is the best, or perhaps the only, solution to data needs.

EVALUATION OF CURRENT DBMS

As mentioned, none of the DBMS on the market has distinguished itself as preeminent. Each system is designed for maximum benefits in some, but not all, areas. In fact, there are major differences even in the approach to data management itself, the most obvious cleavage being between physical linkage and data inversion.

A further complicating fact is that the operational characteristics of a given system depend not only on the hardware configuration of an installation but also on the nature of the organization's application data. By its very design, a data base management system is extremely data dependent in performance. This does not imply that any current system falls below minimum standards in basic data handling; rather, it means that each installation has a unique set of application circumstances, which must be taken into account when selecting the best DBMS package.

Hardware systems, of course, immediately restrict choices among DBMS, especially for the non-IBM user. Table 4 classifies DBMS by hardware. One of the more interesting recent developments in the data base field has been the cross-mainframe implementation of several DBMS, most notably TOTAL by Cincom Systems and SYSTEM 2000 by MRI Corp. Another interesting development that may prove very significant for the systems of the future is the implementation of DBMS on midi- and mini-sized computers. Examples are IMAGE/3000 by Hewlett-Packard, TOTAL by Cincom Systems, and DBMS-11 by Digital Equipment Corp. Somewhat the dark horse in the data base field, at least for the present, is the role that the CODASYL specifications for DBMS standardization are to play in the evolution of data base systems. This issue greatly divides current data base thinking.

Table 4: DBMS classified by mainframe hardware family.

Hardware	DBMS
IBM 360/370	IMS TOTAL IDMS SYSTEM 2000 ADABAS Model 204 DATACOM/DB INQUIRE NOMAD*
Burroughs 6700/7700	DMS-II
Burroughs 1700	DMS-II
UNIVAC 1100 Series	DMS 1100 SYSTEM 2000
UNIVAC Series 90	DMS/90
UNIVAC Series 70	DMS/90 TOTAL
Honeywell Series 600, 6000, 60 Level 66	I-D-S/II (I) TOTAL
Honeywell Series 200 and 2000	TOTAL
Digital DECsystem-10, DECsystem-20	DBMS-10 MAGNUM*
CDC 6000/Cyber 70, 170	SYSTEM 2000 TOTAL DMS-170
Sigma 5/6/7/9 (H.I.S.)	EDMS
NCR Century Series, Criterion Series	TOTAL

*Remote computing only.

There are three essential steps in close DBMS evaluation.

1. A list of DBMS evaluation criteria is devised. A sample list is presented in the appendix to this chapter. The first two criteria—consumption of system resources and interfacing with a generalized teleprocessing system—should be singled out for especially close attention.

2. An effective strategy for incorporating the unique needs of the installation into the evaluation process is defined. One such strategy is presented in the appendix, following the list of DBMS evaluation criteria. Its distinguishing characteristic is the weighing of individual criteria according to their importance to the needs of the organization.

3. The DBMS themselves are rated. Information for this rating may come from a variety of sources:

- Vendor presentations and literature. (A demo can sometimes be arranged, though often at a cost to the user.)
- Recent periodical publications and other independent studies.
- Communications with current users of the systems. (The DBMS vendor can be persuaded to supply a list of representative users).

A log of evidence supporting each rating should be carefully maintained for future reference.

The evaluation should be undertaken by a team of people, consisting of representatives from those areas most affected by the data base project: management, operations, and application systems. Ideally, each member of the team should arrive at ratings independently.

One thing to remember in rating a particular DBMS on a given criterion, especially when the evidence consists largely of user comments from other installations, is that every application situation is different; what is good for one organization may not be for another. Another point to keep in mind is that many organizations have benefited from the expertise of outside consultants, most of whom have been through the selection process many times before.

The results of the evaluation process must be accompanied by a detailed cost/benefit analysis. Items in this analysis should include:

- The price for each package, including the projected costs for installation, maintenance, education, documentation, and support. Some DBMS come in a comprehensive package, others come piecemeal; a quoted DBMS price tag can therefore be deceptive.

- The quality of performance and support guarantees. Can the vendor back up the promises he makes?
- Conversion aids. Are they provided, or must conversion programs be written in-house?
- Projected changes in EDP technology. Will they make the hardware and software outmoded?

APPENDIX

DBMS Evaluation Criteria

I Capabilities and Requirements

1. How much core and overall system resources are required for effective DBMS operation?
2. Is the system part of (or easily interfaced with) a generalized teleprocessing monitor?
3. Are integrity and protection features (back-up, audit trail, checkpointing, recovery, etc.) sufficient?
4. How effective is the teleprocessing interface in selective program back-out?
5. Does the system give performance statistics (for performance monitoring and reorganization)?
6. Is the system (easily) complemented by a capable report generator?
7. Is the system (easily) complemented by a capable query language?
8. Are sufficient utilities supplied, especially for file conversion, reorganization, and loading/unloading?
9. Is the system efficient for both batch and on-line processing, or does it handle one at the expense of the other?
10. How difficult is fine-tuning and ongoing maintenance? What resources are required?

II Flexibility of the Operating DBMS

1. Is the system modular, in the sense that when one portion of the data base is down, other operating areas remain unaffected?
2. How well can user access to data elements and records be controlled? Is data independence supported to the data element level?
3. Is a subschema capability supported? What type of access control and retrieval enhancement does it provide?
4. Are multiple data sets per data base supported so that only active portions need be loaded?
5. Are multiple user languages (for instance, FORTRAN and PL/I) supported?
6. What devices are supported for data base storage?

7. Is the system designed for concurrent retrieval and concurrent access?
8. In the absence of the on-line portion of the DBMS, is a copy of the DBMS required for each batch program? Can a single copy support concurrent data base access from multiple batch programs?
9. Where does support for concurrent access fall?
10. How good are search capabilities (for instance, is the language easy to use, and is sufficient expression building supported)?
11. Is the system more efficient for retrieval or for updating? Is performance for the other seriously degraded?

III Standardization of the DBMS

1. Does the system follow CODASYL specifications? Is the system available on other hardware lines?
2. How much is the data base locked into the DBMS?
3. Is the data directory externally readable and/or standardized?
4. Are data encoded/decoded or compressed/decompressed? Is the feature optional? How much storage space can be saved?
5. How dependent is the system on COBOL?

IV Investment of Professional Resources

1. Is the system difficult for the application programmer to use efficiently?
2. How much actual DBMS implementation is done by the user installation?
3. How much DBMS support is provided by the vendor?
4. How much ongoing physical mapping must be done by the user installation?
5. Is the system well documented?
6. How difficult is selective or massive data entry?
7. What type of data dictionary capability is provided? What services are offered? How difficult to use is the data dictionary?

V Design of Storage Structuring

1. What are the limits on the number of:
   - Record or segment types?
   - Searchable fields per record?
   - Occurrences of a single repeating group?
   - Record or segment type per set or hierarchy?
   - Interfile relationships?
2. Is inversion supported? Is the inversion technique actually indexed access or inverted access? Is indexed-random access supported? How difficult is the inversion to use?
3. How difficult is it to add new fields to the data structure?
4. How difficult is it to change data structures? What can be changed? What impact does the change have on existing applications?

5. How "expandable" is the data structuring?
6. Are variable-length records supported by the DBMS? How strong is this support? Is the feature difficult to use?
7. What facilities are provided for supporting sequential processing of data base files? What overhead is engendered?
8. What facilities are provided for supporting ad hoc searching of data bases and for relating previously unrelated files?

An Algorithm for Evaluating DBMS

Step 1. For the individual criteria within each major evaluation area (see the preceding list), assign relative weights based on an average score of 100. Each weight should reflect the importance of the criterion to the overall philosophy and projected hardware configuration of your installation. The accuracy of the evaluation depends on a realistic estimate of these weights.

Step 2. Rate each DBMS package on each criterion, assigning a score of 1 to 10. This score reflects the strength of that system for the given criterion; the higher the score, the better the system.

Step 3. Multiply each criterion's weight by the rating of each DBMS package on the given criterion. This gives an evaluation score for each package on each criterion.

Step 4. Total each system's evaluation scores for every criterion within an evaluation area. This gives the relative strength of each system for each evaluation area.

Step 5. Total each system's area evaluation scores across all areas. The result is an estimate of the overall strength of each package, given your relative criteria weights.

PART II

The Evolution of Data Base Management

Chapter 5
THE CODASYL EFFORT

In this chapter and the next, various evolutionary advances in DBMS are examined. This chapter focuses on the CODASYL specifications, and the next, on the relational model and on mini-DBMS. In contrast to the CODASYL effort, both of these latter topics are only now beginning to have significant impact. The CODASYL specifications have been influential since at least 1971 and perhaps earlier.

Before examining the CODASYL effort, however, a look at a case study in the evolution of one particular DBMS is instructive. Honeywell Information Systems' I-D-S/II is chosen for this study not only because it is a representative CODASYL system (the forerunner of the system served, in fact, as the prototype for the specifications) but because it presents a clear-cut example of evolutionary trends in DBMS development. I-D-S/II can be considered a microcosm in the development of state-of-the-art DBMS.

A CASE STUDY: I-D-S/II

The I-D-S concept of data management goes back to General Electric, Charles Bachman, and 1961. The first actual host language versions of I-D-S (for use within COBOL) were developed and released for the GE-400 and 600 hardware series during 1965 and 1966. I-D-S software supported a number of features fundamental to data base management as now perceived:

1. *A data description language* providing for the definition of records and their integration into logical data structures.
2. *Physical support* for the data structure through maintenance of physical pointers, data buffering, and formatting of storage areas. This support allowed application programming to be independent of physical access methods.

3. *Device independence,* allowing data base files to be moved between device types without impact on application programming. A number of techniques were featured for optimizing direct access performance.
4. *A data manipulation language* (embedded within COBOL programs) for performing logical operations on actual records in the data base.
5. *Various utilities in support of data base administration.* For example, utilities were developed for creating and loading the data base, for auditing data base records, and for journalization and recovery.

I-D-S software, acquired by Honeywell along with GE computer operations in 1969, predates the CODASYL specifications and thus exhibits a number of departures in language syntax from subsequent CODASYL specifications. The most recent effort to accommodate the latest CODASYL specifications is embodied in the release of I-D-S/II by H.I.S. in late 1975.

Reflecting an industry trend, H.I.S. "unbundled" I-D-S/II software; that is, the software is priced separately from the machine and its operating system. Unbundled DBMS software is now widely characteristic of the industry. I-D-S/II exhibits significant advances over its immediate predecessor (designated I-D-S/I), as the following analysis indicates.

Development in I-D-S/II and I-D-S/I

An independent data description language (DDL). In I-D-S/II, schema (data base) definition is accomplished through an independent data description language, which stands apart from all application programs. By this means, a basic measure of data independence is achieved, namely the separation of program logic from data definition. A data base is described only once; this definition is central to all access. Also, the schema DDL is generalized in the sense that interface languages other than COBOL can be supported.

In I-D-S/I, data description is included in each COBOL application program, as extensions to the ENVIRONMENT DIVISION and the DATA DIVISION. Even using COPY facilities, this arrangement compromises data independence since all application programs must be recompiled for any change in the description. Also, under most circumstances, the user's program has access to all parts of the data structure rather than to a subset of record and relationship types.

Since the schema DDL is included in COBOL language programs, interface with other host languages is not possible.

A subschema facility. In I-D-S/II, subschemas for individual application programs are supported, using an independent language facility. This subschema facility greatly improves data independence—for example, by supporting item-level independence.

No direct subschema facility is supported in I-D-S/I.

An enhanced data manipulation language (DML). In I-D-S/II, data manipulation in COBOL is effected using CODASYL-compliant language, supported directly by the H.I.S. compiler. A FORTRAN interface is under development.

In I-D-S/I, each data base access verb is preceded by an ENTER IDS statement; the application program is processed by a pre-compiler before actual compilation. COBOL is the sole host language.

Storage structuring. In I-D-S/II, development of the following enhancements to data base structuring is noted:

- Variable length records.
- Secondary indexes.
- Support for indexed-sequential and sequential structures.
- Support for "virtual" records—that is, data concatenated from separate records in the data base.

In I-D-S/I, basic support for record and set definition is available, but without features as advanced as in I-D-S/II.

Security and integrity. In the I-D-S/II DDL, support is extended to privacy locks (password protection), encode/decode specification for data items, and data base procedures (procedural exits, procedures for data validation, and so on).

Although I-D-S/I supports some of these features, their implementation is much less extensive.

A device media control language. In I-D-S/II, a device media control language (DMCL) is featured; it provides the data administrator with a number of options in mapping the physical structure of the data base to actual storage devices.

In I-D-S/I, the DMCL function is incorporated into the standard job control language.

A central manager. In I-D-S/II, a single copy of data base access routines is shared by all executing data base programs. This arrangement allows buffer pooling, enhanced control over concurrent access, and performance improvements.

In I-D-S/I, each application program has its own copy of many data base access routines, a method that wastes core space and lessens data base control.

Other Developments in I-D-S/II

Several other areas of I-D-S/II development are worth noting.

End-user facilities. Under I-D-S/II, an interactive version of the DML is supported for on-line access to I-D-S/II data bases. Support is also developed for an interface using an on-line user-oriented query facility QRP (Query and Reporting Processor). Such capabilities greatly improve the responsiveness of the data base to user needs, particularly for the uninitiated user.

A relational capability. Announced in June 1976 was the Multics Data Base Manager (MDBM), which incorporates both a relational and a network view of data bases. This announcement is one indication that commercial impact of the relational model has begun.

A total data management facility. A recent move by H.I.S. was to group a number of facilities involved in data management into a single comprehensive package called DM-IV (announced January 1977). The data base manager I-D-S/II is one component of this package; others include on-line transaction processing and communications, interactive inquiry and reporting, concurrent processing support (for both batch and on-line processing), and host language compilation. Significantly, traditional access methods (sequential and indexed-sequential) are included.

Other DBMS vendors—for example Control Data Corporation, with its DMS-170 and Cullinane with its CDMS—have taken similar actions. The total data management concept is often encountered in mini-computer offerings. Among mainframe systems, a somewhat more restricted view is common, as exemplified by the DB/DC (Data Base/Data Communications) approach of IBM's IMS/VS and Insyte's DATACOM. One area certainly destined as a central feature of total data management systems is the data dictionary—one additional feature of H.I.S.'s DM-IV and I-D-S/II.

CODASYL CONCEPTS

CODASYL systems are not set apart from other DBMS by what they do; there are many data management techniques and capabilities that are widely common to DBMS, whether CODASYL-compliant or not. Nor is data structuring under CODASYL DBMS necessarily more thorough or more powerful than under other DBMS; many features are in fact virtually the same for both CODASYL and non-CODASYL systems.

What sets CODASYL systems apart from other DBMS is their adherence to common concepts and language, which have been carefully and thoroughly developed during the last decade. Since these concepts and language must accommodate many approaches to data management and many hardware environments, the CODASYL specifications are perhaps the most succinct currently available for implementing large-scale state-of-the-art data bases on existing hardware lines.

They are worth understanding for this reason alone. The following sections present the basic concepts in CODASYL thinking, first for the definition of data bases, then for using these data bases for application purposes.

It should be remembered that the CODASYL specifications constantly evolve. Also, no existing DBMS *completely* implements the entire range of CODASYL features discussed. Nonetheless, the foundations for the CODASYL model have been firmly established and proven by real systems in real applications.

The CODASYL terminology and notation are reviewed briefly in the appendix to this chapter.

Defining the Data Base

In the following discussion we will consider the data base structures that can be defined using the CODASYL DDL. The starting point is the schema, the overall description of the data base.

The Schema

A CODASYL data base is described by a *schema* using facilities of the data description language. Within a given data base are *areas, sets,* and *records,* reflecting the organization defined by the schema. Data in separate data bases—that is data under the control of separate schemas—are assumed to be unrelated.

Areas, set types, and record types are named within the schema and are thus known to the DBMS. An area is simply a named collection of records and may contain one or more record types. In most cases, an area corresponds to a file. Similarly, a record type is a named collection of *data items* (data items themselves may be grouped into *data aggregates*); each record type describes actual occurrences (that is, records) in the data base. Basic access to the data base by an application program is at the record level.

Records that are related to one another may be collected into sets. A set type is defined to have one record type as *owner* and one or more record types as *members.* In a given set occurrence (that is, in a set), there is one and only one occurrence of the owner record type and an arbitrary number of occurrences of each of the member record types.

Physical support for sets is left to the DBMS implementor, but two basic types of storage structures are most commonly found: chains and pointer arrays. These structures are illustrated in Figure 17. Chaining (physical linkage) has traditionally predominated in actual CODASYL systems, although considerable attention has recently been given to set implementation by pointer arrays, the essential ingredient for inverted structures.

One important observation on sets is that records of a given set need not reside within a single area (file) but rather are often physically located in distinct areas. This is true whether implementation of the set is by chain or by pointer array. A set is a means of associating related records.

Significantly, there is no expressed limit on the number of set types in which a defined record type may participate. Nor is there a restriction on defining the same record type as owner in one set type and member in another. The same record type can be owner of multiple set types and member of multiple set types, but it cannot be both owner and member of the same set type.

These rules make possible the generalized data structure called a *network,* in which many interrelationships between records can be supported. The following section examines network structures and several data structures that can be accommodated in them.

Networks and Other Data Structures: The CODASYL View

A *network* is a generalized data structure on which few restrictions are placed in relating records. In a network, the same record type can be included in more than one set type and, additionally, may be both owner and member (although not in the same set type). A network structure for the school data model is given in Figure 18.

Some DBMS, particularly the older ones, put restrictions on network structures. For example, in Cincom's TOTAL, a record type can participate in multiple set types but must always be either an owner or a member (that is, the record type cannot be an owner

Figure 17: The implementation of sets by (a) chains and (b) pointer arrays, using the school data model.

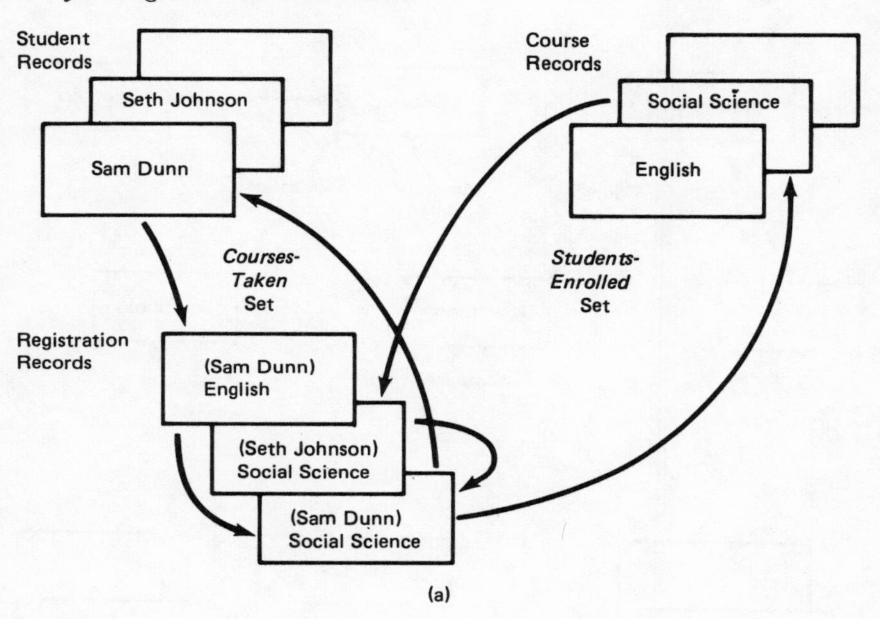

(a)

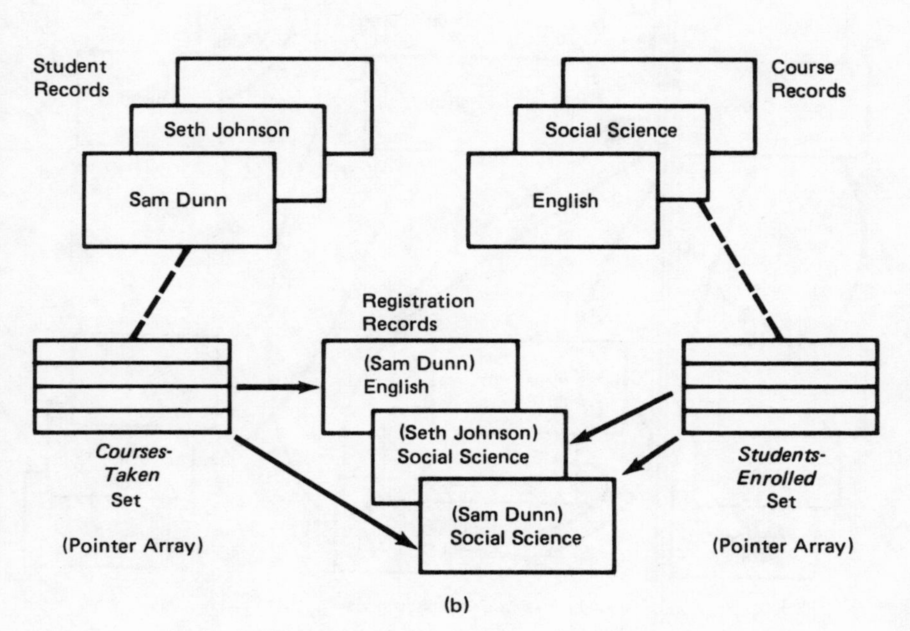

(b)

Figure 18: A network data structure for the school data model.

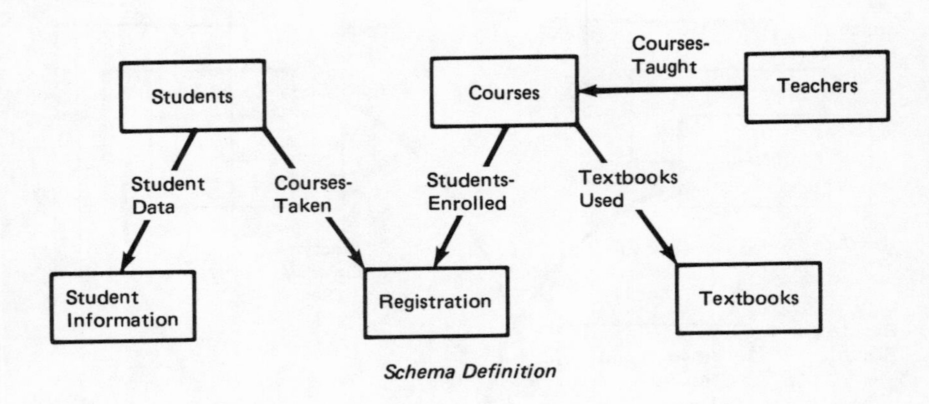

Schema Definition

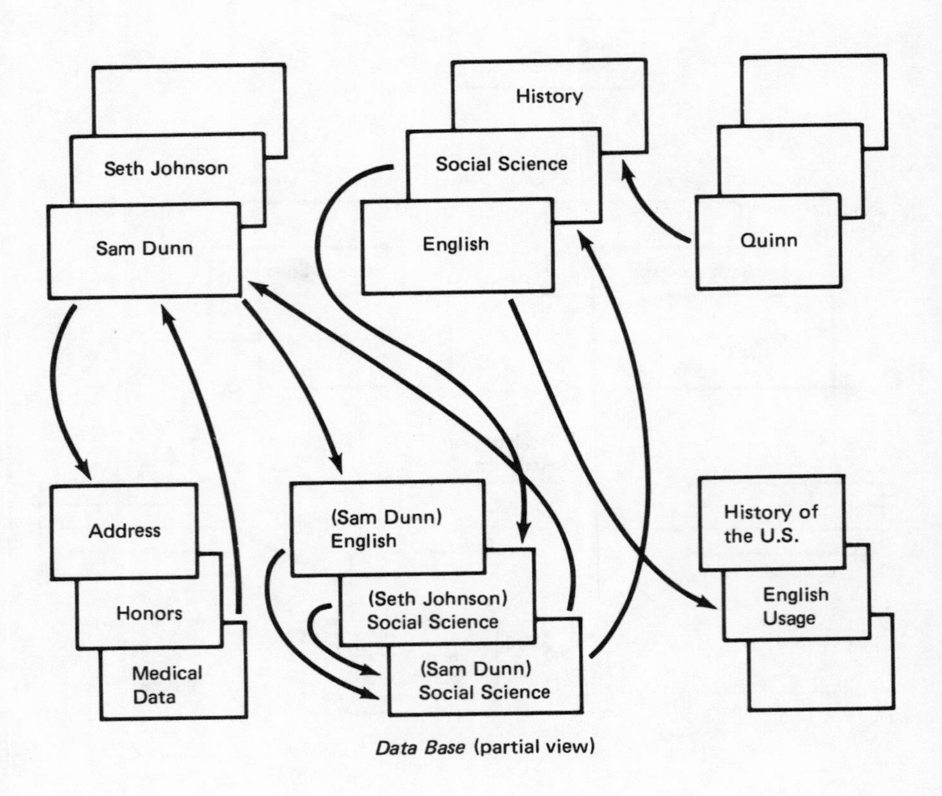

Data Base (partial view)

in one set type and a member in another set type). This rule would invalidate the *courses-taught* set type in Figure 18 because the *courses* record type occurs as a member of this set type but as an owner of two other set types (*students-enrolled* and *textbooks-used*). This type of a restriction is a departure from the CODASYL specifications for networks.

A *tree* or *hierarchical* data structure is one in which each record type is related to exactly one record type above it, except for one "root" record type, for which no higher record type exists. At each lower level in the tree there may be zero, one, or more record types related to a record type at the next higher level. A tree structure is illustrated in Figure 19.

The implication of the hierarchical view is that a record type can participate in one and only one hierarchy at a time so that it must be duplicated if needed in other hierarchies. (It should be noted that DBMS following the hierarchical model have means of circumventing this restriction. IBM's IMS, for example, uses logical relationships between hierarchies in order to avoid duplicating data. An example can be found in Chapter 3, Figure 12.) Trees can be derived in network structures; the opposite is not always true.

A *cyclic* structure results from defining a series of set types such that the owner record type of every set type is a member of the previous set type. An example is given in Figure 20. One difficulty in cyclic structures is determining "where to start" in loading records —that is, which record type is the "original" owner. The CODASYL solution uses "manual" membership, which is an option in defining a set type (for details, see the discussion of manual membership in the next section).

One additional structure is worth mentioning: a *recursive* structure. This is not to be confused with cyclic structures. A recursive structure results when the same two record types participate in two different set types, conserving the owner-member relationship but basing membership on different criteria. An example is given in Figure 21.

Recursive structures are sometimes called bill-of-material structures since their use is common among manufacturing applications. Although difficult in concept, the implementation of recursive structures is not overly complex, and support is widely available in both CODASYL and non-CODASYL DBMS.

Sets: Additional Considerations

Certain operations can be peformed on sets. These operations are illustrated here with examples from Figure 18.

Figure 19: A tree data structure for an organizational data base.

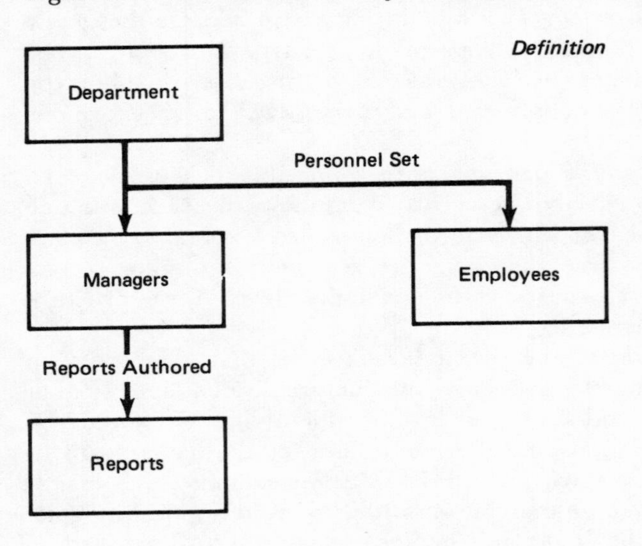

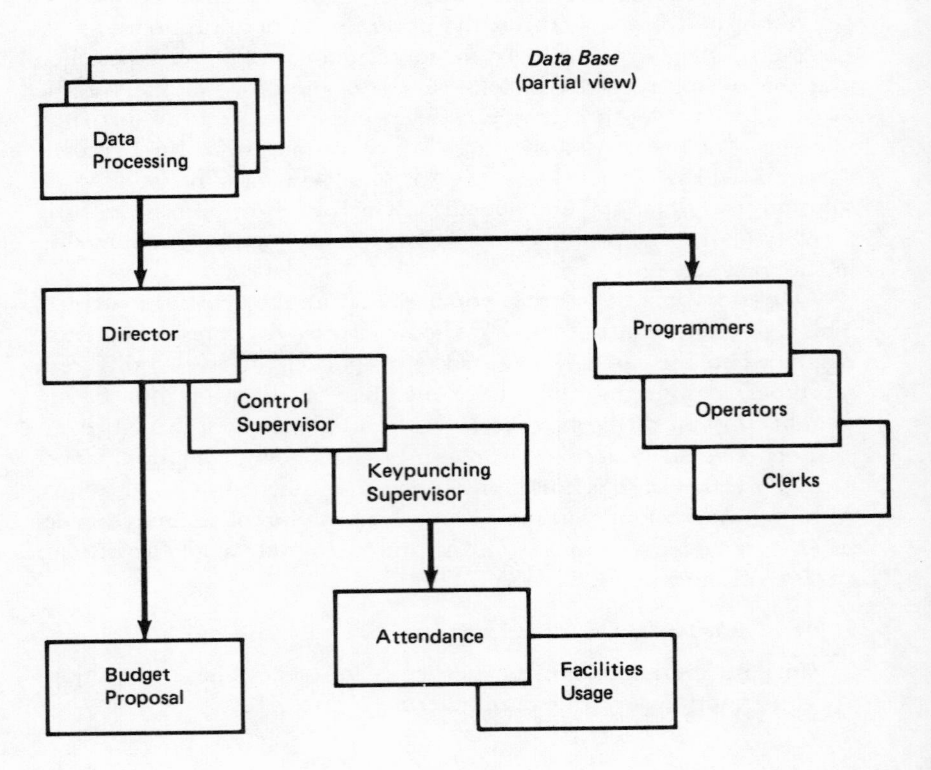

Figure 20: A cyclic data structure for an organizational data base.

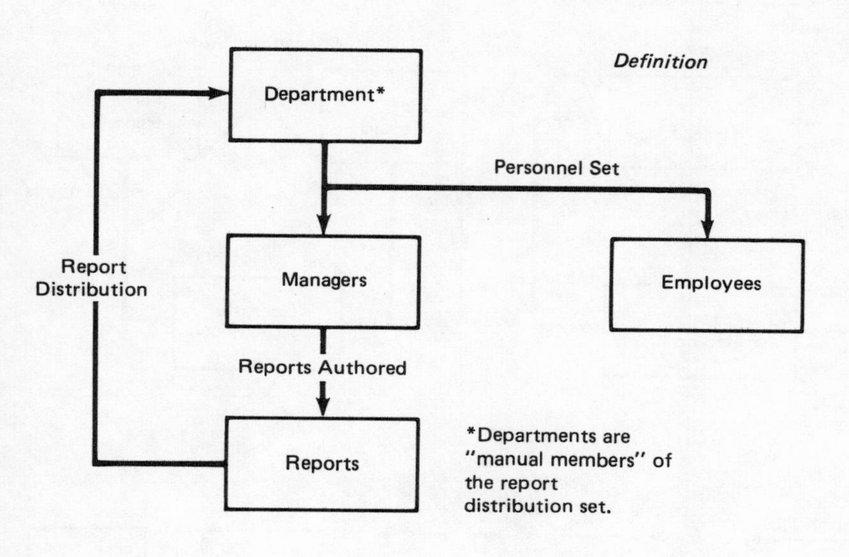

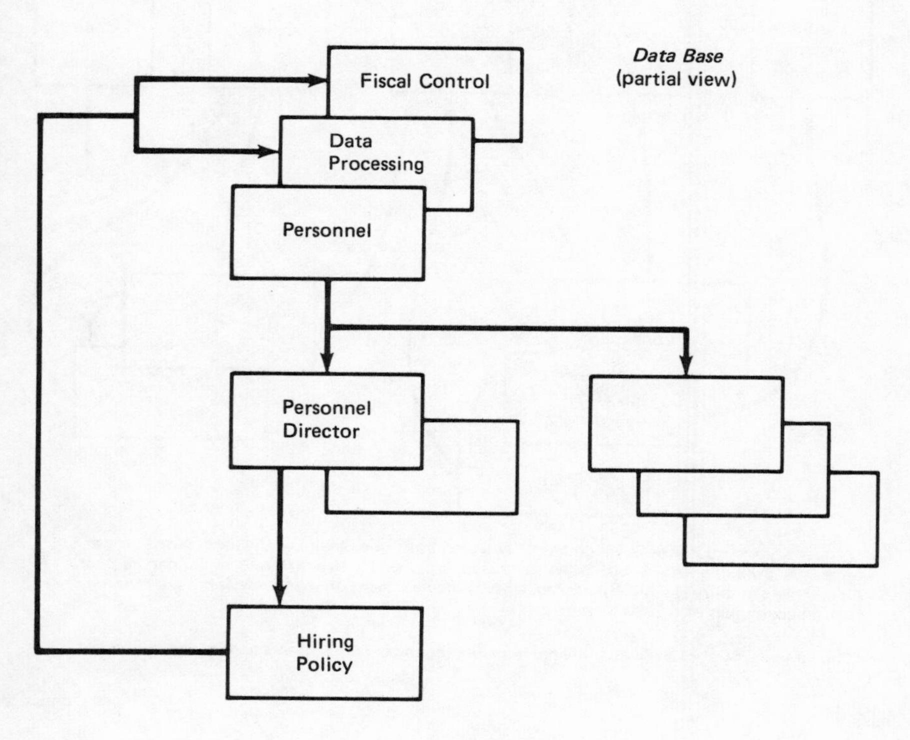

Figure 21: A recursive structure in a manufacturing application.

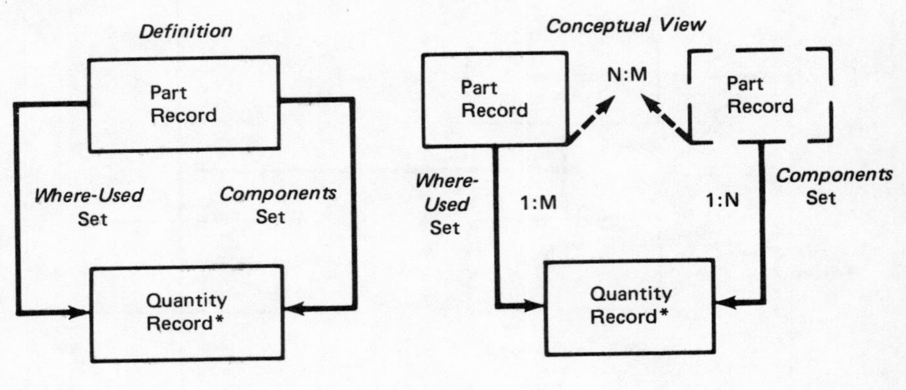

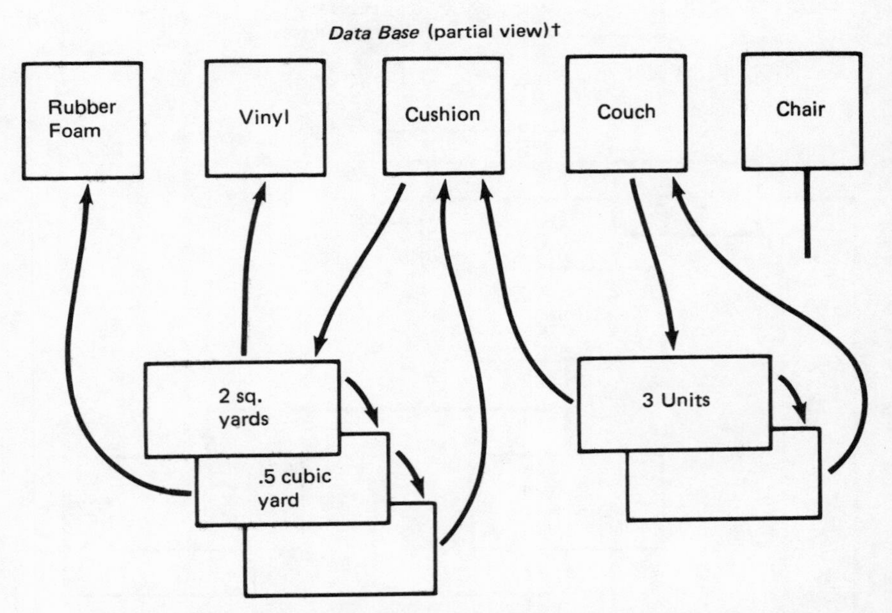

*A quantity record is always a member of two sets, both of which have the part record type as owner. A given quantity record, however, is always owned by two *different* actual part records. A recursive structure is basically a means of supporting a many-to-many relationship between record occurrences of the same type.

†Shown with member chains for the *components* set and owner pointers for the *where-used* set.

Operation	*Example*
Given an owner of a set, access the set's members.	The student is *Sam Dunn* (owner); his registration records are *English* and *social science* (members of the *courses-taken* set).
Given a member of a set, access other members of that set.	A registration record for *Sam Dunn* is *English;* another member is *social science.*
Given a member of a set, access the set's owner.	*History* is a member of the *courses-taught* set; *Quinn* is the *teacher* (owner).

Several additional observations on sets can be made. First, a set represents a one-to-many relationship (1:N) between records since there can be one and only one owner but many members. Where the relationship between records is many-to-many (N:M), a direct relationship cannot be expressed. Typically, two 1:N sets are needed, along with an additional record type. Such a relationship exists between student and course records in Figure 18; for it to be expressed, two one-to-many sets (*courses-taken* and *students-enrolled*) and an additional record type (*registration* records) are needed.

Second, it is often desirable that members of a set be in a specific order and, furthermore, that this order be maintained automatically by the DBMS. For example, it might be convenient for registration records in the *students-enrolled* set to be in alphabetical order of student name (this requires a reordering of the set shown in Figure 18) or for new courses within the *courses-taught* set to be added *first* in the list.

Finally, several special cases of set occurrences are possible. One case is a set without member record occurrences; this is called an *empty set.* For every given owner record occurrence there is always a set, even though that set may be "empty" of member records. Another case is a set type defined to have the *system* rather than an actual record type as its owner. Under this specification there can be one and only one occurrence of the set type, which is called a *singular set.*

The actual mechanics of a record's membership in a set is always the domain of the DBMS; that is, support for storage structures is transparent to the user. (This is simply an aspect of data independence.) At the logical level, however, there are several options in the specification of a set type that effect set membership. These options are discussed below with examples from Figure 18.

The first of these is *automatic* versus *manual* membership, which determines the *storage class* of the member. For automatic membership, the DBMS is required to make a record a member of an appropriate set at the time it is stored in the data base.

For example, it is probably desirable to make registration records automatic members of both the *courses-taken* and the *students-enrolled* set type. It follows that whenever a registration record is stored, it is automatically associated with a *courses-taken* and a *students-enrolled* set occurrence. It is important to note that appropriate owners for both set types must already exist in the data base if this operation is to be successful.

Manual membership, on the other hand, specifies that a record is to become a member of a set not when it is stored, but at some subsequent time when it is explicitly associated with a set by a user.

Manual membership would be appropriate for the *course* record within the *courses-taught* set type. Under this specification, an owner record (a teacher) need not exist when a member record (a course) is stored, but only later, when the given course is explicitly associated with a *courses-taught* set.

Referring back to cyclic structures and Figure 20, it now becomes apparent that at least one of the set types in the structure must have manual members. If all the set types had automatic members, then no record could be stored first, because its owner would already have to exist.

A second option is *mandatory* versus *optional* membership, which determines the *removal class* of the member. Mandatory membership specifies that once a record is associated with a set occurrence, it must always remain a member of that set, or of another set of the same type. A registration record would probably be a mandatory member of both the *courses-taken* and *students-enrolled* set types. Optional membership specifies that the user can not only change membership in particular set occurrences but disassociate a record from all sets of the given type. Optional membership would probably be appropriate for course records in the *courses-taught* set.

Accessing Data Base Records

In a CODASYL data base, every record type has a *location mode*—a specification of how records of that type are accessed. More precisely, the location mode describes the assignment of *data base keys* to records, uniquely one-for-one, at the time the record is stored in the data base. A record's data base key thus corresponds to a unique storage location. Although the data base key is not actually part of a record, it is often available to user program. It never changes so long as the record remains in the data base.

One of four location modes is specified for a record type:

DIRECT Data base keys are supplied by the user.

CALC A randomizing routine is used to store records; that is, record keys are transformed into data base keys.

VIA . . . SET Records are stored in such ways as to optimize their access with respect to sets of a named type (for example, a member is to be stored near its owner).

SYSTEM An implementor-defined method is used to store records.

In addition to these, at least one implementor has added an additional record location mode: INDEX-SEQUENTIAL. (There is actually a way to implement an indexed-sequential structure without this feature, but it is somewhat beyond the present discussion.) The advantage of indexed-sequential access is the compromise it effects between record "lookup" (that is, access to an individual record on the basis of given keys) and sequential access to all records of the given type. More on this topic and on access methods in general is presented in Chapter 9.

A compromise similar to the above can be easily effected using the concept of a singular set—a set type whose owner is SYSTEM. For example, a singular set can be defined to contain a member record type, whose location mode is CALC (randomized). This location mode controls the physical placement of records into the area. The set itself can be defined as SORTED by record keys, in particular by the same key that is used in randomizing. This specification results in a sequentially ordered set consisting of all records of the given type. Figure 22 illustrates these definitions.

It is important to note that "sequentially ordered" implies not *physical* order but rather physical support for a logical ordering. This usually means chaining the records in the sequential order. In summary, a singular set of randomized records can provide both lookup and sequential access on the basis of the same key.

Singular sets can be put to an additional use. An option in set definition allows a sorted set to be *indexed* on the basis of defined keys. Thus, a sorted singular set of all records of a given type can be organized by a secondary index, a means by which lookup and

Figure 22: Sequential access to randomized records, using a singular set.

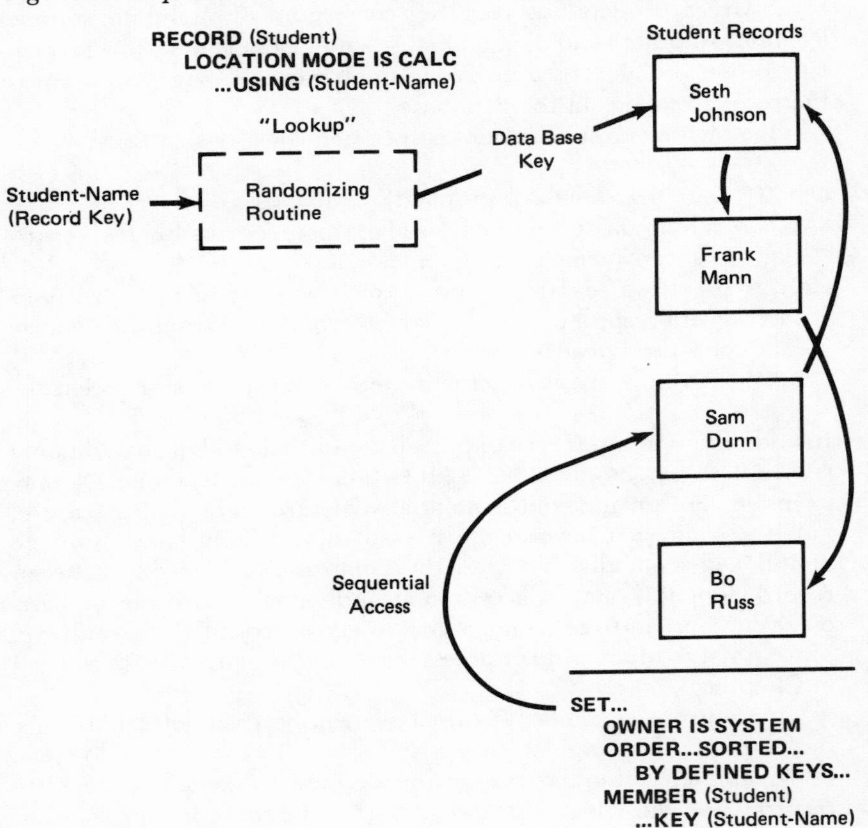

sequential access is possible on the basis of a nonprimary key. This facility is illustrated in Figure 23.

As with the previous example, there is again no *physical* ordering of the records, although logically sequential access is possible. This is, in fact, often the case with *sequential data structures* in the CODASYL specifications—a concept easily misinterpreted. It should be noted that current CODASYL systems by and large only recently began supporting singular sets and secondary indexing as described.

The discussion thus far has centered on access to records of a single given type. In a CODASYL data base, however, it is necessary to consider access to records with respect to records of other types—that is, on the basis of their membership in sets.

Figure 23: Indexing on a nonprimary key.

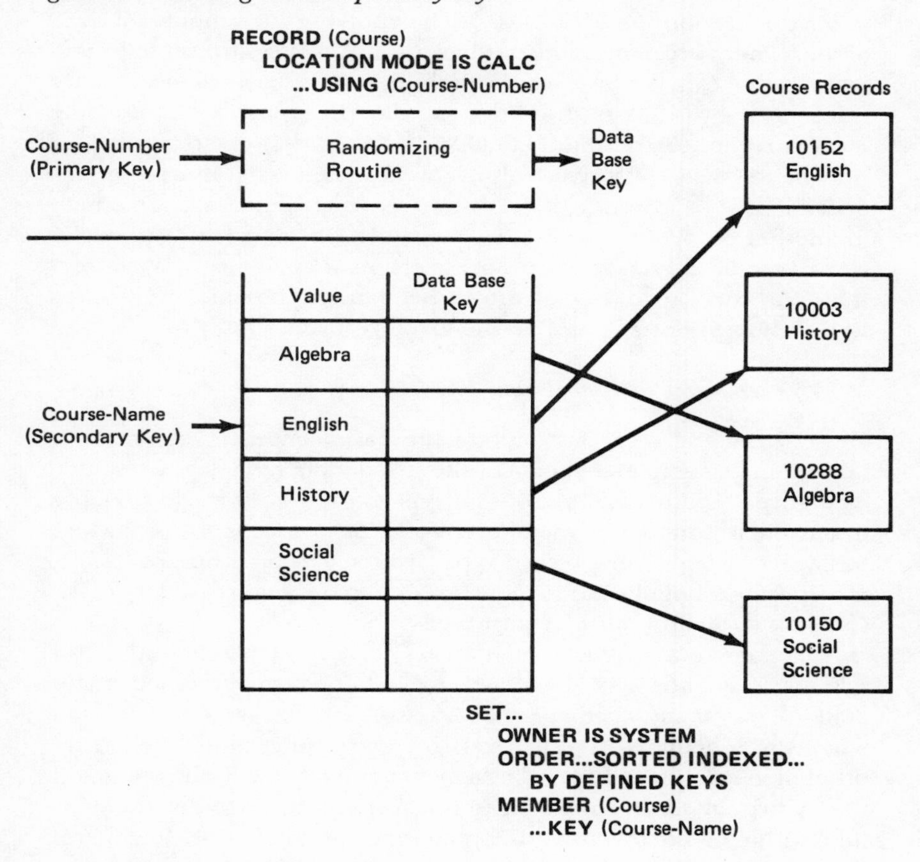

Associating an owner record occurrence with a set presents no problem; by definition, the occurrence of an owner implies the occurrence of the associated set type. For members, however, it becomes necessary to determine with which of all possible owners the given record occurrence is properly associated. This process, which is actually one of finding the owner, is called *set selection.* Every member record type of every set type defined in the schema must have a SET SELECTION clause. Set selection is not to be confused with record location modes; the former has to do with *relating* records and the latter with *placing* records into storage.

There are several relatively straightforward means of set selection. For example, for singular sets (one set occurrence only), set selection is by SYSTEM, since membership is obvious. Where the owner is defined to have a location mode of CALC, then supplying the unique CALC-KEY of the owner (a responsibility of the run-unit) suffices for set selection. Set selection can also be effected on the basis of the last set occurrence referenced by the run-unit (that is, the program can choose the set occurrence) by defining CURRENT OF SET in the schema entry.

The SET SELECTION clause also allows for somewhat more complex operations. For example, if an owner record type is itself a member in another set type (and so on), then several owners for a particular record can be chosen at once. This selection of an owner of a member that is in turn an owner of a member (and so on) may be likened to the choosing of a "path" to the given record.

A Schema for the School Data Model

Set selection is the last among the basic concepts necessary for developing a complete schema of the school data model, as presented in Figure 24. An example of the type of "path" set selection just discussed is found for members of the *students-enrolled* set, which has as its owner a new record type, (course) *sections.* Figure 24 also incorporates singular set types (presented in Figures 22 and 23) for the *student* and *course* record types, respectively.

One new entry type that appears in several places within the schema is *privacy locks.* Two such locks have been specified in the SCHEMA statement. One specifies a password that must be supplied when the schema is used (copied) for processing a subschema; the other invokes a procedure to be run when the schema itself is changed. Other privacy locks appear in the *student* record entry, in the *grade* item within *registration* records, and in the *courses-taken* set. In general, the privacy lock facility provides a greater degree of control over specified operations with regard to the data base.

Using the Data Base

The schema DDL, which creates the data base, is readily identified with the most basic form of data independence: the separation of program logic from data definition. Users need not be concerned with the physical organization of data or with access method per se. The schema DDL is independent of all other languages and creates a data base available to many users for a variety of purposes. The *subschema* DDL, which is likewise independent of other languages, refines that data independence to the level of the individual user.

Figure 24: A schema for the school data model.

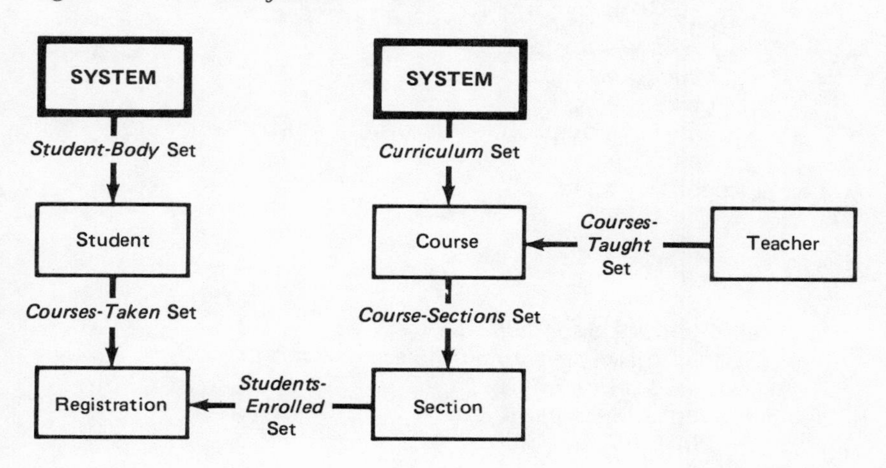


```
SCHEMA NAME IS SCHOOL;
    PRIVACY LOCK FOR COPY IS 'PASSWORD';
    PRIVACY LOCK FOR ALTER IS PROCEDURE SECURITY-CHECK.
AREA NAME IS SCHOOL-AREA.

RECORD NAME IS STUDENT;
    LOCATION MODE IS CALC USING LAST-NAME, FIRST-NAME,
        DUPLICATES ARE NOT ALLOWED;
    WITHIN SCHOOL-AREA;
    PRIVACY LOCK FOR DELETE IS 'DELETE-PASSWORD'.
    02 STUDENT-NAME.
        03 LAST-NAME; PIC. . .
        03 FIRST-NAME; PIC. . .
    .
    .
    .

RECORD NAME IS COURSE;
    LOCATION MODE IS CALC USING COURSE-NO
        DUPLICATES ARE NOT ALLOWED;
    WITHIN SCHOOL-AREA.
    02 COURSE-NO; PIC. . .
    02 COURSE-NAME; PIC. . .
    .
    .
    .
```

```
RECORD NAME IS REGISTRATION;
    LOCATION MODE IS VIA COURSES-TAKEN SET;
    WITHIN SCHOOL-AREA.
    02 STUD-NAME; PIC. . .
    02 GRADE; PIC. . .
        PRIVACY LOCK FOR GET IS 'GRADE-WORD'.
    02 PERIOD; PIC. . .
    02 COMMENT; PIC. . .
    .
    .
    .

RECORD NAME IS SECTION;
    LOCATION MODE IS VIA COURSE-SECTIONS SET;
    WITHIN SCHOOL-AREA.
    02 SECTION-NUMBER; PIC. . .
    .
    .
    .

RECORD NAME IS TEACHER;
    LOCATION MODE IS CALC USING TEACHER-NO
        DUPLICATES ARE NOT ALLOWED;
    WITHIN SCHOOL-AREA.
    02 TEACHER-NO; PIC. . .
    02 TEACHER-NAME; PIC. . .
    .
    .
    .

SET NAME IS STUDENT-BODY;
    OWNER IS SYSTEM;
    ORDER IS PERMANENT SORTED BY DEFINED KEYS
        DUPLICATES ARE NOT ALLOWED.
    MEMBER IS STUDENT MANDATORY AUTOMATIC;
        KEY IS ASCENDING STUDENT-NAME;
        SET SELECTION IS THRU STUDENT-BODY
            OWNER IDENTIFIED BY SYSTEM.

SET NAME IS CURRICULUM;
    OWNER IS SYSTEM;
    ORDER IS PERMANENT SORTED INDEXED BY DEFINED KEYS
        DUPLICATES ARE NOT ALLOWED.
    MEMBER IS COURSE MANDATORY AUTOMATIC;
        KEY IS ASCENDING COURSE-NAME;
        SET SELECTION IS THRU CURRICULUM
            OWNER IDENTIFIED BY SYSTEM.
```

```
SET NAME IS COURSES-TAKEN;
    OWNER IS STUDENT;
    ORDER IS PERMANENT SORTED BY DEFINED KEYS
        DUPLICATES ARE NOT ALLOWED.
    MEMBER IS REGISTRATION MANDATORY AUTOMATIC
        LINKED TO OWNER;
        KEY IS ASCENDING PERIOD;
        SET SELECTION IS THRU COURSES-TAKEN
            OWNER IDENTIFIED BY CALC-KEY.

SET NAME IS COURSE-SECTIONS;
    OWNER IS COURSE;
    ORDER IS PERMANENT SORTED BY DEFINED KEYS
        DUPLICATES ARE NOT ALLOWED.
    MEMBER IS SECTION MANDATORY AUTOMATIC;
        KEY IS ASCENDING SECTION-NUMBER;
        SET SELECTION IS THRU COURSE-SECTIONS
        OWNER IDENTIFIED BY CALC-KEY.

SET NAME IS STUDENTS-ENROLLED;
    OWNER IS SECTION;
    ORDER IS PERMANENT SORTED BY DEFINED KEYS
        DUPLICATES ARE NOT ALLOWED.
    MEMBER IS REGISTRATION MANDATORY AUTOMATIC
        LINKED TO OWNER;
        KEY IS ASCENDING STUD-NAME;
        SET SELECTION FOR STUDENTS-ENROLLED
            IS THRU COURSE-SECTIONS
                OWNER IDENTIFIED BY CALC-KEY
            THEN THRU STUDENTS-ENROLLED WHERE
                OWNER IDENTIFIED BY SECTION-NUMBER.

SET NAME IS COURSES-TAUGHT;
    OWNER IS TEACHER;
    ORDER IS PERMANENT IMMATERIAL;
        PRIVACY LOCK FOR REMOVE IS 'TEACH-WORD'.
    MEMBER IS COURSE OPTIONAL MANUAL;
        SET SELECTION IS THRU COURSES-TAUGHT
            OWNER IDENTIFIED BY CALC-KEY.
```

The Subschema

A subschema, as the name suggests, represents that subset of the overall schema appropriate to a given user (or rather, to that user's program). For a given schema, therefore, there can be an arbitrary number of subschemas—as many as one for each user.

By restricting the user to a subset of all the record types and set types in the data base, not only is user access made simpler, but the rest of the data base is protected from misuse. In addition, user programs are to a degree insulated from *changes* in the schema since changes can often be accommodated within the data mapping that the DBMS performs between schema and subschema (that is, between data base and user program). In other words, if the schema changes but the subschema does not, the new mapping often makes the changes transparent to the user.

What type of data mapping can be performed? Already mentioned was the capacity for eliminating record and set types. The *composition* of individual records can be modified through automatic reordering of data items, by omission of items, by various changes in the "picture" of an item, or even by the creation of new (derived) items. Additional *control* over data retrieval can be achieved; for example, additional privacy locks and changes for set selection can be specified.

An additional feature of the data mapping is that it renders the data base more compatible with the language chosen for data manipulation. This language, which is procedural, need not necessarily be COBOL.

Thus, in contrast to the schema DDL, the subschema DDL is oriented toward a particular user language. This is to say that it takes on something of the character and syntax of the given data manipulation "host" language—in fact, it is considered an *extension* of that language. From this it follows that there is not just one subschema DDL but rather one for each user language. The COBOL subschema DDL was the first to be developed; progress in developing subschema DDL for other languages, especially FORTRAN, has been made.

An example of a COBOL subschema for the school data model is presented in Figure 25. It is important to note that even though the subschema itself is specifically a COBOL subschema, it is nonetheless an independent entity.

The elements shown in the figure are those required for the production of class lists; record and set types not shown are not necessary in this process. The *Stud-in-Section* record is actually the

Figure 25: A COBOL subschema for producing class lists from the school data base.

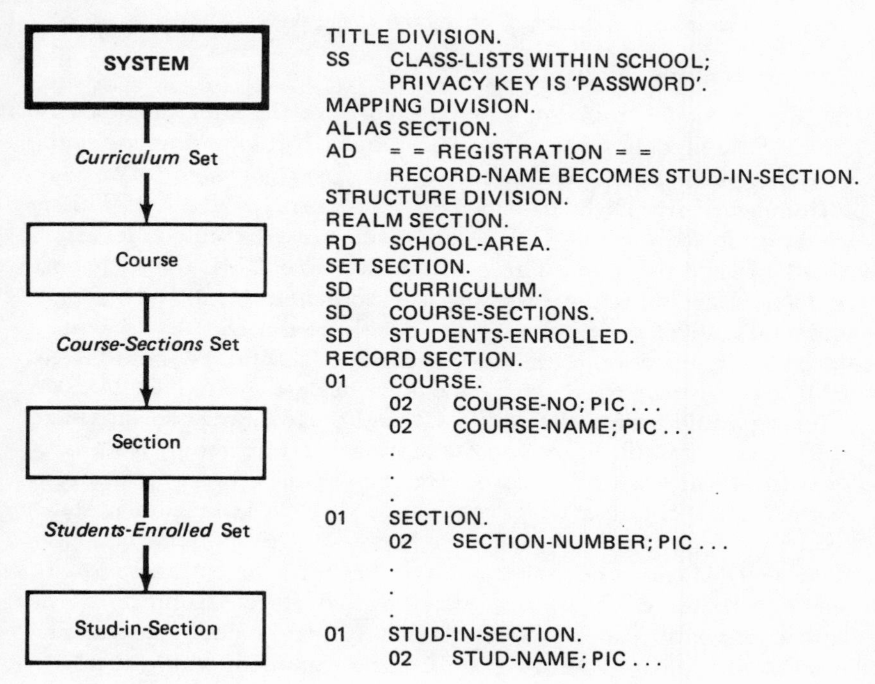

registration record, although it has been renamed in this use.

The subschema (named CLASS LISTS) shown in Figure 25 implements the desired view of the school data structure for a user program. All data items except the student name (STUD-NAME) have been omitted from the *Stud-in-Section* record.

How is a subschema invoked? For a given COBOL program, the name of one and only one subschema is specified in a special area of the DATA DIVISION, namely in the SUB-SCHEMA SECTION. In the subschema, the name of the schema is given so that the correspondence between program, subschema, and schema is established. This correspondence is subsequently followed in the data mapping performed to and from the data base by the data base control system (DBCS).

The actual "fixing" of the correspondence is a process called *binding*. Binding may be thought of as a tying together of the specific data types required by the program with data as physically stored in the data base. It can occur during compilation of the program, during compilation of the subschema, during execution of the program, or at other times prior to data access.

Data Manipulation

In contrast to both the schema DDL and the subschema DDL, the CODASYL data manipulation language (DML) is not an independent language but rather depends on a *host language* to provide a framework from which data base access can be effected. This is to say that the various DML statements must be embedded in a host language program. There is naturally one DML for each host language, and as is the case with the subschema DDL, the syntax and character of the host language is reflected in DML statements.

So far there is only one DML, that for COBOL. A FORTRAN DML is being developed, and others have been suggested. CODASYL thinking would prefer that the DML be supported directly in language compilers, but until recently, most support was effected by *pre-processors.* A pre-processor is a program that scans user code prior to compilation, replacing DML commands with CALLs or similar statements.

The DML is to be understood as record-level interaction with the data base. Records are retrieved and stored, subject to the restrictions of the program's subschema. As mentioned, the subschema is invoked by a COBOL program using a statement within the DATA DIVISION:

```
DATA DIVISION.
SUB-SCHEMA SECTION.
DB CLASS-LISTS WITHIN SCHOOL.
```

A privacy key is supplied if required by the subschema. The effect of the DB statement is normally to bring the data description specified in the subschema into the program so that the data names can be referenced by the DML within the PROCEDURE DIVISION. At the same time, buffer space is established for input and output of the data base records.

From the standpoint of programming, data definition per se is therefore of no concern. The bulk of attention focuses on the PROCEDURE DIVISION, where the framework for interaction with the data base is established. The following are the commands specified for the COBOL DML.

READY The DBCS is instructed to prepare one or more realms (areas) for processing.

FIND A specific record occurrence is sought, subject to certain conditions (that is, a record selection expression is used to establish "position" in the data base).

GET All or a portion of a data base record on which position was previously established is requested; the record is made available to the run-unit.

MODIFY The content of a given record and/or its membership in given sets is changed.

STORE A record is placed into the data base.

ERASE A record is deleted from the data base, and, if it is the owner of a set, possibly certain of the members are deleted.

CONNECT An existing data base record is made a member of one or more appropriate sets.

DISCONNECT The membership of a data base record in one or more sets is canceled.

ORDER Members of a set are reordered; depending on the option specified and restrictions in the schema, the reordering can be permanent.

IF Certain conditions related to the data base are tested—for example, whether a set is empty or whether a record is a set member.

USE Special procedures are specified for execution in case a data base exception condition occurs or a privacy key is needed for an operation.

ACCEPT The contents of specified currency indicators are accessed (that is, the run-unit is informed of its "position").

KEEP A record is placed into extended monitored mode, whereby the run-unit can be informed of updating by other run-units (monitored mode is discussed later in this section).

FREE One or more records are released from the extended monitored mode.

REMONITOR A period of monitoring for one or more records is ended and a new one begun.

FINISH The DBCS is instructed that the run-unit has completed its use of one or more realms.

Much of the nature of data manipulation under the CODASYL specifications can be understood by looking at the following areas.

Record selection expressions. A record selection expression is a means of defining the criteria to be used in locating a record under the FIND command. There are seven general expression types:

1. The run-unit supplies the data base key of the desired record.
2. The run-unit supplies the value(s) necessary to access a randomized (CALC) record.

3. A record of a given type in a named set type is sought with values of given items equal to those of a previously accessed record in that set type (that is, a duplicate is sought).
4. The position of a desired record (in a set or a realm) relative to the current record is specified (for example, NEXT).
5. The current record is sought, for a given record type, set type, and realm.
6. The owner of a set of a given type is sought.
7. A record of a given type within a set is desired, optionally with values equal to those of a previously accessed record. (In some systems the values need not equal those of any previously accessed record.)

Status indicators. The execution of a DML command causes the DBCS to return a code indicating the outcome of the desired action. If the action was successful, a value of zero is returned; if not, codes indicating the type of the erring statement and the type of error encountered are returned. (This is called a *data base exception condition.)* In the event of such error, the name of the realm, the set type, the record type, and other information is often made available to the run-unit.

An application program can establish standard procedures for handling exceptions by USE statements within the DECLARATIVES portion of the PROCEDURE DIVISION. For example, the statement:

USE FOR DB-EXCEPTION ON '0502400'

followed by one or more processing statements establishes a procedure to be executed should the DBCS be unable to locate a record satisfying the given record selection expression in a FIND command. It is important to note that this condition may or may not have been anticipated; that is, it may or may not represent a failure of the program.

Currency indicators. One of the functions performed by the DBCS is the maintaining of currency indicators for the run-unit. These indicators may be thought of as defining "position" in the data base. An executing program (run-unit) has an indicator for each realm, one for each set type, and one for each record type to which it may have access under a given subschema. There is also an indicator for the run-unit itself.

The value of currency indicators changes as appropriate for the successful execution of given DML commands and their options; it consists of the data base key for the "current" record within each indicator type. A run-unit accesses currency values using the ACCEPT command. The current record of the run-unit can often be the implied object of certain DML commands.

Monitored mode. The concept of a monitored mode arises from the sharing of the central data base by two or more run-units. It is a means of preventing the loss of data integrity that would occur should several run-units attempt to update the same record at the same time.

Unlike most current DBMS, the CODASYL specifications do not call for record locking, but rather specify that run-unit is to be *informed* of an access conflict. That is, should a run-unit read a record and then try to update it, the update will be rejected if another run-unit has updated that record in the meantime. A data base exception condition occurs, information about the "other" update is made available, and the run-unit must take appropriate action. The record itself is said to be in monitored mode (the current record of the run-unit is always in monitored mode).

More than one record can be monitored if necessary using the KEEP command, which places the current record into *extended monitored mode.* Records can be released from this mode using the FREE command. Periods of monitoring for records are ended and renewed using the REMONITOR command.

Device Media Control Language

The device media control language (DMCL) is a language specified to be independent of other data base languages (in particular the schema DDL) so that the physical aspects of data storage can be separated from logical definition. In practice, a DMCL (which is always implementor-defined) serves to map areas into files known to the operating system. For this reason, the DMCL is often incorporated into the control language for the hardware line.

Why the data base itself might be segregated into distinct areas is a topic that has not been covered in this presentation; for example, in the school data structure (Figure 24) only one area was used. Generally cited as reasons for dividing the data base into areas are enhanced security and various performance improvements. Subdivision can also be used to lessen operational costs; for example, data that are seldom accessed can be placed on slower devices.

THE HISTORY AND FUTURE OF CODASYL

The Conference on Data Systems Languages (CODASYL) is composed of representatives from computer manufacturers and users, whose goal since its formation in 1959 has been the creation of standardized languages for data management. CODASYL is perhaps best known for its development of COBOL (Common Business-Oriented Language), which contributed tremendously to the evolution of computing during the 1960s. The scope of COBOL and of CODASYL itself has advanced significantly since these early beginnings; during the 1970s, it has focused increasingly on data base management.

The concept central to the CODASYL effort, whether for COBOL or for data base management, is that *standardization* of user languages is crucial to productivity within the industry. Standardized languages provide natural bridges between hardware generations and between the configurations of different hardware manufacturers. It means that application systems are *portable*—that is, that the investment in application programming is not inextricably tied to the survival of any given machine. It also envisions that application programmers, once trained, can produce application code irrespective of changes in hardware lines. These considerations come under the general category of *machine independence.*

CODASYL is not a government agency; its specifications do not carry the weight of law. Other organizations—primarily the American National Standards Institute (also not government-associated) and the National Bureau of Standards within the U.S. Department of Commerce—are typically responsible for the creation of standards in the United States. The former of these is responsible for ANS COBOL, which has become the industry standard. Similar action has not been taken on the data base management proposals, although both groups are active in the area. There is also considerable international interest in standardization, evidenced by international contributions to the CODASYL effort.

CODASYL and Data Base Management

The vehicle for CODASYL proposals is the *Journal of Development* (*JOD*), which is issued periodically (approximately once every two years) and is definitive for language specifications. There are actually separate *JOD*s for data description and for data manipulation: the *CODASYL Data Description Language JOD* and the *CODASYL COBOL JOD.* As the name of the latter suggests, its specifications cover the entire COBOL language, and only in the most recent issue (1976) have language proposals for data base interfacing been included. Also included in the 1976 *COBOL JOD* were the initial proposals for a subschema language.

The first *CODASYL Data Description Language JOD*, which sets forth the language specifications for schema definition, was produced in June 1973. By many accounts, however, an earlier work, the April 1971 *Data Base Task Group* (DBTG) *Report*, was the actual watershed for the development of the specifications. This report generated considerable interest in the industry, and at least two existing implementations were begun in its wake.

The report covers data manipulation language and subschema definition, in addition to the data description language. There were many influences in the development of the report (the report itself had an important predecessor in 1969); the most significant are considered to be the I-D-S DBMS and one of its chief architects, Charles Bachman.

The work of CODASYL is done by committee; these committees have been organized since 1974 in the form shown in Figure 26. The two committees on the left are responsible for the respective *JOD*s mentioned earlier.

Significantly, the Data Description Language Committee was formed in 1971, some months after the release of the April 1971 report. Its status as equal with the Programming Langaage Committee is consistent with its charter: to develop specifications for a common DDL *independent* of any programming language.

The FORTRAN DML Committee, newly created in 1974, has as its purpose the creation of specifications for a FORTRAN DML interface, using existing American National FORTRAN Standards.

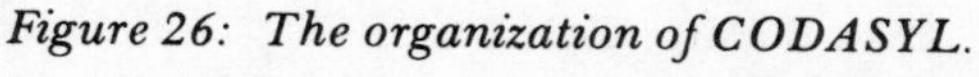

Figure 26: The organization of CODASYL.

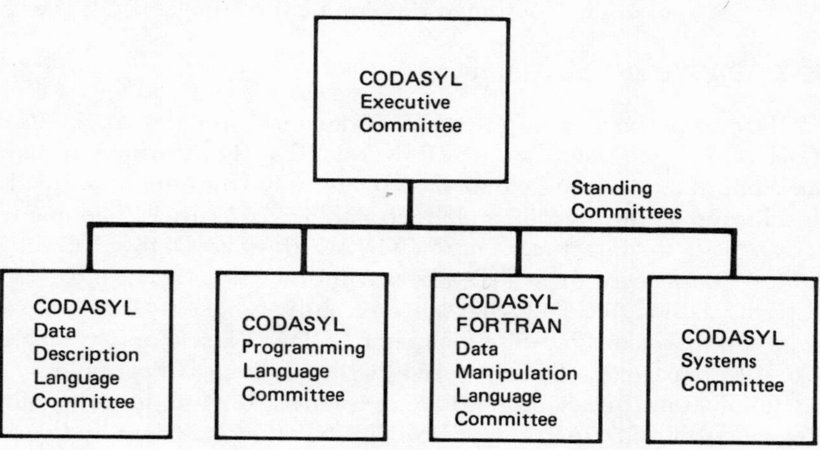

The fourth group, the Systems Committee, is officially charged with the development of languages and techniques for automating as much as possible the tasks of systems analysis, design, and implementation. It is responsible for one recent work of interest, entitled *Selection and Acquisition of Data Base Management Systems* (March 1976).

Two new committees have recently been chartered; they are the End Users Facilities (EUF) Committee and the Common Operating System Control Language (COSCL) Committee. The former has as its purpose the development of facilities to allow untrained users to interact naturally with computerized data bases. The COSCL Committee aims at developing specifications for a standardized job control language.

Each of the CODASYL committees creates ad hoc task groups as their need becomes apparent. These task groups include the following:

Data Description Language Committee (DDLC)
- Sub-schema Task Group (SSTG)
- Purpose: The continued development of subschema facilities
- Data Base Administration Working Group (DBAWG)
- Purpose: The development of facilities for data base administration (for instance, development of a DMCL). (DBAWG is based in the United Kingdom and is associated with the British Computer Society.)

Programming Language Committee (PLC)
- Data Base Language Task Group (DBLTG)
- Purpose: The continued development of the COBOL DML.

CODASYL and the Future

Two organizations opposed the endorsement of the April 1971 *Data Base Task Group Report*: IBM and RCA. The former to date has continued to keep its data base focus away from the CODASYL specifications; the latter is no longer within the industry. The major CODASYL manufacturers are UNIVAC with its DMS 1100 and DMS/90; H.I.S. with its I-D-S/I and the new I-D-S/II; and DEC with its DBMS-10. DEC has also recently released DBMS-11, a mini-DBMS for its PDP-11. One major CODASYL system is available for IBM hardware: IDMS, offered by the Cullinane Corporation.

Of manufacturers other than the above, Burroughs originally marketed the CODASYL-like DM6700 but now has departed with

DMS-II. Xerox offered EDMS, a system acquired by H.I.S. upon Xerox's exit from the industry. CDC has struck out on a course of its own with DMS-170, which shows similarities with, but also departures from, the specifications. Of the mini-manufacturers, only DEC and PRIME Computers have thus far released CODASYL-like systems (1976 and 1977, respectively), although a number of others have begun to come out with significant data management facilities.

Since about 1970 a number of independent software companies have marketed DBMS, particularly for IBM hardware. This development was made possible by IBM's unbundling in the 1960's, a move that was followed by all manufacturers except UNIVAC and has contributed significantly to vitality in the software marketplace. Most notable among the DBMS independents are Cincom Systems (with TOTAL), MRI Corporation (with SYSTEM 2000), Cullinane Corporation (with IDMS), and Software AG (with ADABAS). Several other independents have also had recent successes, but Cullinane's IDMS remains the sole major CODASYL DBMS for IBM hardware.

In looking at the IBM user base, it quickly becomes evident that DBMS usage is overwhelmingly non-CODASYL. This is certainly one factor in the lack of official standardization to date under the CODASYL specifications. A number of other factors are also often cited, among them the fear that hardware advances will render the proposed standards obsolete within a short period and that adoption of the standards would thus retard evolution within the industry. This point is debatable.

Another factor is the increasing influence of the relational model, which after a somewhat slow start now seems to be gaining acceptance. Whether the CODASYL standards can be made compatible with a relational view is an open question. (There are efforts in this direction among actual DBMS implementors, for example, CDC and H.I.S. The relational model, which seems to have the attention of IBM, is discussed in detail in the next chapter.)

Finally, it should be noted that significant portions of the specifications have been officially defined only recently—as late as 1976 for the COBOL DML and subschema facility—and that development within CODASYL continues. Standardization is necessarily a slow process, and sure footing is required at each step of the way

The CODASYL specifications produce workable systems; this has been proven by many successful data base systems under existing CODASYL DBMS. One criticism certainly appropriate, however, is that the specifications are too dependent on COBOL, a language noted for neither its brevity nor its syntactical power.

Put simply, there is a feeling that monolithic COBOL systems are not exactly the wave of the future. Desirable substitutes are interfaces to many languages rather than to COBOL alone, in particular to high-level, user-oriented language facilities. (This latter is an area where the relational model is particularly strong.)

A second, and related, criticism is that the navigational access required to negotiate a network structure (particularly a physically linked structure) is at once too complex and too restrictive. It is complex in the sense that undue structural awareness is required on the part of the user; it is restrictive because of path dependence. Physically supported paths are highly favored; unanticipated "paths" are not.

CODASYL is aware of the criticisms and is moving to act on them. One particularly interesting area is the continuing development of the subschema concept, which, since it is oriented toward individual users, is in an ideal place to support user-specific enhancement of data retrieval. For example, a record type might be defined that actually represents a concatenation of records (or data items) from the data base. Such a device simplifies user processing and begins to provide a degree of structural independence.

In actual DBMS implementations there is growing support for full subschema capability, an area somewhat neglected in the past. In other areas, various CODASYL groups are working toward a FORTRAN interface and toward end-user facilities, such as a self-contained DML (a query language).

There is some effort to make the DDL, which is supposed to be independent of other languages, less COBOL-like. Several implementors—among them UNIVAC, H.I.S., and Cullinane—have begun to move toward support for inversion so that improved query facilities are to be expected from several actual systems.

The future of the CODASYL specifications in an unbundled and diverse industry is at this time an open question. Undoubtedly they have provided an important forum for both the discussion of standardization and the evolution of data base thinking; but as yet there is no official adoption. Whether or not this development comes to pass, the CODASYL specifications are certain to remain a major influence on the data base field for years to come.

APPENDIX

CODASYL Terminology: A Quick Look

schema—the description of the data base and its structure and content, using data description language (DDL) entries.
data base—interrelated data under a given schema.
subschema—a description of the data base, or of a portion thereof, as appropriate for one or more given users.
area—a named collection of records (corresponding in most cases to a file).
realm—a named logical subdivision of the data base; an area (or file) as it is known in a subschema.
record type—a named collection of data items or data aggregate types.
record—an occurrence of a record type.
data aggregate—an occurrence of a named collection of data items within a record (for example, a repeating group).
data item—an occurrence of the smallest unit of named data.
set type—a named collection of records, with one and only one owner record type and one or more member record types.
set—an occurrence of a set type.
owner—the record that owns a set; a set has one and only one owner.
member—in a set, records other than the owner; a set can have zero, one, or more occurrences of each of the member record types.
empty set—a set that has no members (all sets have at least an owner).
singular set—a set type defined to have the DBMS (SYSTEM) as owner so that only one set occurrence is possible.
network—a data structure characterized by the membership of records in sets, as owners and members.
alias—the renaming of an area (realm), set type, or record type in a subschema (the alias is known to the user).
data base key—a unique identifier for a record, corresponding to a storage location.
CALC—randomized access to records of a given type.
VIA—storage of records of a given type in such a way as to optimize access through a given set.
data base procedure—a special computation required for a specific data base (for example, for checking privacy keys).
privacy lock—a value or a procedure which, as specified in the schema (and subject to the subschema), is used to check user passwords for specific operations.
privacy key—a password (or other appropriate data) applied to a privacy lock (usually by a run-unit).
run-unit—the execution of a program.
DBCS—the data base control system—that portion of the DBMS which actively (and centrally) supports user access to the data base(s).

currency—data base position with respect to realms, set types, and record types. Currency indicators are kept by the DBCS for each run-unit.

DMCL—the device media control language—a language that, independently of the DDL, is used to map data onto storage media.

CODASYL Notation

Charles Bachman is generally credited with developing the graphic notation for CODASYL-like data structures. This notation has two basic components.

Student

A rectangle denotes a record type in the data base. A record type is assumed to have zero, one, or more occurrences (records).

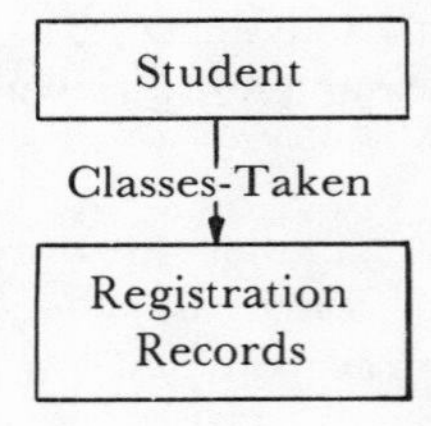

An arrow connecting two or more record types denotes a set type in the data base. Set types are likewise assumed to have zero, one, or more occurrences (sets). The tail of the arrow denotes the owner; the head(s), the member(s).

Chapter 6

DATA BASE MANAGEMENT: NEW DIRECTIONS

In this chapter, several of the most significant areas of development in data base technology are presented. Although the impact of these developments has not yet been felt by the user community on a large scale, data base systems prevalent in the 1980s will certainly feature as a matter of course much of what is discussed here.

The first area of development to be discussed is the relational model; following that, the topics of mini-DBMS, back-end processors, and distributed data base systems are reviewed.

THE RELATIONAL MODEL

A point of departure for the relational model from traditional systems is that the complexity of storage structures is kept to a minimum. In theory, a data file in a relational system consists of a table of records, each of which may consist of one or more data elements, but without repeating groups (for instance, an OCCURS in COBOL). Data structuring, if it can be said to exist at all, is closely associated with data modeling. It does not assume the significance that it has in traditional DBMS.

The concept basic to interrelating data arises from the fact that the same element may appear in several different files. These files can be mapped together on the basis of the common element in order to produce new informational formats. Considerable attention in relational systems is directed toward providing the user with powerful high-level languages that can be used to effect this mapping.

In contrast to traditional DBMS, particularly physically linked DBMS, the interrelating of data takes place largely during execution rather than before execution of a program. A pure relational system would be notably devoid of pointers and other types of fixed linkages.

The relational model is revolutionary in concept and to many delimits new territory in the development of data independence.

In the discussion that follows, the major features of the relational model are presented. The model has its own terminology, which, although seemingly complex, nonetheless translates to relatively simple concepts. (For a brief summary of relational terminology see the appendix to this chapter.)

Much of the credit for the development of the relational model goes to E. F. Codd, whose 1970 paper "A Relational Model of Data for Large Shared Data Banks" was a landmark in the field. This paper also laid the groundwork for two of the foremost families of relational languages, the relational calculus and relational algebra.

Describing Relations

A *relation,* the starting point for all thinking in the relational model, may be pictured as a simple table. Table 5 presents a *courses-taken* relation from the school data model. Within the table, each row describes something about which information is kept. For example, Sam Dunn, whose student number is 1099, is registered for the courses English and social science. Each row in the table, properly called a *tuple,* contains similar information, but no two rows are exactly the same. This is to say that the *components* of the tuple (the data values making up the row) do not exactly match those of any other tuple.

The columns of the table are called the *attributes* of the relation; each column is labeled to denote its *role name* within the relation. The role name describes the meaning of the attributes to the relation. The relation in Table 5, for example, would be quite different if the role name assigned to the third column were "courses-failed" rather than "courses-taken."

A rigorous mathematical definition of a relation follows.

Table 5: The courses-taken relation for the school data model.

	Student Number	Student Name	Courses-Taken
Courses-Taken	1016	Frank Mann	History
	1099	Sam Dunn	English, Social Science
	1861	Bo Russ	Algebra, History
	1902	Seth Johnson	Social Science
	2006	John Kitt	Geology

> Given sets $S_1, S_2, ..., S_n$, a relation R is a set of n-tuples each of which has its first element from S_1, its second from S_2, and so forth. The sets $S_1, S_2, ..., S_n$ need not be distinct. A given set S_i is called a *domain.* R has a *degree,* given by the number n, and a *cardinality,* which is the number of tuples. In the relation R, the following rules hold:
>
> 1. No two tuples are exactly the same.
> 2. The order of elements within a tuple is significant and must remain consistent with other tuples.
> 3. The order of tuples themselves is not significant and need not be maintained.

Applying that definition to our example in Table 5, we can see that the *courses-taken* relation has a degree of 3 and a cardinality of 5. Attributes have been selected from three distinct domains: the set of all student numbers, the set of all student names, and the set of all course names. The *courses-taken* relation need not necessarily be a stored relation; it could in fact be the end product of operations on other relations, or even an intermediate or transient relation.

A *candidate key* is one or more data item types (columns) whose values uniquely identify rows or tuples of the relation. In Table 5, the student number represents a candidate key. Although rows in the relation have been physically ordered on the basis of values for this key, this is not required. A relation can have more than one candidate key (the student name is another); one is usually designated the *primary key.* A relation always has at least one candidate key since no two tuples can be identical. The term "candidate key" is sometimes shortened simply to "key."

A *foreign key* is one or more data item types (columns) whose values correspond to those of a candidate key within another relation. For example, the *course-taken* attributes constitute a foreign key to the *curriculum* relation (shown in Table 6) since that relation has attributes in the *course name* column taken from the same domain.

Table 6: The curriculum relation for the school data model.

	Course Number	Course Name	Room Number	Teacher Name	Office Hours
Curriculum	10003	History	A76	Quinn	11-12
	10150	Social Science	B101	Shaw	9-10
	10152	English	H299	Shaw	9-10
	10288	Algebra	A92	Aaron	3-4

Foreign keys provide the basic building block for effecting data interrelationships in the relational model. Several points are worth noting. First of all, a foreign key need not be a candidate key of its own relation. Secondly, the role names for the foreign key and corresponding candidate key need not be the same. Finally, neither candidate keys nor foreign keys imply the existence of any particular physical structure for storing relations. This last point is crucial. The relational data base may be supported by any number of physical means, but no matter how it is done, such devices always remain transparent to the user.

Improving the Format of Relations: Normalization

Certain relations yield better performance than others; the process by which optimal formatting is achieved is called *normalization.* A relation in *first normal form* has no tuples with components made of multiple items. This requires a conversion of the *courses-taken* relation in Table 5, resulting in the first normal form presented in Table 7. The first normal form is likened to a single-level record array, often called simply a flat file.

Successive improvements in relations are achieved by converting first normal forms through the second normal form (a transitory stage) and into *third normal form.* It is instructive to review the failings of the first normal form in order to understand the advantages of the third. These failings—or "anomalies," as they are called—fall generally into three categories, which can be illustrated using the *curriculum* relation in Table 6.

Each of the anomalies arises from the fact that the relation carries information not only about courses (course number, course name, room number, and teacher name) but about teachers as well (office hours).

Table 7: The courses-taken relation in the first normal form.

	Student Number	Student Name	Courses-Taken
Courses-Taken	1016	Frank Mann	History
	1099	Sam Dunn	English
	1099	Sam Dunn	Social Science
	1861	Bo Russ	Algebra
	1861	Bo Russ	History
	1902	Seth Johnson	Social Science
	2006	John Kitt	Geology

Update anomalies. The teacher Ms. Shaw needs to change office hours because of a scheduling conflict. This information does not appear in a single place in the relation but rather once for each course she teaches (that is, the information appears once for each tuple; note that there are two courses listed for this teacher in Table 6). This "redundancy" requires multiple operations for updating her office hours (each tuple must be located and modified), a process that may tend to be cumbersome and error-prone.

Insertion anomalies. A new teacher, Mr. McGraw, has been assigned to the school. Although he does not yet have courses to teach, he has picked office hours. To enter this information into the relation, null values must be assigned to the tuple components of course number, course name, and room number. The presence of such values would be undesirable, particularly for the candidate keys.

Deletion anomalies. An existing teacher, Mr. Quinn, has decided not to teach courses this term, but he retains normal office hours. If his history course is dropped from the relation (that is, if the tuple is deleted), the information about his office hours is lost.

It can be seen from these illustrations that the failings of the relation in the first normal form arise from the mixing of two different types of information in the curriculum relation: information about courses and information about teachers. In the third normal form there is one and only one type of information in any given relation. Thus the curriculum relation must be split apart into separate curriculum and teacher relations.

A rigorous definition for the third normal form is as follows:

> Given a relation R with attributes A and B, where A and B may also be sets of attributes, the attribute B is *functionally dependent* on A if each value of A is always associated with only one value of B. This relationship is expressed A→B, where A is called the *determinant.*
>
> From the definition of a candidate key, it follows that every relation has at least one functional dependence: all attributes are dependent on the candidate key, which is thus a determinant.
>
> A relation is said to be in third normal form if *every* determinant is a candidate key. Since a relation may have more than one candidate key, a relation in third normal form may thus have multiple determinants.

Under this definition for the third normal form, it is found that the teacher name in our example is a determinant of office hours

Figure 27: Relations for the school data model in third normal form.

Curriculum

Course Number	Course Name	Room Number	Teacher Name
10003	History	A76	Quinn
10150	Social Science	B101	Shaw
10152	English	B299	Shaw
10288	Algebra	A92	Aaron

Teacher

Teacher Name	Office Hours
Aaron	3-4
Quinn	11-12
Shaw	9-10

Student

Student Name	Student Number
Sam Dunn	1099
Seth Johnson	1902
John Kitt	2006
Frank Mann	1016
Bo Russ	1861

Courses-Taken

Student Name	Courses-Taken
Frank Mann	History
Sam Dunn	English
Sam Dunn	Social Science
Bo Russ	Algebra
Bo Russ	History
Seth Johnson	Social Science
John Kitt	Geology

but not a candidate key of the relation. The necessary revision is shown in Figure 27, in which the *courses-taken* relation from Table 7 has also been revised.

Using Relations

Much of the developmental activity in relational systems has focused on languages, called *data sublanguages,* to be used in interacting with a relational data base. The term data sublanguage originally referred to a facility meant to be embedded in a host language but now is sometimes used to refer to both embedded and stand-alone languages. The relational model is generally held to be particularly well suited for the latter of these, which envisions high-level, user-oriented query languages. In general, data sublanguages for the relational model tend to be rigorous in their mathematical foundation yet rather easy to use.

Examples for three operators from relational algebra are presented in Figure 28. Although the syntax is hypothetical, it could closely resemble that found in a given data sublanguage.

The full flavor of these operators is brought out when several are used in succession in order to retrieve certain information in a particular format. An example is given in Figure 29. It should be noted that the results of both intermediate and final expressions (which might well be nested into a single expression) are *tables* of data (that is, relations) rather than individual records or tuples. In fact, since relations constitute both the "input" and "output" to the operators of typical relational languages, the term data manipulation language is perhaps inappropriate in describing data sublanguages. A DML is normally record and data structure oriented; a data sublanguage is not.

Finally, it should be noted that updating in the relational model is an eminently simple operation from the user's point of view. There is in fact no data structure; "position" and "set selection" are irrelevant. The equivalents of simple read, write, and delete commands suffice since a user is not concerned with anything more than creating, replacing, or eliminating tuples in a relation.

The Relational Model and Data Independence

Keys in the relational model denote properties of information content. A key implies a candidate key or a foreign key; there is no required relationship between data content and actual physical storage of tuples.

This orientation is in sharp contrast to the familiar network and hierarchical views of data, in which keys are as much physical as logical agents. In physically linked DBMS, for example, keys are used to order records in actual storage structures and to establish linkages between like-valued records. Even in inverted DBMS, a "keyed" item is invariably one for which a physical index is created. In all, the relational model insists only on flat files—an exceedingly simple concept in storage structures.

Figure 28: An illustration of three operators (PROJECT, SELECT, and JOIN) from relational algebra.

PROJECT

Problem: List teacher name by course number.

User expression: Project curriculum over course number and teacher name, giving teacher- list.

Teacher-List

Course Number	Teacher Name
10003	Quinn
10150	Shaw
10152	Shaw
10288	Aaron

SELECT

Problem: Find all courses taken by Bo Russ.

User expression: Select courses-taken where student name = Bo Russ, giving schedule.

Schedule

Student Name	Courses-Taken
Bo Russ	Algebra
Bo Russ	History

JOIN

Problem: Include student numbers in a courses-taken list.

User expression: Join courses-taken and student over student name, giving comp-list.

Comp-List

Student Name	Courses-Taken	Student Number
Frank Mann	History	1016
Sam Dunn	English	1099
Sam Dunn	Social Science	1099
Bo Russ	Algebra	1861
Bo Russ	History	1861
Seth Johnson	Social Science	1902
John Kitt	Geology	2006

Figure 29: A problem requiring use of several operators.

Problem: List the courses taken by Bo Russ, and include teacher name and office hours.

User expressions and results:

1. Select courses-taken where student name = Bo Russ, giving Step-1.

Step-1

Student Name	Courses-Taken
Bo Russ Bo Russ	Algebra History

2. Join Step-1 and curriculum over (course-taken = course name), giving Step-2.

Step-2

Student Name	Courses-Taken	Course Number	Room Number	Teacher Name
Bo Russ Bo Russ	Algebra History	10288 10003	A92 A76	Aaron Quinn

3. Project Step-2 over course-taken and teacher name, giving Step-3.

Step-3

Courses-Taken	Teacher Name
Algebra History	Aaron Quinn

4. Join Step-3 and teacher over teacher name, giving Step-4.

Step-4

Courses-Taken	Teacher Name	Office Hours
Algebra History	Aaron Quinn	3-4 11-12

The absence of physical implications for keys in the relational model is one example of how the task of data structuring is circumvented. By definition, a data structure translates logical relationships within the data into physical structures; these structures are unnecessary in the relational model.

Furthermore, the concept of navigational access is meaningless for relational systems. The user does not traverse a relational data base a record at a time; he transforms it table by table into formats he desires. When storing a record he is unconcerned with "related" records; there is no operation equivalent to the CODASYL concept of set selection or to the IMS concept of parentage.

The relational model brings to bear the computing power of the machine to effect the interrelating of data through a mapping process that occurs at the time of the actual execution of the request. This mapping can be as flexible as the user requires; it does not depend on preestablished "paths" within the data.

The absence of these paths implies several types of improvements over traditional systems. Not only is periodic data base reorganization less a factor, but the absence of "data structure" means more flexibility in evolving with changing user needs. To many observers, this represents a higher form of data independence to which conventional systems cannot lay claim.

Also, data independence in the relational model extends convincingly to the level of individual data elements, because relational operators are often selective with respect to items rather than entire records. Nonetheless, retrieval is powerful beyond even the record level since the unit of interaction is a table of records rather than anything less.

Finally, by supplying powerful operators to the user, a relational system eliminates, at least in theory, the need for intermediary programming—an area of considerable investment in conventional systems. Thus, in a number of ways, the relational model elevates information usage from the level of the machine, which is the central concept in data independence.

Relational Systems and the Future

What does the future hold for the relational model? One significant problem that relational DBMS will face is that of supporting concurrent access, an area that promises to be particularly troublesome, given the volume of ongoing file mapping that occurs under relational operators.

There are dimensions to this problem beyond what has been discussed in this presentation. For large relational data bases, it is easy to envision the substantial computing power necessary to support user access; it is in fact generally agreed that full-scale relational DBMS will be forced to await a new generation of computer hardware. According to some observers, however, this generation is not distant. Widespread speculation is currently concerned with the possible emergence of associative memories (capable of addressing by content rather than strictly by location). Such a development would be of obvious use to relational DBMS.

The rapid growth of microprocessor technology may prove significant in this regard since "intelligent" storage configurations would represent a profound advance over current disk technology. One unfortunate side effect of the third normal form is the inflation of storage space requirements (a look back at Tables 5–7 and Figure 27 is convincing in this regard). Whatever the storage technology, relational data bases do not promise modest use of storage facilities.

Existing experimental implementations of relatively "pure" relational DBMS number perhaps several dozen, but most have been limited to smaller, single-user data bases. The best-known implementations are the MACAIMS system at M.I.T.; the PRTV system (formerly IS/1) at the IBM Scientific Centre in Peterlee, England; the RDMS system of General Motors; and the SEQUEL system of the IBM Research Laboratories in San Jose, California.

One potentially significant project is System R, a relational DBMS developed at the IBM San Jose Labs, which is purported to be the first truly large-scale facility capable of handling many concurrent users and a large volume of requests. System R is one indication of the emphasis that IBM seems to be placing on the relational model.

Of other manufacturers, H.I.S. (with MDBM) and CDC (with DMS-170) have incorporated certain aspects of the relational model within current systems. Several independent vendors of inverted DBMS, among them Software AG (with ADABAS) and Infodata Systems (with INQUIRE), increasingly describe their systems in relational terms. (This fact coincides with a view held by some observers that inversion is the optimal technique for implementing a relational-like system under current technology.) The relational model has had notable impact on systems newly offered by remote-computing companies. Examples include MAGNUM by Tymshare, Inc., and NOMAD by National CSS.

The prospect is that the relational model will have increasing commercial impact during the next five years and, given hardware advances, significant impact on future data base management practices. A number of performance-related problems are currently being addressed; in all, the relational model is providing one of the most vigorous sources of alternative thinking for the evolution of future DBMS.

MINI-DBMS, BACK-END PROCESSORS, AND DISTRIBUTED DATA BASE SYSTEMS

Intense development of data base management facilities has been widely characteristic of the mini-computer industry during the past several years. This activity is testimony not only to the power and attractiveness of the data base concept but also to the increasing range of computing now within reach of mini-machines. Significant technological advances may come of this activity; we will be looking at two of them—back-end processors and distributed data base systems—later in this chapter.

Mini-DBMS

Before discussing mini-DBMS themselves, it is appropriate to review the exact capabilities of the hardware marketed by the mini-computer manufacturers in the second half of the 1970s. The term "mini" is certainly no longer an appropriate designation for the computers supporting mini-DBMS applications. Because of their capabilities, many observers now use the terms midi-computer or supermini to denote machines of this class.

An appropriate example is Hewlett-Packard's HP 3000 II Model 9, with 320K to 512K bytes of main memory and a variety of software, including a COBOL compiler, a DBMS, and a query language. Similar offerings are found in DEC's PDP-11/70, in Data General's Eclipse series, and in UNIVAC's V70 series. These machines are increasingly indistinguishable from the lower end of the large mainframe lines—for example, the IBM 370/135, Burroughs B 3700, Honeywell 2050, NCR Century 251, and UNIVAC 90/60.

This similarity suggests that data management in the mini environment is becoming increasingly similar to that within comparable mainframe systems. For example, a user of the IMAGE DBMS on the Hewlett-Packard 3000 II is involved with virtually the same tasks as a user with a corresponding large mainframe system—say, TOTAL on the IBM 370/135 or DMS/90 on the UNIVAC 90/60. An important feature of this correspondence is the availability of COBOL on the mini-machines—a development that has come about only in the last several years.

Furthermore, it is evident that both the mini manufacturers and the mainframers are increasingly aware of the data management needs of small to medium-sized users—especially business users—who until now have constituted a virtual frontier within the industry. The competition in this arena is wide open; manufacturers of both mini and mainframe machines are converging on this target with significant software offerings. Although emphasis on software is new to the mini manufacturers (powerful hardware at economic prices has been their traditional strength), current industry developments seem to indicate that the new emphasis is permanent.

In reviewing the market for mini-DBMS, several distinct classes of potential users are evident.

Small to medium-size organizations. Many smaller organizations have sophisticated data management requirements but lack the processing volume to justify a traditional mainframe machine. The cost of a mini-DBMS and a mini-machine (roughly $100,000) is within reach of such organizations; the price of a mainframe ($1 million plus) is not. At the other end of the spectrum, the potential small user has requirements beyond the scope of typical small business computers—for example, the IBM System/3, IBM System/32, NCR 499, and DEC Datasystem 310.

Large organizations with mainframe overloading. A mini-DBMS has been suggested as one means of easing the processing load on large mainframes operating in the data base environment. Under the suggested configuration, the data base management function is segregated into a separate mini-computer processor. This arrangement creates a *back-end DBMS.*

Large organizations with decentralized usage. Many organizations are characterized by relatively minor functional overlap between constituent groups, especially in terms of their data management requirements. In the past, such groups have nonetheless been serviced by a central data processing facility in order to exploit the economics of scale. This strategy, although viable from an economic standpoint, often results in conflicts of scheduling, priorities, and standards. In addition, a loss of responsiveness to given users often occurs. Observers are now noting that the concept of decentralized or distributed processing, featuring mini-computers with data management software, is becoming increasingly attractive pricewise. Distributed processing is particularly well suited to organizations that are geographically dispersed, which is characteristic of many organizations in transportation, manufacturing, government, and retailing.

Commercial software currently available for data management on mini-computers is presented in the list below.

MINI-DBMS

System	*Vendor*	*Type*
TOTAL	Cincom Systems, Inc.	Network
Varian TOTAL	Sperry UNIVAC (formerly Varian Data Machines)	Network
Harris TOTAL	Harris Corp.	Network
IMAGE	Hewlett-Packard	Network
DBMS-11	Digital Equipment Corp. (DEC)	CODASYL
Prime DBMS	Prime Computer, Inc.	CODASYL

OTHER DATA MANAGEMENT SOFTWARE

System	*Vendor*
ADMINS/11	Admins, Inc.
BIS/3000	Data Base Management Systems, Inc.
DataBoss/2	Florida Computer, Inc.
DRS/2	A.R.A.P.
Enscribe	Tandem Computers, Inc.
IIS DBMS	Interactive Information System
INFOS	Data General
Product 3	ELS Systems Engineering
Reality	Microdata, Inc.

Mini-DBMS can be classified by hardware as follows.

Machine	*DBMS*
DEC PDP-11	DBMS-11, TOTAL
HP/3000, HP/1000	IMAGE
UNIVAC V70 series	Varian TOTAL
Harris 100 and 200 series	Harris TOTAL
Interdata 7/32, 8/32	TOTAL
IBM System/3	TOTAL
Prime 500	Prime DBMS
Honeywell Level 62, Level 6	TOTAL

One of the most significant mini-DBMS is perhaps DEC's DBMS-11, which was released for the popular PDP-11 line during 1976. DBMS-11 is an adaptation of IDMS software. DEC is foremost in size among traditional mini manufacturers, with slightly better than one-third of the total market. DEC's nearest competitor, Hewlett-Packard, beat DBMS-11 to the market by several years with its own DBMS, IMAGE. Both DBMS-11 and IMAGE feature network data structures, but the former follows the CODASYL model whereas the latter closely resembles Cincom's TOTAL.

TOTAL itself, possibly the most widely used of all DBMS, is implemented on a number of mini lines, including those offered by DEC, UNIVAC (Varian), Harris, and Interdata. Versions are also operational for the IBM System/3 and Honeywell Level 62 and Level 6 machines. Of all the independent DBMS vendors for IBM mainframes, Cincom Systems has so far made the most vigorous entry into the mini arena. Cullinane Corporation has been involved with the DBMS-11 system; activity is also reported for M.R.I. Systems Corporation (SYSTEM 2000), Software AG (ADABAS), Insyte Corporation (DATACOM), and the Computer Corporation of America (Model 204).

Observers are particularly interested in the implementation of these latter four systems, because implementations to date (DBMS-11, IMAGE, TOTAL) have leaned toward physical linkage rather than inversion. The reason for this emphasis on physical linkage is not difficult to discern: physically linked DBMS tend toward modest space overhead in basic structural tasks (for example, they use randomized and chained access to records rather than access via indexes). This is important on the relatively small minis. Nonetheless, inversion offers a number of inviting capabilities, and its use in mini-DBMS seems inevitable. There are reports that the recently released CODASYL-like Prime DBMS uses inversion extensively.

The implementation of established mainframe DBMS on minis is particularly significant for two reasons. The first is that migration paths are thereby established for smaller users to move toward larger machines should growth warrant this. The second is that the mini-DBMS is available to mainframe users for a back-end configuration, which can be implemented without extensive impact on existing applications. Both of these reasons define new dimensions to the meaning of machine independence.

There are other mini-systems that, unlike the systems discussed thus far, fail to fall neatly within mainframe DBMS categories. Two basic groupings can be identified among these systems.

The first features software that supports powerful data access but limited data independence. These systems, represented by Data General's INFOS and ELS Systems Engineering's Product 3, are essentially enhanced access methods.

The second group, best represented by ADMINS/11 and Microdata's Reality, comprises highly user-oriented systems, featuring concepts of total data management. These systems have been labeled boxlike systems in some quarters since virtually all details of storage structuring are invisible to the user.

The future of mini-DBMS is not without potential constraints. Some of the most significant are discussed below.

1. A number of vendors have had difficulty with the implementation of COBOL compilers and DBMS within the size of existing hardware lines, forcing upward expansion. Increased size translates into increased price, a critical factor to smaller users. The implementations of COBOL compilers and DBMS are by many accounts relatively primitive, especially in contrast to mainframe offerings. This gap may be difficult to close, especially as increased resources are focused on developing facilities for distributed processing.

2. The problem of constrained size also affects the application environment: for example, there is less to draw on for heavy peak-time usage, for enhancement in data structuring, for extensions in application processing, and so forth. Application programming is no less difficult in the mini environment than on mainframes; in fact, it is often more so.

3. The mainframe companies are aware of the potential of the small-user market and of distributed systems and have already made significant moves toward the market. IBM, for example, has recently released its first true mini-computer, the Series/1, and an impressive new small business computer, the System/34. NCR and Burroughs have been traditionally strong in these areas. UNIVAC acquired the Varian line in 1976. The mini manufacturers are posing a direct challenge to the industry leaders and are likely to meet with significant competition. Although the former currently have the price advantage, the mainframers have long-standing capabilities in the areas of marketing, customer service, and software development.

4. An area not discussed thus far is the move of the remote-computing industry toward data management and DBMS. Many attractive data management facilities have begun to appear over remote-computing services; examples include NOMAD by National CSS and MAGNUM by Tymshare. In addition, many remote-computing companies offer established DBMS software; SYSTEM 2000 is especially notable in this regard. Remote-computing companies

and mini-computer vendors define relevant markets along much the same lines, and competition is inevitable. The remote-computing companies have proven capabilities in dealing with small users and in providing user-oriented software.

5. Mini-DBMS are pioneering a new market, always a risk for technology-intensive products. The concept of distributed processing meets with opposition from many segments of the data processing community, which has something of a vested interest in centralized processing.

Back-End DBMS

One of the more intriguing uses of mini-DBMS is their potential for easing the processing load on central mainframes in large data base environments. A *back-end DBMS* envisions a dedicated processor "behind" the mainframe to which all or most DBMS functions are relegated. In particular, the back-end DBMS controls all actual access to data base files.

A similar arrangement has been used successfully in teleprocessing. In this environment, all communication functions are segregated from the mainframe into a *front-end processor,* to which many user terminals are connected. The front-end processor eases the burden on the mainframe by freeing it of terminal support, line control, transaction queuing, and so forth. A front-end configuration, like its back-end counterpart, is one form of *multi-processing*—the sharing of processing functions by interconnected processors.

Under the back-end configuration, application programs run within the mainframe processor (called the host) and issue regular DML commands for data base access. These commands are passed by the host to the back-end DBMS, where actual data base access occurs. The results of this access, including data and/or codes to indicate success or failure, are passed back to the mainframe and thereby to the appropriate application program. This arrangement is illustrated in Figure 30.

What does the back-end configuration require? For organizations with existing data base applications, the foremost requirement is a mini-DBMS with facilities matching those of its mainframe counterpart. Compatibility along CODASYL lines (for instance, IDMS matched with DBMS-11) is one means by which this match-up can occur; implementation of the same DBMS (for instance, TOTAL) on both machines is another.

Another requirement is the existence of special access methods

Figure 30: A back-end DBMS configuration.

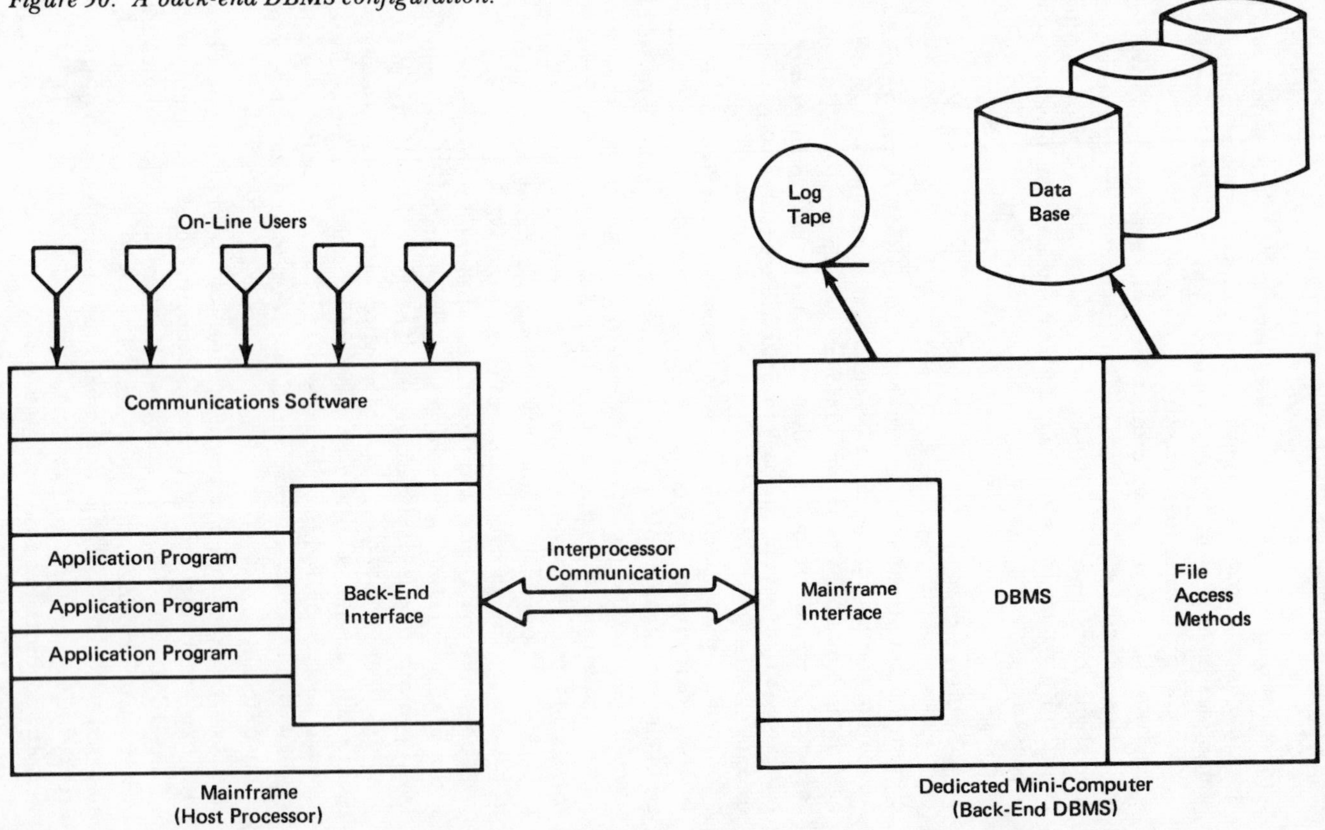

to effect communication between the processors. (These access methods are indicated by back-end and mainframe interfaces in Figure 30.) Actual data transmission between the processors takes place over a high-speed link; an adapter is often required since the processors are likely to be of distinct origin.

What does the future hold for the back-end concept? Complete back-end DBMS support will become commercially available only in 1978 or perhaps slightly later. It will be several years before more complete development makes widespread use possible. Also, many mainframe DBMS do not yet have a mini-DBMS version—a necessary prerequisite for configurations of the type examined here.

The back-end concept does not preclude the use of machines other than mini-computers to support DBMS functions; indeed, the coupling of *mainframes* to accomplish this goal is a likely possibility. Such an arrangement would be well suited for IBM's IMS, for example, because of its size and lack of machine independence.

The benefits and disadvantages of the back-end concept are summarized in the following lists.

Benefits

- Overloading of the host processor is relieved, which results in improved response time for all tasks.
- Space in the main memory of the host is freed; I-O channel contention is lessened.
- The relatively good cost/performance ratio of mini-computers is exploited.
- Recoverability is improved through isolation of the data base management function, a feature also resulting in improved security.

Disadvantages

- The presence of multiple processors somewhat increases the probability that some major component of the overall system will fail.
- Predicting and measuring performance in a back-end configuration is relatively complex.
- Incompatibilities between mainframe and mini versions of the DBMS, or limitations within the latter, may restrict options in data structuring or in migration between configurations. The back-end processor is an additional expense and often raises problems of multi-vendor support. The interface between the processors may be difficult to support adequately.

The fate of back-end DBMS is additionally important in the sense that they are a proving ground for the concept of distributed data base systems. Using back-end processors as a building block, more complex configurations can be conceived. Examples include the following:

- Multiple mainframes intercommunicating with a single back-end processor.
- Multiple back-end processors, each supporting separate data bases.
- A partially free-standing back-end processor, capable of handling certain types of access (for example, requests in the DBMS query language) directly. Other types of access, for example access within COBOL programs, would be handled through the host.

Increasingly complex networks can be derived using combinations of these configurations.

Finally, back-end DBMS may encourage the development of a *data base machine*—a processor in which data base support (including file access methods) is implemented largely within hardware rather than by software. Such a machine exploits the fact that the processor has to run only one program (the DBMS) rather than a changing array of programs, such as supported within the host. Although no data base machine is yet available, the increasing focus of the industry on data base management may well encourage development in this area.

Distributed Data Base Systems

During the decade and a half of user experience with data base systems, the concept of large, corporate-style data bases has evolved to become more or less the ideal for a substantial portion of implementations. Such a concept typically envisions support by ever larger machines, with an increasingly centralized perspective on how the system is to be managed and whom it is to support. The "distribution" of processing (and of the data base), if any, means that geographically dispersed users are given terminal access to the central machine, in a manner only simulating a localized resource.

This approach has had definite advantages. Although the economic reasons for centralization of the data processing function are now held suspect, this was not the case in the past. From the perspective of data base systems, the concepts of data integration, of data

Figure 31: Data usage in the school data model.

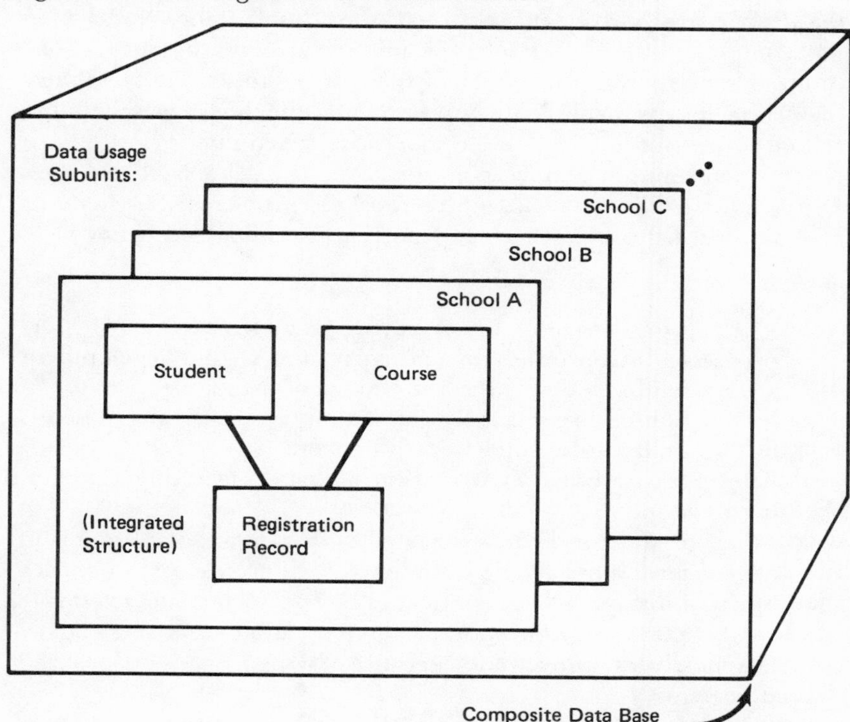

independence, and of data as a valuable resource have had a definite positive impact on general data management practices. Some observers see corporate-style data bases as a realization of old MIS goals.

There are now predictions, however, that processing capability is to become increasingly distributed; that is, that the large, centralized machine will be partially or completely replaced by many smaller machines, located physically near actual users. These machines would probably intercommunicate, forming a network of processors. The data base itself may become physically distributed over this network.

Proponents of the distributed concept argue that the centralized approach simply does not fit the functional makeup of many organizations. The school data model illustrated in Figure 31 is an appropriate example.

Under current DBMS, data for each of the schools would probably be aggregated into a composite data base, even though usage of the data is largely distinct for each of the schools. Moreover, under the composite model, schools are unduly affected by the actions of other schools, and the extent of their access to data outside their own sphere is probably inappropriate. The timeliness of school-by-school processing is likely to be poor since scheduling priorities are largely determined by factors external to the schools themselves. Distribution of the data base addresses these problems. The benefits and disadvantages of such an approach are summarized below.

Benefits

- The responsiveness of a distributed system is potentially better; processing turnaround, data integrity, and system development are more intimately tied to the actions of actual users.
- System failures are relatively isolated; not all processing depends on the welfare of a single, central system.
- The artificial isolation of a central data processing function is eliminated.
- Much of the overhead associated with multi-programming in a large machine is avoided; under current economics, a network of small machines has significant cost/performance benefits.
- Under many configurations, communication costs are actually lessened by decentralization because of the emphasis on localized processing.

Disadvantages

- A geographically distributed system is relatively difficult to support and manage; the technology for interfacing many machines of varying types is new and relatively untried.
- A sophisticated communications network is required; special problems of inter-processor deadlocks and multi-processor recovery must be addressed.
- There is a danger of duplication in effort and of fragmentation of development in the overall network.
- Under some configurations, a potential for renewed data redundancy and undesirable restraints on data base sharing may arise.

How might a distributed data base system be implemented? Several configurations commonly suggested for distributed processing are presented in Figure 32. It is important to note, however, that distributed processing alone does not necessarily imply a distributed data base; the latter occurs only where physical data base files are

Figure 32: Two possible configurations for distributed processing. In a star configuration (a), a hierarchy of processors is established such that every station can communicate with zero, one, or more substations but with only one station above. There is one station at the center of the star that has no station above it. In a network configuration (b), each station communicates directly with every other station.

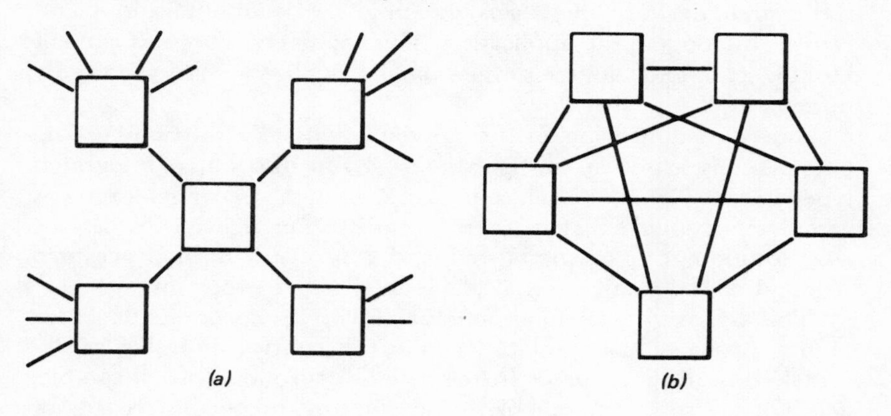

distributed among geographically dispersed processors. The fullest expression of a distributed data base system can be achieved only where these processors readily intercommunicate.

There are several important dimensions to the implementation of a distributed data base. The first is determined by the means of locating data in the system. In a *distributed independent* system, all processors are more or less independent agents, responsible only for their own portion of the overall data base. The task of locating data outside the processor's sphere is an application task; that is, an application program must be aware of the location of data in the overall network. To access "outside" data, the application program issues a request to the appropriate processor through the communications network.

This type of arrangement is largely possible under today's technology. There is, however, disagreement on whether or not a distributed independent configuration is a true distributed data base system. It has been argued that the system does very little to provide an integrated facility to the user or to prevent renewed data redundancy. It would in fact sometimes be easier for an application within a given processor to have its own data base rather than search for data among other processors within the network.

A *distributed integrated* system corrects these deficiencies by incorporating the task of locating data into the DBMS function. Under this configuration, an application program is unaware that portions of the data base physically reside at distinct locations; instead, it views the data base as a completely central or integrated resource. When a request for data is issued, the system locates the data in the overall network, performs the necessary communication, and returns the data to the application. This capability is beyond current DBMS technology, but the development of such systems is reportedly under way.

A second dimension in the implementation of distributed data base systems arises in configurations of the distributed integrated type. In one form of such a network, each processing location is completely "open"; that is, there is no manner in which access by *other* locations can be monitored and controlled. Each processor's segment of the data base is available to all other processors.

This arrangement, while compatiable with the corporate data base model, probably does not reflect the full control desirable in decentralizing the data base. In the school data model, for example, it is not desirable for schools to be able to update the records of other schools to have access to confidential student information.

Many applications can be identified where it is appropriate to limit the sharing of distributed data bases. It is in this area that substantial rethinking of the corporate-style data base model will have to be undertaken as distributed data base systems become prevalent.

Distributed data base systems are conceptually complex and will require significant advances, not only in communication and hardware systems, but in operating systems and DBMS software as well. The school data model discussed earlier is a relatively simple one since there is no interrelationship of data *across* hardware boundaries. Such relationships can be conceived, however, as in the following case.

A teacher teaches courses at separate schools; in CODASYL terms, a *courses-taught* set type is defined, where members cross processor boundaries. The DBMS must be able to access this set and to resolve any conflicts that might arise in concurrent usage between the processors.

Once capabilities such as these are developed, distributed data bases will make possible information systems of an unprecedented sort—systems that will expand current notions of data base management in significant ways. The administration of these systems will be a difficult task requiring pervasive modification in current practices; nonetheless, these systems hold great potential for users of computerized systems.

APPENDIX

Relational Terminology: A Quick Look

tuple—an ordered group of several data items, corresponding to a simple record.

component—a data item in a given tuple.

degree—the number of data items in a tuple.

relation—the set of all tuples of a given type.

cardinality—the number of tuples in a relation.

attributes—the values for a given data item type in a relation.

domain—the set of all possible values for a data item type; attributes are chosen from this set.

candidate key—one or more data item types in a relation, whose values uniquely identify tuples in a relation.

foreign key—one or more data item types in a relation, whose values correspond to those of a candidate key in another relation.

data model—the set of all relations; all data stored in the data base.

data submodel—those relations available to a given user.

normalization—a process of altering the format of relations in order to improve their performance in user operations, particularly in update operations.

flat file—a relation in normal form; a single-level record array with only one record (tuple) type.

determinant—an attribute or set of attributes on which the value of one or more other attributes depends.

data sublanguage—a language for interrogating and updating a relational data base, usually without computational capability.

PART III

The Implementation and Management of Data Base Systems

Chapter 7

THE DATA BASE ADMINISTRATOR: WHAT IS HIS PLACE?

Over the past several years data base management systems have opened a new round of change in basic data handling. This change has not, however, been easily managed, nor have simple migration routes always been available. Out of the implementation of data base systems, and perhaps the confusion and counter-purposes that have followed in their wake, the position of data base administrator has appeared.

The implications of this position are important enough to be considered carefully. As it happens, many organizations that have tried to do without the position at first have found that they could ill afford to continue without it. Vendors of data base management systems, while publicly maintaining a diplomatic hands-off posture, appear to be widely in favor of it. Their sales and support literature cites a data base administration function, with implications of a central person or team.

The immediate result of implementing a DBMS is centralization of physical data control, away from individual application programs or groups. While the degree of control may approach completeness, in most cases it does not. For example, actual data base *content* at the data element level is always under logical control of one application area or another. Logical *access* is for the most part controlled by the data base administrator (DBA), but in that capacity his role may be that of a technician more than of a policeman. That is, he may or may not get final say in who gets what data.

It is evident that there are several interpretations of the DBA position and that different situations require different degrees of central control. The major areas of responsibility in data base administration are (1) data base description; (2) control of data access; (3) system support, protection, and tuning; and (4) information enhancement.

DATA BASE DESCRIPTION

The DBA serves two masters in data base description. On the one hand, he must model logical relationships between data as they exist in the organization. This means optimal organization of data, measured by their availability for evolving information needs. On the other hand, the data organization must be physically implemented in ways that ensure minimal consumption of system resources.

These two functions are not isolated from each other; in fact, they are often at cross-purposes. Trade-offs between the two are complex to the point that data base description, beyond technical basics, is said to be more of an art than a science.

A typical data base application, which serves as an example for data base description, is in the payroll/personnel area. The goal of the data base approach is a single interconnected data base system that serves both applications, payroll and personnel, with equal facility. By describing a single system rather than separate files for each application, data redundancy is reduced so that individual data are more easily kept current.

Other uses of the data may be required by the organization. In the case of the payroll/personnel data base, a skills inventory application might be of value. In this case, the DBA looks to the existing data base system to determine whether adequate data exist to meet the requirement, perhaps using an indexing technique. If not, a new data base structure may be in order, interconnected with the existing payroll/personnel system.

Within all three applications the DBA must ensure that each is served with the entire set of data elements that it requires, in sequences that lend themselves to the application processing. Describing a physical structure that meets this objective *efficiently* is difficult under all DBMS, but more so under some than others. Structuring data bases is something akin to designing buildings: each DBMS offers materials to the DBA for the construction he has in mind.

Under inverted DBMS such as SYSTEM 2000 or ADABAS, a structure is built using relatively large blocks whose internal composition is not under DBA control. Design is greatly simplified using these blocks, but often there are many rough edges to the structure when measured in terms of performance and expandability.

Other DBMS—for example, TOTAL and IMS—furnish the DBA with the girders, plates, and bolts to structure his system from the ground up. In this manner, the rough edges in the system can be eliminated and a tailored structure completed. At this level, however, a much greater investment in manpower is required, both to put the structure up and to maintain it later on.

IMS probably presents the worst of this latter case. A sample of DBA activities in the design of an IMS data base includes the following:

- Selection of an access method (HSAM, HISAM, HDAM, HIDAM).
- Definition of files (ISAM, VSAM, etc.).
- Delineation of the hierarchical structure and selection of inter-segment pointer types.
- Definition of secondary indexes.
- Delineation of interfile logical relationships, plus selection of pointer types.

One last point in data base description that should be kept in mind is that effective data base design is a largely iterative process. As such it may tend to consume the bulk of the DBA's time, especially during the initial stages of data base implementation.

DOCUMENTATION, APPLICATION ANALYSIS, AND DATA BASE DESIGN

A temptation in data base design is to strike out with physical structures before adequate analysis of application requirements has been accomplished. This is especially true where data base structures exist that are perceived to satisfy or nearly satisfy the information requirements of a new application. Even in this case, severe access conflicts may arise unless sufficient analysis is undertaken, especially where the volume of transactions for the new application is high.

Actual documentation of application requirements is a task performed in part by a systems analyst, often with collaboration by the DBA. In practice, the division of tasks between application analyst and DBA is largely a matter of convenience and circumstance, within the following general guidelines. The systems analyst is responsible for documentation of the application itself, the DBA, for adequate documentation of the data base design. The DBA specifies the *type* of information necessary for translating system requirements into data base design considerations; then the two collaborate in producing this information.

The initial step in the analysis of application requirements as well as in data base design is definition of all data elements. In reality, this differs little from traditional definition practices, except perhaps in the degree to which it is pursued. Element-naming conventions, no longer sole domain of the analyst, are likely to be established jointly with the DBA. Additional efforts may be desirable to locate corresponding data elements (that is, duplicate or common elements) existing in other applications. Where the information requirements for a new application are satisfied completely by an existing data base system, no additional data element definition is usually necessary.

A widely accepted method of identifying data relationships and potential data base structures is the data usage matrix, known also as a frequency matrix. This method involves the mapping of data elements against relevant applications in order to pinpoint conjunctive usage.

An example, again from the payroll/personnel area, is shown in Figure 33. In this matrix the nature of transactions for each data element is estimated. This involves overall estimates for retrieval, replacement, insertion, and deletion frequencies so that the data base system may be optimally tailored to meet these processing requirements.

Several other areas must be investigated before final design decisions can be made. These areas include the following:

The existence and use of historical data.
The relative frequency of random vs. sequential processing.
Requirements for alternative processing sequences.
Projected data volume.

Much of the documentation related to the data base system may eventually find its way into a data dictionary system. A data dictionary is essentially a repository of all documentary material concerning data elements within the data base system, including where-used and where-located specification. As such, it is a subset of the total data base system documentation and may in fact include information about physical and logical structures.

The data dictionary presents an interesting opportunity for improving in-shop data base skills. Some vendors and other sources suggest that a data dictionary should be among the first applications to be implemented under a data base system. This requires an investment in man-hours and resources but tends to ensure that adequate documentation is maintained. An automated data dictionary has several other advantages:

Figure 33: Data usage matrix for payroll/personnel.

DATA ELEMENTS

APPLICATION:	Employee No.	Name	Address	Telephone No.	Age	Sex	Date Hired	Position(s)	Department	Salary	Vacation Accum.	Sick Days	Soc. Sec. No.	No. of Dependents	Race	Skill Type	Experience	Educ. Level	Comments
Payroll	✓	✓							✓	✓	✓	✓	✓	✓					
Employee History	✓	✓	✓	✓	✓	✓	✓	✓	✓						✓	✓	✓	✓	✓
Employee Directory	✓	✓	✓	✓				✓	✓										
Budget Interface								✓	✓	✓									
Skills Inventory	✓	✓						✓	✓							✓	✓	✓	✓
TRANSACTION:*																			
Retrieve	7,500	7,500	500	1,000	100	100	350	5,000	6,000	1,500	50	200	500	100	100	2,500	1,000	250	750
Replace	M	5	15	20	10	Y	Y	40	80	20	20	100	M	1	M	100	40	3	25
Insert	10	10	10	10	10	10	10	30	150	10	10	10	10	10	10	100	50	10	100
Delete	2	2	2	2	2	2	2	10	100	2	2	2	2	2	2	10	10	2	50

*Frequency per day (M= monthly; Y= yearly).

- It provides the DBA with practice in data base design and support in an area not immediately critical to production.
- It provides a training facility for programmer interface with a live data base system.
- For on-line systems, it provides data base documentation wherever terminals are available.
- It provides input for certain types of aids in data base design.

Control of the data dictionary is in all cases the responsibility of the DBA.

CONTROL OF DATA ACCESS

The capability to define selective access privileges for user programs is an important feature of DBMS. In shared file systems, such as the payroll/personnel example, it is essential to prevent certain types of transactions from taking place against given data elements. For instance, it might be undesirable for the skills application (that is, users of the skills programs) to access the sex or race data elements or for a user of the employee directory to change the salary element.

The DBA, with the perspective that cross-application exposure provides, is in an ideal position to define and implement access prerogatives. The levels of prerogatives for each data element are the following:

0. No retrieval.
1. Retrieval only.
2. Retrieval and addition.
3. Logical content control (retrieval, addition, change, and deletion).
4. Description control (that is, change in the content description).

Level 4 involves data base description and is therefore normally reserved for the DBA. Level 0, no retrieval privilege, is always the default option when no other level is specified. Prevention of extra-DBMS data access is a separate topic, to be discussed in the following section.

Levels 1 through 3 represent overt specification by the DBA for program access privileges. For the most part, implementation of these privileges is a relatively simple process, except for Level

3, which in network and hierarchical data structures can involve conceptual difficulties.

In some organizations, especially those having highly integrated data bases or significant amounts of sensitive data, the DBA retains strict control over the definition of access privileges. More often, the DBA, the systems analyst, and even users collaborate in an analysis that arrives at a mutually acceptable set of privileges. In this situation, the DBA's role may be essentially that of a technician, but it remains his responsibility to evaluate overall data base access privileges for effectiveness and potential conflict.

SYSTEM SUPPORT, PROTECTION, AND TUNING

The DBA is involved in an assortment of activities that have as their focus the well-being of the data base system.

Under support functions a number of activities are included. Some of these are the following:

- Generate DBMS software and apply enhancements.
- Define and implement utility programming (for example, statistical reporting and transaction error interception) for data base support.
- Monitor the conversion of files into the data base system.
- Ensure optimal use of physical devices.
- Implement appropriate procedures for recovery from various types of system or program failure (this recovery normally involves use of facilities provided by the DBMS, such as audit trail and back-out).
- Provide assistance to programmers and analysts for effective use of the data base system.
- Provide assistance for the interfacing of the data base system with on-line processing.

DBA involvement in system protection involves actions to prevent access to data by means other than through the DBMS itself. By preventing unauthorized access, it is assumed that no contamination or destruction of data values will occur. Commonly cited measures in this area include the following:

Invoking encode/decode routines for protecting data on storage media.

Assigning passwords for sensitive transactions.
Implementing procedures for logging unauthorized transaction attempts.
Maintaining user area security.
Controlling distribution of data base documentation.

Activity in data base protection reflects recognition of the system's importance to the continuation of effective operation of the organization.

The last activity in data base system support is tuning. This is perhaps the most complex and intuitive of all tasks. Effective tuning requires the collection of appropriate statistics and intimate knowledge of physical storage techniques, especially for handling insertion and deletion of element values. A high volume of transaction activity in these two areas causes destabilization of data base files over time, which must be corrected by reorganization.

Unfortunately, automatic generation of adequate statistics is a weak area in most DBMS. A resourceful DBA may be able to capture or sample some of the following:

Amount and distribution of free space within data base files.
Program transaction frequencies by type, by data element, and by time of day.
Length of data element chains.
Data volume growth rate.
Rate of decline in transaction response time.
Average number of physical I-O's per transaction.

Armed with statistics like these, the DBA is able to spot trouble areas and take appropriate action: reorganize data base files, redesign data base structures, or initiate changes in programming usage standards. In some instances, better training of users is the appropriate solution.

CENTRALIZATION OF THE DBA FUNCTION

The DBA acts as coordinator in the development of organizational information systems. This role requires familiarity with several levels of organizational activity: (1) management planning, policies, and goals; (2) application design and development; and (3) inter-area use of system resources. From exposure to these areas, the DBA distills information needs, both present and future, and directs the orderly development of relevant data base systems.

To accomplish this objective, the position of DBA is centralized, with sufficient authority to obtain that information *and compliance* necessary for designing and supporting an effective data base system.

The DBA should not, however, be a member of a central systems support group. An analysis of DBA functions reveals a small percentage of overlap with the duties of an internal systems group as typically defned. This is detailed in Table 8. The essence of the distinction between the DBA function and internal systems work is the emphasis of the former on information structuring, which is not of direct concern to systems support.

Concentration of DBMS knowledge within a central DBA group produces the best results in terms of the level of in-shop DBMS proficiency that can be achieved and eliminates wasteful redundancy

Table 8: Data base administration tasks and their overlap with internal systems work.

Tasks with full overlap	Tasks with partial overlap	Tasks with no overlap
Implementation and support for on-line monitor program.	Data base system tuning.	Description of data base files.
DBMS system generation.	Data base performance evaluation and configuration analysis.	Definition and implementation of program access prerogatives.
DBMS software support.	Application programming support.	Consultation and support for system analysis.
Evaluation and tuning of system software interface.	Development of data base related standards.	Data definition support.
	Security support.	Coordination of multiple data base use.
	Establishment of recovery procedures.	Direction of the data base structure as an evolving information resource.
Approximately 10% of total data base administration tasks overlap fully with internal systems work.*	Approximately 25% of total data base administration tasks overlap partially with internal systems work.*	Approximately 65% of total data base administration tasks do not overlap with internal systems work.*

*Subject to variation depending on the DBMS and its application.

of training and function across groups. In short, a central DBA team is the best solution for in-house DBMS support.

DEFINING THE ROLE OF THE DBA

Organizations using DBMS find themselves in one of three application situations: transition, expansion, or corporate. These situations can be described as follows.

Situation 1: Transition. This situation is characterized by the initial implementation of the DBMS within one major application area. The groundwork for data base administration is laid: expertise in data base technology is acquired, standards are established, and a trend toward centralization is begun.

Situation 2: Expansion. This situation is characterized by the expansion of data base organization into many application areas and the integration of partially redundant master files within each of these. New applications are usually implemented under the DBMS. A relatively minor integration of data between major application areas is achieved. Data base systems account for a significant portion of production processing.

Centralization of data base administration tasks necessitates an administration team, with a moderate degree of data base control.

Situation 3: Corporate. This situation is characterized by the integration of data into central data base files that are used by many application areas. A trend toward management information systems is evident since there is heavily centralized use of data. Data base systems are party to virtually all data processing activities. A fully empowered data base administration team becomes necessary for most organizations in this situation. This team not only oversees data base activities but coordinates and controls much of the information flow within the organization.

Even in Situation 2, it is evident that data base implementation involves a cross-application perspective, in which several or more existing master files are integrated into a single structure. Situation 2 reflects the fact that users of the system are in disparate organizational locations or that *usage* is not heavily centralized as in a management information system (MIS). Situation 2 also has relevance to distributed processing and to the concept of distributed data base systems, both of which are likely to increase in importance to general data processing.

It is sometimes possible to evolve from Situation 2 to Situation 3, although successful strategies of this type require considerable foresight. The reverse would be much more difficult. Situation 3 reflects an orientation toward central management and toward the coordination of activities between highly interrelated groups. Situation 3 is often interpreted as the fullest expression of the benefits associated with the *centralization* of computing within the organization, a long-standing trend among many contemporary organizations.

Whereas it is fairly easy to see where the corporate model fits, it is perhaps more difficult to understand Situation 2. Data processing for school district administration will serve to illustrate the latter. This environment is characterized by the following functional areas:

1. School information processing (student records, scheduling of courses, and so on).
2. Payroll/personnel administration.
3. Maintenance and development for the physical plant.
4. Inventory of teaching aids (for example, films).
5. Library purchasing and control.

Each area is relatively distinct, and there is little or no overlap between them. Moreover, the first area, school information processing, varies from school to school; there is only a limited amount of districtwide processing activity. Thus a "corporate" school data base encompassing *all* students fits poorly with data *usage.*

Several points should be emphasized. First, "integration" and "centralization" are distinct concepts and in no way synonymous. "Integration" refers to an approach to data organization and is characteristic of all data base applications; "centralization" refers to data usage and to a philosophy of management within the organization. Both have their impact on data base design, but they are nonetheless distinct.

Secondly, the three situations discussed (transition, expansion, and corporate) do not inevitably define an evolutionary path toward a corporate-style data base. In most cases, a choice must be made between Situation 2 and Situation 3 in recognition of their "fit" to the needs of the organization. If a corporate-style approach does not fit the organization, then that approach should be rejected, just as Situation 2 should be rejected where its only "fit" is that it is simply closer to existing organizational practices. Chapter 8 presents material on the design of data base systems that may be useful in making this choice.

In almost all cases, however, omission of the transition situation is a mistake. Despite pressures for immediate return on heavy DBMS investment, an initial period of adjustment and trial and error is important for the eventual success of the data base project. A transition period allows a relatively painless shaping of data base administration tasks to occur.

The distinction between Situation 2 and Situation 3 sets the stage for two alternative interpretations of the functions of the DBA. These functions are detailed in the appendix to this chapter. In many cases the differences between interpretations is a matter of degree, but in some there are also qualitative differences. This is especially true for control of data access, in which the DBA simply implements and advises under the first interpretation but defines and coordinates in the second. Within either interpretation the scope of the DBA's duties is sufficiently far-reaching to make disruption of established organizational patterns almost unavoidable.

There are several dimensions to this disruption. First, by centralization of data definition, many degrees of design freedom are removed from individual application analysts and programmers. A second factor is the centralization of data access control, which opens a multitude of questions concerning responsibility and ownership for data in the data bases.

Additional factors may be at work. Data base technology is complex, and when problems arise, application personnel therefore have no place to turn except to the DBA.

THE PLACE OF THE DBA

An organization implementing data base systems and faced by the need for creating a central DBA position is likely to ask the following three questions.

When should the DBA position be established? In many organizations, creation of the DBA position comes as an afterthought, when the organization is already deeply committed to the data base approach. This is not the best practice, especially if it is known from the beginning that eventual evolution to the corporate stage is likely. The ideal time for establishing a DBA position is during the transition stage, well before data base systems become critical to organizational production.

Where in the organization should the DBA position be established? It is clear from the analysis of data base administration tasks that a centralized and independent DBA position is necessary. Only from this type of vantage can the DBA effect the cooperation and compromise needed for successful data base projects. The DBA should report directly to a high level of data processing management and should direct a team of at least two well-trained individuals.

What type of person should fill the DBA position? A point worth mentioning, at the risk of stating the obvious, is that the DBA must have data processing experience. A data base system, if it is to fulfill its role as an organizational resource, deserves an administrator who can adequately support its growth and enrichment. The ideal candidate is a person equally comfortable with the roles of technician, administrator, and diplomat. The selection of a qualified DBA is in fact one of the most crucial steps in establishing successful data base projects.

APPENDIX

The Functions of the Data Base Administration Team

The outline on the following pages describes the functions of the data base administration team. These functions are categorized into four major areas of responsibility: data base description; control of data access; system support, protection, and tuning; and information enhancement.

For each function there are three possible entries. The first two entries define alternative interpretations of the role of the data base administration team. The first interpretation contains a relatively limited set of functions and is most appropriate for organizations identifying with Situation 2 (expansion stage) in data base usage. The second interpretation expands these functions into more complete data base control and is thus more appropriate for Situation 3 (corporate-style data base usage; see pp. 132–134 for a discussion of application situations).

The second interpretation is inclusive of all functions defined within the first. The third column in the list outlines functions not deemed appropriate for the data base administration team under either interpretation. These functions are best performed elsewhere or are not meaningful in the data base context.

Data Base Description

Interpretation I	Interpretation II	Inappropriate Functions
Evaluate application requirements and develop effective design of data base systems. This involves translation of perceived information needs into the format required by the physical structuring routines of the DBMS.	Identify organizational information requirements by review of all existing and projected application systems.	
Eliminate the storing of redundant data between applications wherever feasible under the given DBMS.	Coordinate efforts to identify and remove data redundancy between major application areas.	
Assist in the definition of unique names for data elements within the data base system. This may involve implementation of a central data dictionary system.	Assign names to all data elements within the scope of the data base system and document them in a centrally controlled data dictionary system.	Maintain a formalized data dictionary system of all data elements used in any form within the organization.
Implement any desired modification to the description of existing data base systems. Evaluate the inclusion of additional data elements into existing data base systems for potential impact on performance.	Approve all modifications to the description of existing data base systems. Evaluate and approve, where appropriate, the inclusion of additional data elements to ensure compliance with the organization's overall objectives.	

Control of Data Access

Interpretation I	Interpretation II	Inappropriate Functions
Assist in the establishment of standards to facilitate and control the acquisition of information from the data base system.	Establish and police all standards regarding acquisition of information from the data base system.	Humanize the interface between users and the data base system. (This is primarily the responsibility of analysts or consultants).
Assist in the definition of user (i.e., program) prerogatives concerning individual data elements, especially for retrieval and update. Implement	Define user prerogatives concerning individual data elements.	Unilaterally define all information access by organizational groups. (This the domain of management.)

Control of Data Access (cont.)

Interpretation I	Interpretation II	Inappropriate Functions
such prerogatives as appropriate under the given DBMS.		
Assist in the monitoring of user access to data.	Police user access to data.	
Provide special data base testing and training facilities.	Ensure the complete segregation of program testing from production data base systems.	
Assist in the identification of costs for data access through the DBMS.	Assist in user cost distribution for data access through the DBMS.	Manage cost accounting to users.
Implement encode/decode routines to ensure the security of stored data, where appropriate.	Develop special-purpose encode/decode routines.	Unilaterally define data elements sufficiently sensitive for special encoded storage.

System Support, Protection, and Tuning

Interpretation I	Interpretation II	Inappropriate Functions
Facilitate and monitor the conversion of files into the data base system. Assist in the identification of the impact on related programming.	Evaluate and oversee the conversion of files into the data base system. Assist in the analysis of the impact on related systems.	Plan and direct the conversion of application systems into the data base environment. (In some cases it may be appropriate for a data base administrator to perform related system analysis, but this is not a regular function of the position.)
Monitor the performance of the data base system by inspection of DBMS statistics, making adjustments where necessary. Establish procedures for transferring data base files between physical devices.	Develop and administer measurements for evaluation of data base performance.	
Establish procedures for data base recovery and reorganization, especially through back-up dumps and reloads, audit trails, etc.	Provide the facilities to ensure the security of the data base system. Evaluate and/or design special procedural and physical protective devices.	Maintain special security personnel (exceptions to this rule may exist in certain highly sensitive areas).

System Support, Protection, and Tuning (cont.)

Interpretation I	Interpretation II	Inappropriate Functions
Assist in the development of procedures for verifying the validity of data element values over time (i.e., for identifying gradual erosion of data value due to subtle software bugs).	Develop and administer validity checking routines.	
Monitor user programs for inefficient data base related code.	Establish and enforce data base code standards.	
Identify the need for utility programming, especially for user convenience and description enhancement. Obtain or design such programming as necessary.	Evaluate all software interfaces related to the data base system to ensure that there is no interaction detrimental to overall system performance.	Correct and enhance DBMS software. (This is appropriate only for certain cases in sophisticated environments.)
Provide technical assistance and instructional support for programmers and analysts using the data base system.	Oversee and direct all technical assistance and instruction in data base use.	Develop in-house instruction on a large basis. (In most cases, adequate instruction is externally available.)
Analyze and evaluate the effect of planned systems on data base system design and performance (and *vice versa*).	Assist in the analysis of software and hardware configurations for their responsiveness to data base requirements.	Unilaterally determine optimal software and hardware configuration.
Assist in the integration of the data base system with on-line systems; evaluate software packages facilitating high-level user interface.	Evaluate and monitor all on-line systems using data base files.	Oversee implementation of all on-line systems.
Ensure that adequate documentation of the organization and use of the data base system is available to users.	Police access to data base documentation.	Oversee documentation of all data base related systems.
Communicate with the DBMS vendor in order to keep abreast of enhancements and software developments.	Encourage the enhancement of DBMS software for specific system requirements.	Ensure that contractual obligations are met by the DBMS vendor.

Information Enhancement

Interpretation I	Interpretation II	Inappropriate Functions
Design and implement means for ensuring responsiveness of the data base system to ad hoc user requirements so that minimum standards of system performance are not violated.	Monitor *ad hoc* user information needs.	
Assist in the delineation of responsibility for data in the data base system, especially for keeping data current and accurate.	Define responsibility and ownership for data in the system.	Assume responsibility for data element content in all cases.
Assist in the identification of application systems' requirements for common information so that information processing and storage can be consolidated and integrated.	Establish short- and long-term strategies for data integration.	
Provide the technical groundwork via the data base system for evolving user information needs.	Anticipate and direct evolving information needs. Coordinate efforts toward a management information system where appropriate.	Unilaterally establish projected information requirements.

Chapter 8

THE IMPLEMENTATION OF DATA BASE SYSTEMS

The purpose of this chapter is to review considerations relevant to the design and implementation of application systems under a DBMS. These considerations may be envisioned within a stage-by-stage progression toward an implemented system, such as outlined in Figure 34 (see p. 142). We will focus here on the initial stages—that is, on the creation of a data model—but material on the character of data structuring and operational systems will also be presented.

In Figure 34, the overall process of implementing a data base system is conceptually divided into two portions: considerations relevant to the DBMS and considerations relevant to the application. It is particularly significant that Stage I is an application-oriented period; it is here that a data model is created which is translated into a data structure only later.

Although perhaps tempting, it is not entirely accurate to identify the left portion of the chart, DBMS considerations, with the duties of a DBA and the right portion, application considerations, with those of a systems analyst. Especially during Stage I, the DBA is heavily involved in system research and performs many tasks that are highly application-oriented.

Worthy of special note is the documentation for the data structures created in Stage III. This documentation is best accomplished with structural diagrams and should be accompanied by an explanation of how the structure meets the processing requirements of the application.

In considering data base implementation, the concepts of a data model and a data structure must be distinguished. A data model is the conceptual representation of the data associated with an organization; it specifies where the data are used in that organization and how they logically fit together. A data model is independent of machine and software. A data structure, by contrast, is the rendering of that data model in the data description language of a DBMS; it is the translation of logical requirements into a physical organization. In practice it represents a compromise between these two considerations: data requirements and physical limitations.

The creation of a data model is an analytical process, which should in all cases *precede* data structuring. Although this point appears straightforward, it is often a stumbling block in the implementation of data base systems. DBMS offer such impressive structural capabilities that it is sometimes tempting to concentrate on data structuring rather than on models—a mistake for which a price is paid subsequently.

The creation of data model is really nothing more than becoming well acquainted with the application. It means extensive user contact, where "users" are not only in the data processing department but in "end user" departments as well. In the implementation analysis (Figure 34), a data model is associated with Stage I; data structuring with Stages II, III, and IV.

In contrast to traditional systems, however, becoming acquainted with the application does not mean familiarization with just one application. A data base system eliminates the partially overlapping master file schemes of traditional systems, in the process eliminating the artificial boundaries between "separate" applications. For example, in a data base system there are no separate master files for payroll, personnel, and skills applications; there is one data base serving all.

Integration, then, is a foremost feature of data base implementation. Integration implies qualitatively different approaches to data handling; it is a mistake to think that existing files can be simply converted to a data base system. Such conversions have been tried; they usually end in partial or complete failure. Data base systems are a genuine departure from master files, not simply more powerful master file schemes.

Knowledge of this fact encourages greater attention to the analysis of the data model. Since integration of applications is a goal, it must be determined to what extent existing applications "speak the same language." The identification of common data elements is one way in which the required "translation" can be achieved, but beyond that, it also is a foremost means of becoming acquainted with the data model. Data element definition is the first step in the implementation analysis.

Figure 34: Implementation analysis for data base systems.

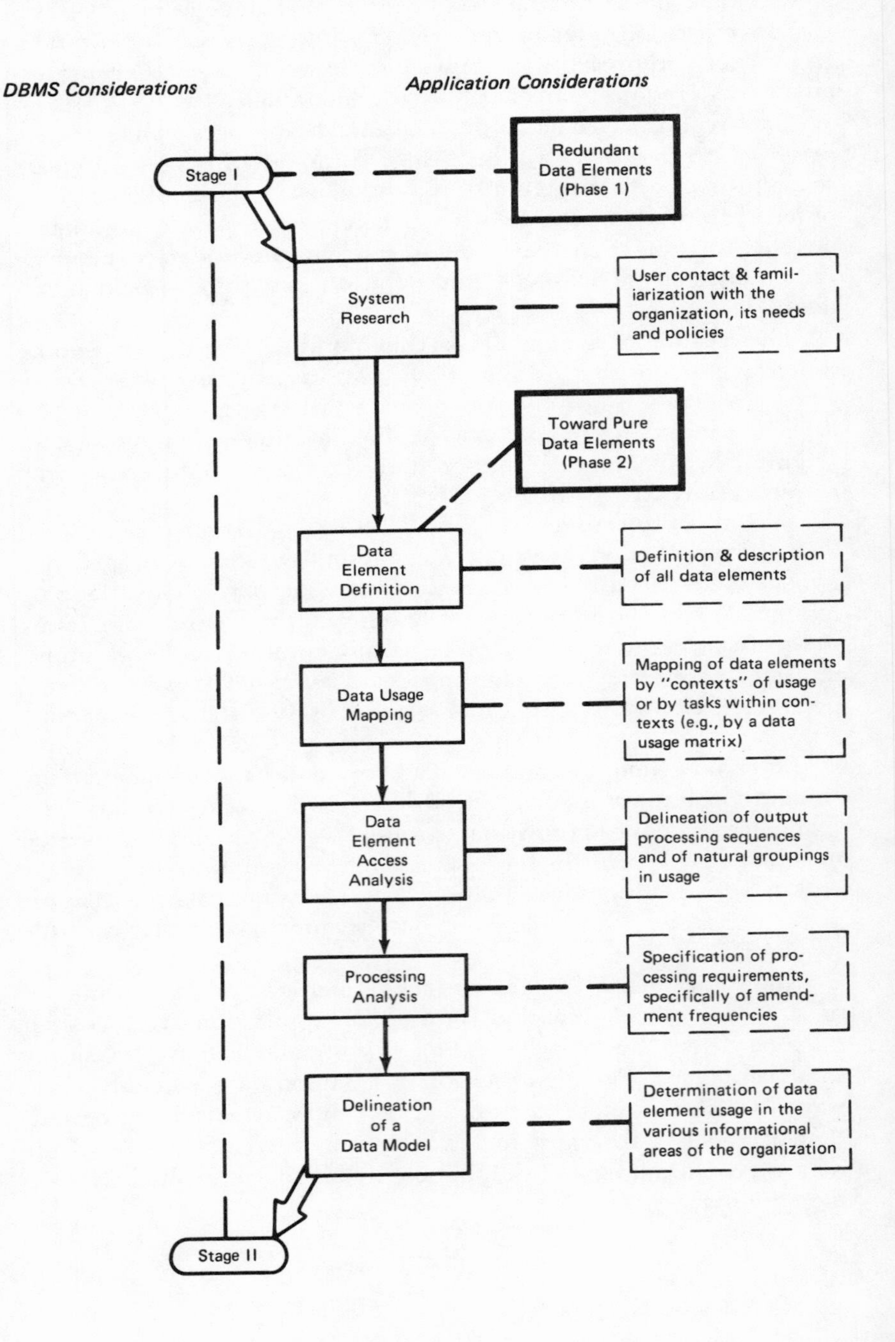

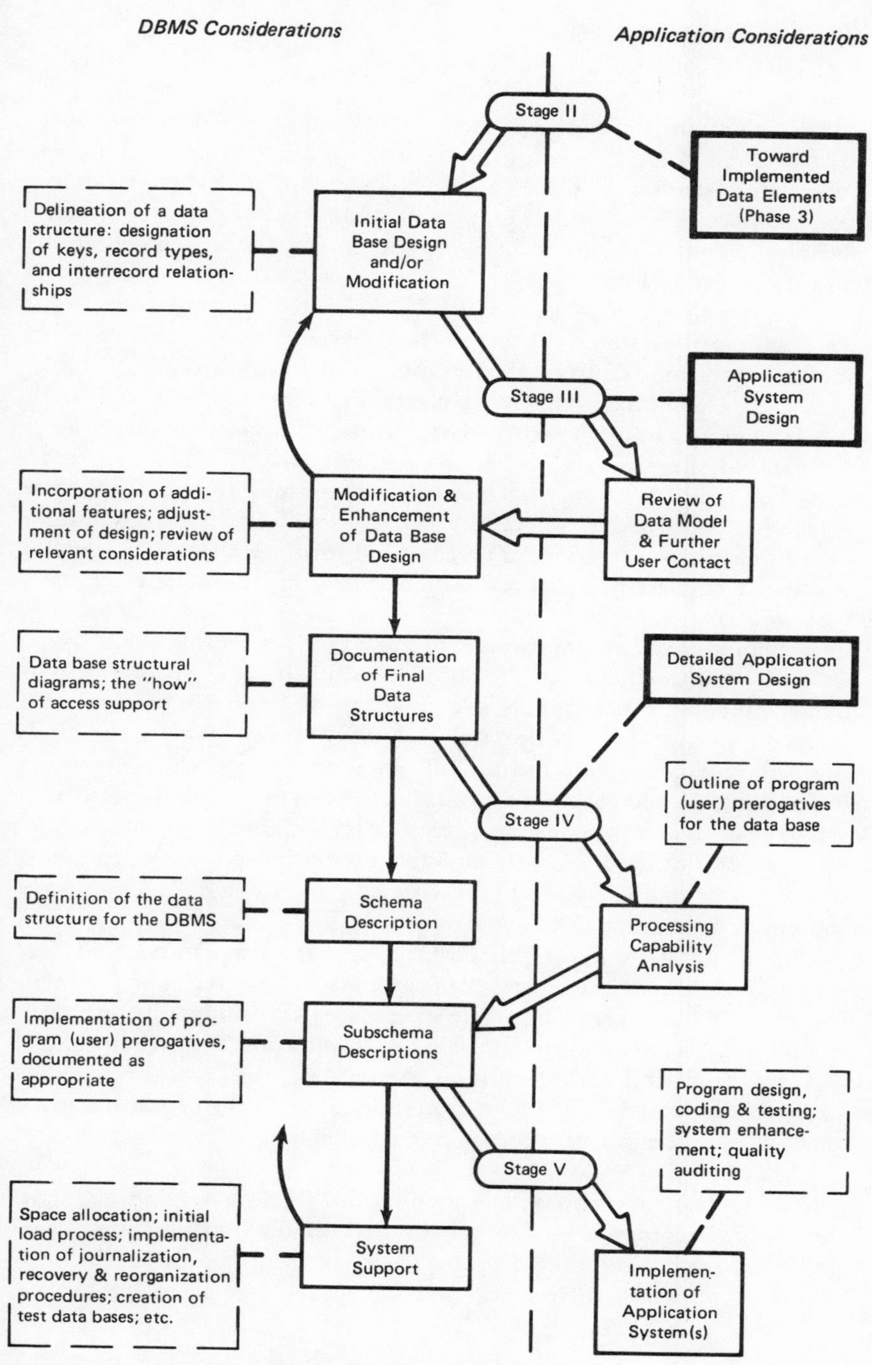

Adapted from *Government Data Systems,* December 1975/January 1976.

DATA ELEMENTS AND SYSTEM DESIGN

A data element is simply one item or unit of data, which becomes a field when contained within a record. A data element commonly refers to a person, a place, a thing, an event, a characterization, and so forth, any of which may have various values. Data element definition goes through several phases during the implementation of a data base system.

Analyzing for redundancy (Phase 1). Prior to the implementation of a data base system, the same data element often exists within several applications, although definition and format may vary. Each item may be updated by distinct sources, or there may be straightforward cross-updating between master files. Although values largely correspond, there may be variation in editing rules and in interpretation. For numeric items, permissible ranges may differ; for items represented by codes, different schemes may be in effect. Some items thought to correspond may actually be distinct; those in manually produced reports may correspond to those in automated reports. The goal for analysis at this stage is to ascertain the *meaning* of data elements and to determine commonality between applications.

Conceptualization (Phase 2). Subsequent to the analysis of existing data elements, "pure" items are uniquely defined for the overall application and are appropriately named. A pure item is one that is distilled from many redundant ones and for which "context" dependence is removed. For example, a student's name is just that, regardless of its usage in one place as "legal-name" and in another as "student-enrolled." Or in an inventory application, a product's name is distinguished from the contexts in which it might mean "component-product" or "ordered-product."

By distilling items in this fashion, it has been found that for many environments, the number of original data items can be reduced by 80 to 90 percent. For numeric items, definitive ranges are established; for items requiring codes, applicationwide schemes are devised. Once the item definition is complete, the goal for analysis becomes the modeling of the information needs of the organization—that is, a modeling of the *contexts* in which pure data items are used.

Implementation (Phase 3). In the third and final phase, data element definition becomes a tool in the process of data structuring. Data items are organized into groups (that is, records), which have a collective meaning to the organization. Some items are chosen as "keys" in order to physically implement the data structure. A degree of item redundancy is reintroduced; that is, the same "pure" data item must in some cases be defined in several places in the structure. The most obvious reason for this is to provide a correspondence between keys so that different record types can be related by common value. In some cases where usage cannot justify the overhead associated with interrelating records, there may be a need for storing some data redundantly. New data items occasionally appear; control totals in particular often become desirable. The goal for analysis during this phase is to map data elements into structures effectively and to use a degree of controlled redundancy for improved information and better system performance.

The evolution of data element definition is often difficult to manage for even moderately sized data base projects, given the volume of information required for successful implementation. The management of this information is one important function of data dictionary systems, to which the next section is devoted.

DATA DICTIONARY SYSTEMS

It is often difficult to understand exactly where data dictionary systems fit in with data base systems or, indeed, how they differ from them. A data dictionary is essentially a repository of data about the *informational* content of a data base. One of its most fundamental aspects is a definition of all data elements. Since this definition is basic to the delineation of data models, a data dictionary is an important aid to system analysis and data base implementation. The most fundamental purpose of a data dictionary is the identification of what data are where.

How does this differ from a DBMS? Relative to a data dictionary system, a DBMS may be characterized as a set of computer-oriented access methods specifically attuned to the translation of a data model into storage structures. A data dictionary system, by contrast, is *user*-oriented in the sense that the particulars of storage structures are translated into a form more immediately useful and understandable to the user of the data base. Data dictionary systems often *use* DBMS to store information *about* the data base.

Data dictionary systems also offer a number of potential productivity aids for the implementation of data base systems:

- ○ The generation of record descriptions in programmatically usable form (for example, in COBOL).
- ○ The mapping of data elements to actual records and structures, and *vice versa.*
- ○ The cross-referencing of data elements with application programs or modules (that is, a where-used mapping).
- ○ System and data base documentation, often automatically generated from the same data used to support production systems. (This ensures that documentation is kept up to date with system changes.)
- ○ The provision of information for automatic data editing, input validation, report generation, and so forth.
- ○ Assistance in generating various DBMS control blocks (for example, schemas and subschemas).
- ○ The translation of item or record names, in particular of user-oriented names to internal names, such as in the processing of a user query.
- ○ The provision of information on program data requirements, for optimization of run scheduling.

An automated data dictionary system is a popular "first" application among organizations newly arrived to DBMS; there are also a number of commercial packages available, as listed in Table 9. There is a

Table 9: Commercial data dictionary systems.

Data Dictionary System	Vendor	DBMS
ADABAS Data Dictionary	Software AG	ADABAS
Cincom Data Dictionary	Cincom Systems	TOTAL
CONTROL-2000	MRI Systems Corp.	SYSTEM 2000
Data Base Directory	Eastern Air Lines, Inc.	TOTAL
Data Catalogue	Synergetics Corp.	IMS, TOTAL, ADABAS
DATACOM Data Dictionary	Insyte Corporation	DATACOM/DB
DATAMANAGER	Management Systems and Programming	IMS, TOTAL, ADABAS, IDMS
DB/DC Data Dictionary	IBM	IMS
Integrated Data Dictionary (IDD)	Cullinane Corp.	IDMS
LEXICON	Arthur Andersen & Co.	IMS
UCC TEN	University Computing Co.	IMS

growing feeling in some quarters that the omission of an integrated data dictionary feature among almost all currently available DBMS is in fact a deficiency and that vendors should move toward support in this area. The offering of separate (and separately priced) facilities is currently the rule.

One final point: since a data dictionary is a central repository for information about a data base, it is in an ideal position to serve as a focus in enforcing standards (for instance, naming conventions and editing rules) for the data base system. This possibility argues for a highly *integrated* data dictionary system.

DATA MODELING

Data element analysis has long been the focal point of data base implementation, a position rightly deserved. During the past several years, however, it has become increasingly evident that data element analysis alone is insufficient. An additional dimension of analysis is required: the delineation of the *contexts* in which the data elements are used.

Unfortunately, this type of analysis is something that the data processing department, because of circumstance or custom, is not particularly wont to do. It is, in fact, a more comprehensive function than typically assigned to data processing and implies involvement of operations research, management information systems, and production control, all combined into a special information-oriented mix. In short, it is the modeling of what the organization *does,* with an emphasis on how information fits in.

Is this extensive involvement with modeling organizational activity really necessary? The answer is yes, for several reasons.

First of all, data models are basically "created": given the same set of data elements, many data models can be derived. Although each data model lends itself well to certain types of "meaningful" information use, the data model with the highest productive value is the one that best lends itself to the "meaning" of the context.

Secondly, the success of a centralized data resource depends on its relevance and usefulness to end users; unless the needs of these users are served, their participation in the project will falter. User participation is a must for a successful data base project.

Finally, data structures must be attuned to processing requirements; an appropriate data structure is possible only where the data model is well considered.

What is meant by an organizational context? The concept refers to an area in the organization where decision making and the control of resources are exercised. It is an area where specific *tasks* are performed. Inventory, billing, and ordering can be conceived as a context; payroll and personnel constitute another. In the administration of a school, the matching of students and teachers with courses is a central context. In each of these examples, the context has a specific orientation, which is discovered only by detailed analysis.

An example will illustrate this. In resource management for a large organization, two areas of interest are identified: "equipment" and "departments." In modeling the context, the following relationship is identified:

This relationship indicates that items of equipment are requested by departments. Given a department, it is possible to determine what equipment is needed; likewise, given an item of equipment, it is possible to determine by what departments it has been requested. The relationship between equipment and departments, however, is subordinate; it is possible to identify "requests" only from the vantage of a given department or item of equipment.

This modeling, although perhaps reasonably accurate, may not correctly reflect the context in which the information is used. For example, if there exists a group within the organization that is specifically charged with resource management, its orientation is probably not toward departments or equipment per se but rather toward requests, which are *items* of direct import to the group's activity. The group will have specific *tasks* associated with the requests for equipment. This is appropriately modeled as follows:

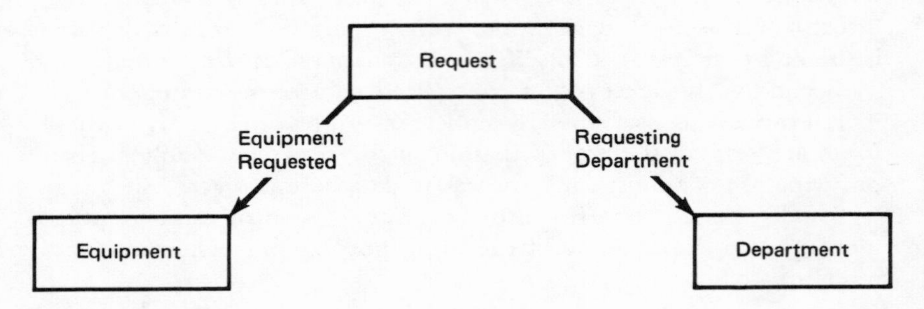

Under this modeling, requests are given a status appropriate to their importance to resource management; that is, a request becomes a "thing" easily accessed and managed. This "thing" is commonly referred to as an *entity;* the collection of all like entities (for example, requests) becomes an *entity class.* Data elements (for instance, *date-requested*) that describe the entity are called attributes. In the context of resource management, a *request* entity is required that is subordinate to neither equipment nor departments.

This example illustrates two points. First, strict attention to data elements, without considering the context of usage, would probably not have arrived at the appropriate model. Second, contexts have definable orientations, which reflect meaning and usage—that is, actual tasks performed. To model resource management information, it is necessary to consider what resource management is about and how related tasks are performed. This type of analysis goes far beyond that typically pursued in application-oriented master file systems. (This is an important point to remember in looking at existing systems during the process of creating a data model.)

One thing that aids in data modeling is that contexts are fairly stable over time. For example, even though actual equipment, requests, and departments change, the *context* of resource management does not.

Even so, as demonstrated in the example, it is sometimes difficult to determine when a "thing" should be an entity and when it is more accurately a relationship. In the school data base example, for instance, the equivalent of *equipment-requested* is *courses-taken.* But should *courses-taken* become a course schedule, as requests became an entity in the resource management example? Probably not. The essential difference is that, unlike in the case of equipment requests, there are no *tasks* associated with course schedules. In the school data base example, *courses-taken* should therefore remain a relationship between students and courses and, in a sense, somewhat subordinate in the model.

ADDITIONAL CONSIDERATIONS

Although the goal of data base implementation is an integrated structure serving two or more applications, the implementation of the system by stages, as resources and requirements permit, is not precluded. A successful strategy of this sort follows an analysis of the *total* data model, by which an integrated structuring is identified, and then proceeds in stages to achieve it. It does not, however, identify a piece of the data model associated with one application, then implement it, then identify the next piece, and so on.

Where this latter strategy is followed or where a stage-by-stage implementation occurs too slowly, the danger arises that unsupported applications will develop (or continue to support) their own "parallel" systems in order to meet informational needs. Once this tendency is set into motion, a trend toward renewed data redundancy is begun that is often difficult to counteract. More than one data base project has eventually failed in this manner. The actual problem, however, is not so much with data redundancy as it is with lack of user participation; in order for a data base project to succeed, users must participate in the design and have a stake in its implementation and continued welfare. Commitment to a "parallel" system inevitably detracts from commitment to the data base system.

Another important consideration is *how much* is to be integrated into the data base structure. A simplistic answer is that all processing (or rather, all data) should be integrated that currently overlaps under master file organizations. Unfortunately, in most organizations there is no effective end to the overlap; in fact, it quickly becomes evident that there is a degree of correspondence in *all* the information-related activity within the organization.

Also, for data base systems implemented from scratch, there is no redundancy that can be used as reference points for the process of integration. Even where this is not the case, existing deficiencies in informational support may be so significant that integration alone is not an adequate solution. Decisions must be made on how and where the data model is to have its focus.

Two interrelated questions serve to define this focus. First, what are the central information areas within the organization? Where are the data most heavily interrelated; where are natural boundaries between the content of various outputs needed by the organization? What are the *contexts* of major usage?

Secondly, who are the users of the information? Where in the organization are they located; how centralized is their perspective? How do they use the data?

An example will serve to illustrate how these questions are answered. In the school data model, three existing master file systems are identified as having significant overlap: the student and course master files for each school and a districtwide curriculum master file. Although there is overlap with other application areas (for example, with teachers in the districtwide personnel master file and with students in the budget area), it is decided that this information represents a "central" informational area (that is, a context with a set of tasks) in the school data model, which by comparison renders other overlap of minor consequence. The data model is to have as one focus the school administration area, and integration can begin at least with the three master files mentioned.

Who are the users? Is it the central district administrators, with their state reporting requirements and their need for planning and coordination; or is it the personnel of individual schools, who are responsible for scheduling, report cards, and so forth? Who puts the bulk of the data in? Who has the biggest stake in its usefulness?

It is tempting to push integration to the limit—that is, toward a highly centralized MIS-like "corporate-style" organization—but this may not reflect the bulk of processing and information activity within the overall application. This concept of usage and centralization was shown to be relevant to "situations" in data base administration (see pp. 132–134); it is equally relevant to determining the appropriate limit to integration.

A highly integrated corporate-style data base has its price as well as its benefits. The more completely integrated a system, the more widespread disruption will be if any one part fails. Where the stability of a functional area is more critical than centralized usage (for example, where efficient school administration is more important than districtwide data usage), less complete integration may be wise.

Also, it is often more difficult to make a highly integrated system responsive to the individual user; in some cases, many users are unnecessarily penalized for the careless actions of one. Such considerations demonstrate that many factors must be weighed in determining how much to integrate; the final decision is necessarily a compromise.

In conclusion, it becomes clear that the persons responsible for implementing the data base are much more than technicians. They find themselves, in fact, in a politically sensitive environment where a firm grasp of what the organization is about is necessary. In contrast to the traditional data processing environment, where an analyst implements a single file structure needed by a small group of users and knows perhaps little about its contents, the data base environment requires the analyst or administrator to have extensive knowledge of the overall organization and of the meaning of its data. Also, a successful data base project requires the firm and continuing commitment of management and users alike.

THE IMPLEMENTATION OF DATA BASE SYSTEMS

It is difficult to characterize the implementation of data base systems for all DBMS; indeed, this implementation is dependent on the nature of individual DBMS. Also, data structuring in particular requires some familiarity with concepts of storage structuring, the topic for Chapter 9.

Nonetheless, several general features are worth noting. First of all, data base systems tend to be more transaction-oriented than their batch-oriented master file counterparts. This is to say that master file systems tend to be more oriented toward batch-sequential reporting tasks. While data base systems must frequently support this type of processing, very often *on-line* access to individual records is a requirement. Thus the balancing of these access types (and the elimination of batch-sequential access wherever possible) is a major concern in data base implementation.

Why eliminate batch-sequential reports? For one thing, the data are out of date as soon as they are printed (a printed report is merely redundant data in disguise). For another, usually only a small subset of the report, which may be voluminous, is ever used. On-line access solves these problems. On-line systems, of course, have implications of their own for both programming and recovery and add a dimension of complexity to the data base environment.

Another consideration, related to the first, is that wherever possible, the *sorting* of records to produce outputs (or to process inputs) is to be eliminated. DBMS offer capabilities of data structuring (for example, interfile relation, inversion, and randomization) that eliminate the need for sorting, a process whose overhead is largely unacceptable in the on-line environment.

Several examples of the facilities of DBMS for eliminating record sorting were presented in Chapter 2. Since these facilities are those of data structuring, required processing sequences must be identified beforehand and are therefore to be considered part of the data modeling task. In the implementation analysis (Figure 34), delineation of processing sequences is identified as one step in Stage I.

Data bases are often also characterized by the *segmentation* of data—that is, the grouping of data items that have similar patterns of usage. Especially among physically linked DBMS there are methods for placing the resulting segments or records into the data structures so as to optimize access performance. Also, since some DBMS lack element-level security support, segmentation of data elements must additionally reflect a commonality of security requirements.

Information on usage patterns and security requirements must of course be gathered prior to data structuring. Also, it is recommended that once segmentation is affected, records should be analyzed and documented in much the same manner as data elements themselves; that is, naming conventions should be established, usage frequencies traced, access prerogatives defined, and so forth. This information is often most comfortably supported within a data dictionary system.

For the foreseeable future, all data structuring under current DBMS will be dependent on *keys* to provide physical access to and between records. Careful attention to the specification of keys to identify entities, access individual records, facilitate output sequencing, aid in content searching, ensure uniqueness, and relate records is thus of primary importance in data structuring and programmatic access. This task should not be overrated, however, because the definition of keys often falls neatly into place once "contexts" are fully delineated and the facilities of the individual DBMS mastered.

SUPPORT FOR IMPLEMENTED SYSTEMS

The remainder of this chapter focuses on those features of data base systems that are aimed at keeping an implemented data base up and available to users. These features recognize that machines and software are imperfect and that events occur that make *recovery* necessary.

Journals and Recovery

Fundamental to recovery capability is the *journal,* also referred to as a *log tape,* wherein an audit trail of changes to the data base is kept. As the latter name suggests, this journal is normally kept on magnetic tape and is largely automatic for many DBMS.

Common to journals are two basic types of information: *before-images* and *after-images.* These images refer respectively to data before a change is applied and to the same data after the change. The actual unit of data (for example, record, page, or item) recorded for the image varies among systems and circumstances of usage.

Additional information is kept in order to identify the source of the transaction that initiated the change, although the transaction itself is often not stored. Other information is also recorded: for example, the initiation and termination of tasks, checkpoint data, and so forth. In some cases the log tape is not one but several actual files.

The existence of before- and after-images makes possible several basic types of recovery, as discussed below.

1. Where a user program (or more properly, a *run-unit*) terminates abnormally or is otherwise unable to complete successfully, the before-images of the data changed by that program are applied to the data base. By this means the changes effected by the program are reversed and the data base is restored to the original condition. This type of recovery is called *roll-back* or *back-out,* often with a preceding modifier *selective* to indicate that only those changes made by a given program are to be reversed. In some cases, selective roll-back of one or more given *transactions* can be effected if it is determined that the entire run was not in error.

2. Where a disk-resident file is lost due to failure of the device itself, after-images are applied to the last intact copy of the data base (for example, in a *data base dump* on magnetic tape) so that the copy is brought up to date with intervening changes. The reapplication of changes is commonly called *roll-forward,* and the overall process, *dump-restore.* Where only a portion of the disk-resident file is lost (for instance, if a given record cannot be read), it is sometimes possible to effect selective restoration, using the most recent after-image on the log tape for the record. Intelligent mapping of structures across devices (via the device media control language) can often reduce the overhead associated with a dump-restore.

3. Recovery from other machine failures, such as power loss, can often be effected using *checkpoint* and *restart* facilities. A checkpoint is the recording of the complete state of the machine at a given point in time (often on the log tape) so that all processes can be restarted from that point should failure occur. Normally, restart implies a complete roll-back for all changes made to the data base since the last checkpoint. It follows that the more frequently checkpoints occur, the less time it takes to restore the system to a usable form. In addition, the more recent the checkpoint, the less processing is required to redo processing lost *after* the checkpoint was taken.

Especially in on-line systems, however, checkpointing is complicated by the presence of many concurrent processes, which exist in varying states at the time chosen for the checkpoint. Often these processes must be allowed to complete their current transaction (and be prevented from initiating new ones) so that the machine can be "frozen" long enough to take the checkpoint. This action translates directly into loss of response time to terminal users (even over and above the time taken for the checkpoint itself). The frequency of checkpointing must therefore be balanced against the delay caused to users. A checkpoint can often be initiated by either the computer operator or the DBMS itself, and under many systems, it is the operating system rather than the DBMS which performs the actual checkpointing.

Log tapes or journals serve one additional purpose: they are inputs to *quality-auditing* (also called *quality assurance*). By inspection of before- and after-images for given transactions, the loss of data accuracy or consistency (that is, the loss of *data integrity*) can often be traced to a specific erring program so that corrective action can be taken. In such a case the "recovery" is from poor data base usage.

Often, recovery is required for not just one but several failures occurring within a short period of time. This necessitates a combination of recovery procedures, complicating overall support. One final point: the trend in DBMS is toward the elimination, wherever possible, of operator intervention to effect recovery. This is in fact an area in which significant progress has already been made.

Concurrent Access and the Deadlock Problem

By supporting access to data bases by many concurrently executing tasks, DBMS are faced with conflict between these tasks, in particular where updating is requested for the same record at the same time. This potential for conflict is not restricted to on-line tasks; the same situation can occur between an on-line and a batch program, or even with several batch programs in a multi-programming environment.

Many DBMS use the concept of *record locking* to prevent harmful interactions between the tasks (actual physical locking is sometimes at the block or page level rather than at the record level). By record locking, all tasks except one are prevented from updating a given record until the original task is completed.

While locking successfully prevents harmful interactions between tasks, it also raises problems of its own. The most obvious of these is delay for the other tasks: if the first task "holds" a record for a lengthy period, response time for the other tasks may noticeably degrade.

Some DBMS provide strategies for limiting the holding period; for example, the first task may be forced to relinquish control after a certain number of access attempts by other tasks. This strategy can complicate user programs, however, by requiring additional status checking after update attempts.

A more serious side effect of record locking is the problem of deadlock, a situation that can occur between two or more concurrently executing tasks. Deadlock is most easily understood as follows: Task 1 locks Record A, then tries to read and lock Record B before updating Record A; Record B, however, is already locked by Task 2, which is trying to read Record A before updating Record B. In this situation, neither task can proceed, and both are said to be *locked out.*

One solution to this problem is to allow a task to lock only one record at a time, which prevents an interlock situation such as described. This solution is held to be unsatisfactory because it restricts the processing capability of individual tasks.

Another solution is to effect a *selective roll-back* of one of the deadlocked tasks in order to allow the other(s) to complete their processing. This solution solves the conflict but results in delay for all tasks since the journal (where the before-images necessary to effect the roll-back are recorded) is temporarily unavailable for recording other changes to the data base. Also, the roll-back solution requires a degree of sophistication on the part of the DBMS because the deadlock problem must not only be solved but *detected* in the first place.

One final observation on concurrent access support: optimum performance is to be expected where the DBMS is fully *multi-threaded;* that is, where the I-O for different tasks can be overlapped rather than processed one at a time (*single-thread*). This requires that the DBMS be written in largely *re-entrant code*—again an additional level of sophistication. Other aspects of support in the DBMS are relevant to performance, for example, the ability to exploit re-entrancy in user code and the ability to dispatch multiple copies of the same program where high transaction volume is detected.

Storage Structures and Reorganization

The organization of data into storage structures is a complete topic in itself and is therefore reserved for the following chapter. A general characteristic common to many structures, however, is the degrading of access performance over time, as updating causes disorganization relative to the original state of the data base. Chains become distended, overflow is filled, sequential records are separated, and so on; the overall phenomenon can be likened to entropy.

Given this tendency, *reorganization* becomes a task periodically relevant to all data base systems, although to some (for example, physically linked DBMS) more than to others. Utilities are commonly supplied to support reorganization; more often than not, the major problem associated with reorganization is downtime, which sometimes is measured in hours.

Some DBMS are claimed to be *self-reorganizing;* that is, any potential disorganization of storage structures is detected and corrected during actual updates. Although this strategy avoids subsequent deterioration of performance and postpones a separate reorganization, the update process itself is notably slowed. A significant degree of complexity is also added to the DBMS.

The impact of reorganization is one consideration in determining the degree to which data should be integrated; it is also an area relevant to maintaining performance in operational systems. Reorganization presents an opportune time for various types of support activities: for example, taking data base backup copies (dumps), altering data structures or access methods, collecting statistics, or even modifying record content.

Chapter 9

THE BASIC PRINCIPLES OF STORAGE STRUCTURING

The concept of *structure* is central not only to understanding the rendering of data on storage media but to many areas of data base thinking in general. In an important sense, every input and output of a computerized information system represents a "structuring" of data, even though that particular structuring or format may not exist as a structure *per se* in computer storage.

In contrast to data base systems, simple information systems serving a single application often do exhibit a file structuring where each record looks very similar to actual input and output data formats. In data base systems, many application purposes are served by a central data organization, which must support inputs and outputs that differ in significant ways from the physical storage of the data.

Presented in Chapter 2 was the concept of a *data model,* which in essence aggregates all actual and possible informational inputs and outputs into a comprehensive conceptual representation. All data—and, significantly, all their interrelationships—are captured by the data model. A *data structure* is the rendering of that data model through the data description language of a DBMS. Examples of data structures include hierarchical and network structures.

A *storage structure* refers to the configuration of data as they reside in computer storage, including the physical means for access—that is, an *access method.* Thus data structures map into one or more storage structures, as determined by the DDL and by the DBMS itself. An access method may be defined as any scheme used within a storage structure to store or retrieve records. A number of access methods are discussed in this chapter.

BASIC ACCESS METHODS

Following is a discussion of the access methods most commonly used for initial entry into data base structures—that is, of those access methods that support the "first" access to data base files. A record that may be accessed by the first user command is called an *entry point;* the access method used to support the command is commonly referred to as an *entry point access method.*

Physically Serial Access

Physically serial access is the most rudimentary of access methods since no reference is made to record keys. In physically serial access, records are stored (or retrieved) by virtue of the "next" *physical* location on the storage media.

Physically serial access characterizes almost all access to magnetic tape (whether or not records happen to be in sequential order) and is often used in conjunction with other access methods on direct storage devices. Physically serial access to an indexed-sequential file, for example, retrieves records in sequential order. (With overflow or free space, however, the access is complicated.)

It is important to note that "sequential" does not refer to an access method per se but rather means that records to be accessed (for example, by physically serial access) are logically ordered by key value.

Direct Access

In the direct access method, record keys correspond one to one with physical addresses; that is, given a record key, access is predetermined (whether for storage or for retrieval) to a unique storage location. The direct access method is particularly effective where the ratio of record keys to available storage addresses is high—that is, where keys "map" nicely onto storage. In some DBMS, records are assigned *arbitrary* keys (that is, keys unrelated to record content) that automatically map records into available storage locations. Especially for the initial loading of a file, this amounts to assigning the "next" storage location so that record storage becomes physically serial.

An important feature of the direct access method is that no type of table or index "lookup" is required prior to record access; the physical location of the record is derived directly from the key itself. Access methods that use tables of record addresses (that is, indexes) are properly "indexed" or "inverted" even though indexes may contain "direct" addresses.

Randomized Access

Randomized access is similar to the direct access method in that storage locations are derived directly from record keys; it is dissimilar in that storage locations are not available on a one-to-one basis with possible key values. Instead, a transformation algorithm of some nature is used to map a large number of potential key values into a smaller number of available storage locations.

A typical example is the use of social security numbers as record keys: in most applications only a small percentage of all possible numbers are represented by actual records in the file. In this circumstance the direct access method results in considerable waste of storage space since a record location must be allocated to every possible key value. The randomized method allows a tailoring of the file size to the expected number of records, without significant loss of access speed, because the record location is still derived from the key.

The problem arises, however, of what to do with records whose key values randomize or "hash" to the same location in storage. The most common method for handling this situation is the use of linked lists, whereby "synonym" records are linked to the record occupying the original hashed location. As these linked lists become extended, record access times degrade sharply. This situation occurs if the file becomes full or if the randomizing algorithm yields a poor distribution of records over available locations.

An additional consideration in randomized structures is that the order of the randomized file often does not match the sequence of the randomized key, which makes sequential processing of the file problematic. An illustration of a randomized file structure is presented in Figure 35.

Indexed Access

The indexed access method is one of two comprising the general access method inversion. Storage structures implementing inversion are characterized by the segregation of key values into separately maintained tables or indexes. Access to the inverted file is effected by a lookup of key value within the index, where pointers to the actual data are stored. (More on inversion in data structuring can be found in Chapter 3.)

In the indexed access method, an index consists of key values paired on a one-to-one basis with pointers to the indexed records.

Figure 35: A randomized file structure.

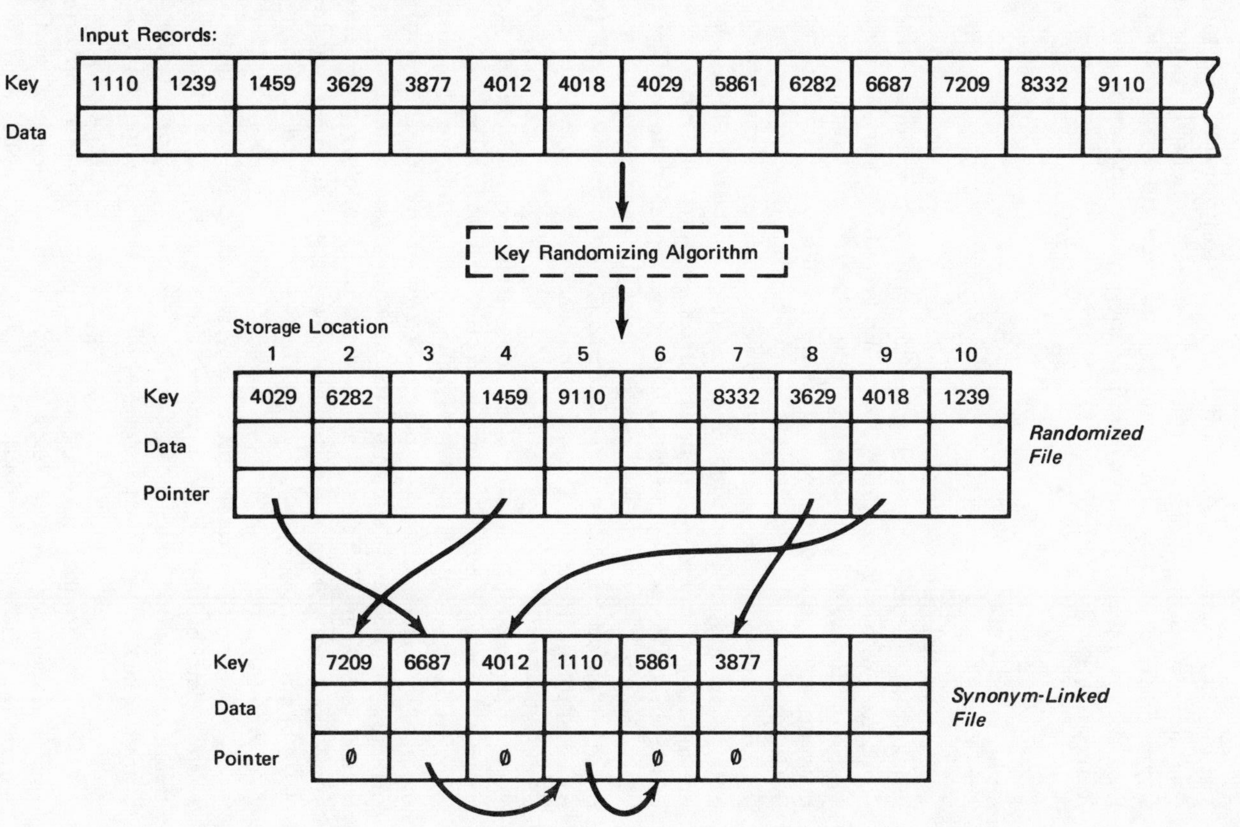

Various organizations are possible for the index itself; the most commonly used in DBMS is probably indexed-sequential. Indexed-sequential is one of two variations of indexed storage structures; the other is indexed-random. Both of these variations are discussed in separate sections later in this chapter.

Inverted Access

In inverted access structures (the second type of inversion), indexed key values are stored once and only once within an index. Associated with a given index key value are pointers to all records within the indexed file having that value for the key. The difference between inverted and indexed structures is illustrated by Figure 14 in Chapter 3.

The most common use of the inverted access method for file entry is in conjunction with system-assigned arbitrary keys, which are stored as pointers within index entries. As noted in the discussion of the direct access method in an earlier section, this allows efficient space management and rapid record access. In most cases, the order of an index under the inverted access method does not match the order of the indexed file, a situation that corresponds to indexed-random organization.

Numerous structures for the index itself are possible; in fact, there is surprising variation among inverted DBMS in index construction. In DATACOM/DB, for example, entries for the same data element inverted within distinct record types are intermingled in order to form a composite index for an entire data base. Associated with inversion in SYSTEM 2000 is structural modeling (in essence, structural information is inverted along with data values). A matched list scheme (coupling) used by ADABAS was presented in Chapter 3 (see Figure 14).

These examples suggest that there is considerable potential for *relating* data by use of the inverted access method, beyond entry point access alone. This is in fact the second topic of interest in storage structuring: how to access *related* data after initial data base entry has been effected.

One final point on inverted access structures: the term "inverted file" is sometimes used to refer to fully inverted files (that is, files where every field is inverted). This infrequently applies to files of inverted DBMS; for these systems, "inverted file" means partially inverted.

VARIATIONS OF INDEXED ACCESS

Indexed-Random

In indexed-random organization, the order of the indexed file is *not* the same as that of the index itself. This situation results where the indexed field is not the primary key of the indexed file or where the indexed file is basically unordered (that is, "random"), such as often occurs in randomized files. Especially in this latter case, indexed-random structures provide a sequential processing capability otherwise unavailable except by sorting.

Because primary access to the indexed file under indexed-random organization is normally by a key other than the indexed-random key, this access method is sometimes referred to as *secondary indexing.* Values for the indexed-random key are often nonunique for a given file, whereas primary keys normally are unique. Especially for physically linked DBMS, the indexed-random key field provides an important "alternate" or "secondary" key for entry into data base files. Indexed-random access support is in fact an important criterion in determining the state of the art among systems of that class.

Indexed-Sequential

In indexed-sequential organization, the indexed file and the index itself are both sequentially ordered on the basis of the same key field, usually called the primary key of the file. Since there is strict correspondence in record order, not all records in the indexed file need actually be represented by an index entry. Instead, indexed file records are often grouped into "blocks"; the highest key value in the block is then indexed.

This arrangement is illustrated in Figure 36, which also presents an indexed-random indexing for the same file. In comparing the size of the respective indexes, it is evident that the indexed-sequential index is relatively compact. Furthermore, since both indexes are sequentially ordered, an indexed-sequential organization for the indexes themselves is possible; that is, index records can be grouped into blocks, which can then be indexed. For large files, this arrangement can be repeated a number of times, a scheme that greatly speeds record access.

The strict sequential ordering of the indexed file poses a number of problems for indexed-sequential structures, in particular for file

Figure 36: An illustration of indexed-sequential and indexed-random organizations.

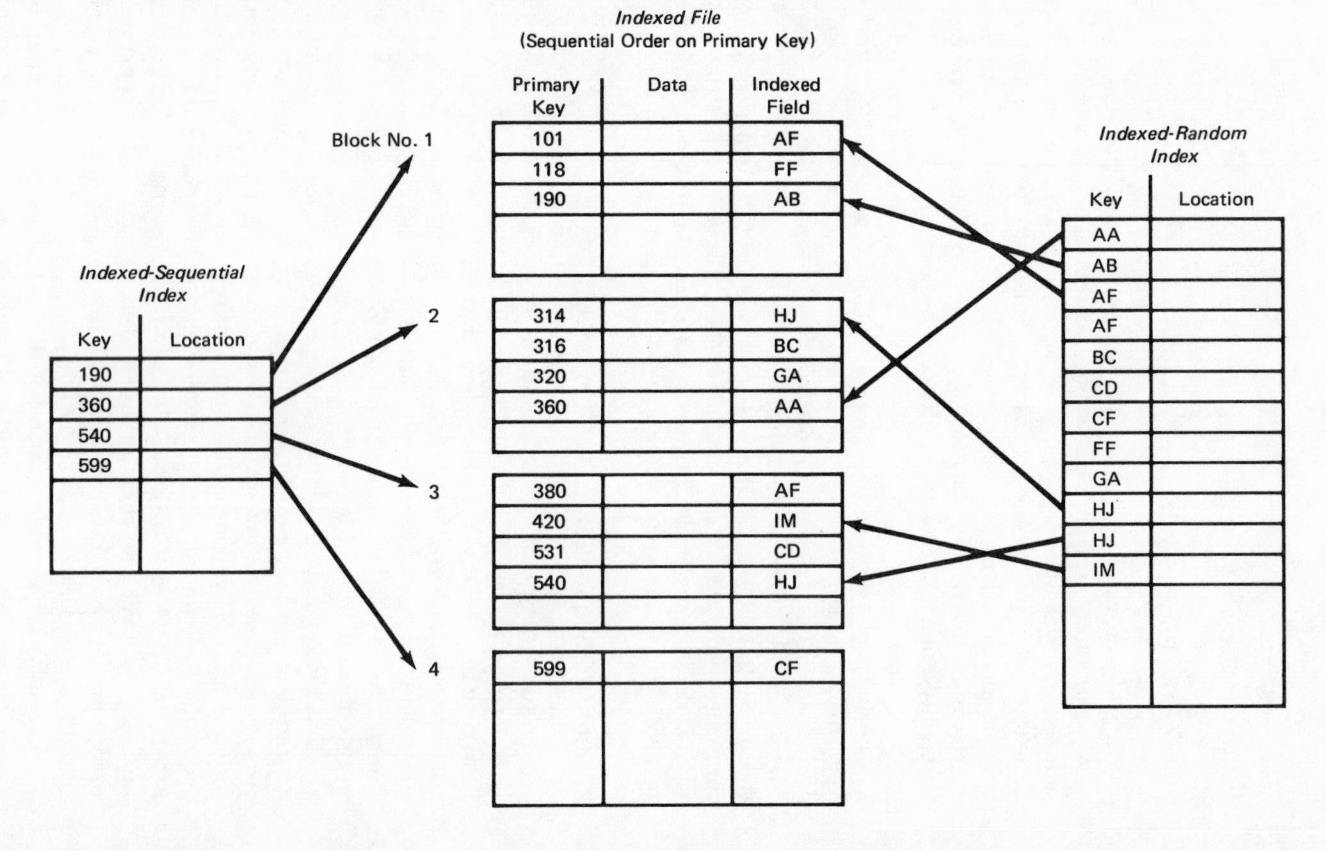

growth. Space can be allocated in individual blocks for file growth, but at some point "overflow" becomes inevitable. One method for handling additional records is by chaining them to the appropriate block; another is by the creation of a new block, which is then indexed. Neither method is completely satisfactory, and occasional file reorganization becomes necessary, in particular if chaining is used.

Indexed-sequential organization provides a compromise between individual record lookup and sequential processing of the indexed file, an activity that becomes largely physically serial. A similar compromise is possible under indexed-random structuring for a randomized file; this compromise works somewhat better for lookup than for sequential processing. Where no indexed-random capability is supported (a situation common among network DBMS), sequential processing of randomized records is sometimes possible by chaining—that is, by definition of an ordered set on the basis of the randomized key.

ACCESS SUBSEQUENT TO ENTRY

As suggested earlier, there are several ways in which storage structures support access to the next sequential record after initial entry into a file. In indexed-sequential organization, where sequential ordering is largely a physical characteristic of the indexed file, access to the "next" record is relatively straightforward. Alternatively, chaining records (as is common in physically linked DBMS) in sequential order serves the same purpose. For indexed-random and inverted structures, the "next" record is defined by the next entry within the index.

Access of types other than the above—specifically access to records *related* to the "current" record—becomes somewhat more complex. In CODASYL terminology, all such "related" records become a set; storage structuring must provide the means for accessing some or all *members* of the set—that is, all records in the data base that "belong" to the set.

The abstractness of the concept of sets tends to obscure its simplicity; a set is nothing more than a collection of records that have a commonly valued field (the field itself is not always stored). In hierarchical data structuring, a set corresponds to a "tree" (there may actually be a number of sets within a tree); in inverted DBMS, particularly where interfile relation is supported, a set is defined by all records that can be accessed by a matching of index values.

The implementation of sets—that is, support for access to related records—thus becomes a central concern in storage structuring for data bases. Some of the most common means for implementing sets are discussed in the following.

Lists and Chains

In a linked list, each member of a given set is stored with the address of the next record in the list; in a chain (or ring), the last member is linked back to the first. Variations allow for linkage to the previous member (backward pointers) and linkage to the owner record from within each member.

Records in a list or chain need not be in any particular order; often, however, sequential ordering lends itself well to various types of access. Lists and chains are the workhorses of physically linked DBMS.

Record Arrays

A record array is similar to a linked list, except that records are physically juxtaposed (as in a table) rather than physically linked. Members of a given set include all entries within the array.

A variation of record arrays is a multiple-level record array, in which each table entry may also have its own record array. This arrangement results in arrays within arrays (or sets within sets) as in a COBOL record description with several levels of OCCURS. (Such description is physically hierarchical.)

Most DBMS allow for multiple-level record arrays to some extent; the relational model (see Chapter 6) does not. A simple record array (without multiple levels) is called a single-level record array.

Pointer Arrays

A pointer array is a collection of record addresses for all members of a set; that is, it contains pointers to all like-valued records. An entry in an inverted index is precisely a pointer array; a pointer array is thus the physical result of inversion.

Pointer arrays are of course prevalent in inverted DBMS; they are relatively scarce as a set implementation technique in physically linked DBMS. Pointer arrays lend themselves well to search-type operations.

Bit Array

A bit array requires one "bit" for every record in a data base; an "on" bit signifies that a record is a member of a given set, an "off" bit, that it is not. Each set requires its own bit array. Since bit arrays for many sets often consist largely of "off" bits, arrays can be "packed" by various techniques. Bit arrays (also called Boolean arrays) are not in widespread use among current DBMS.

Given structural support for accessing a set of records by one or more of the methods discussed, several types of operations on a given set come under consideration. Each storage method shows strength for some types of operations but weakness for others. These strengths and weaknesses are a major concern for mapping data structures into storage structures.

Typical operations on sets are the following:

qualified—A set member is accessed on the basis of supplied information, such as record type or field value.
next (prior)—The next (or previous) member of a set is accessed.
first (last)—The first (or last) member of a set is accessed.
sequential—The next member of a set in logically sequential order (sorted) is accessed.

These operations can often be invoked automatically by appropriate specification within a DDL (for example, by a "rule" for the insertion of members into a set); in addition, comparable operations are often supported for programmatic access to members of a set. For example, a user might specify that the member of interest is the *prior* member of the set or that the member of interest has given field values (the latter is *qualified* access).

Support within DBMS for access of these types results in a reduction of the logic necessary for record processing within application programs. This feature is often associated with the enhancement of productivity in data base systems.

An additional set operation that is often desirable is access to the *owner* of a given set. This capability is useful, for example, where a record is a member of more than one set. Having accessed a record as a member of one of these sets, it is then possible to access the owners of the other sets.

This capability is easily demonstrated within the school data base example presented in Figure 12 in Chapter 3. Given a student name, it is possible to determine the classes for which he or she has registered by accessing members of the courses-taken set (that is, registration records). These registration records, however, are each members of another set, *students-enrolled.* Access to the *owner* of this set from a given registration record retrieves data on the courses taken.

The discussion so far has presented basic set operations. There are of course many variations in these operations, particularly as record access is further divided according to the processing requirements of retrieval, addition, and deletion. These are only some of the many influences on set implementation techniques; another, for example, is the host operating system.

Worth mentioning in this regard is one final, commonly cited, set operation: that which causes a member record to be stored *near* its owner. This operation is especially relevant to performance in "virtual memory" schemes, where a "near" command increases the probability of storage on the same "page" as the owner. The *near* operator also demonstrates the degree of machine intimacy that data bases of this generation still require.

STORAGE STRUCTURES AND DATA BASE TECHNOLOGY

The result of the various storage structures necessary to establish the appropriate relationships between data is well described by the term *network.* A data base organized in this fashion lends itself well to a variety of inputs and outputs while exhibiting minimum redundancy. This accessibility of data is the core of data base philosophy.

Although the concept of network is normally used in connection with the structures derived in CODASYL DBMS (a designation within which theoretical purists would like to stay), a somewhat more general view—that of *data* networking—easily includes the logical relationships of IMS/VS or the interfile relation capability in inverted DBMS. Even the relational model is not exempt; data networks are "there" in the data base even if only for the moment that they are sought out.

This chapter has reviewed the most common storage structure techniques used by currently available DBMS. Many other techniques are possible. A note in closing: hardware advances may within a relatively short period revolutionize storage structuring as now implemented. It is from this source that the raw energy for future data base evolution is likely to come.

PART IV

Data Base Management Systems

Chapter 10
SYSTEM DESCRIPTIONS

The information contained in the following system descriptions was obtained directly from the DBMS vendors. Every effort was made to ensure accuracy.

The system descriptions have been ordered in the manner indicated in Table 10.

INFORMATION MANAGEMENT SYSTEM (IMS)

IBM's IMS is a widely implemented data base management system, rivaled in numbers only by Cincom's TOTAL. It was originally designed in the mid-1960s in conjunction with the Apollo space program.

IMS is actually a generic name for a family of systems, encompassing various levels of compatibility with other IBM systems. Basic data handling under IMS is performed by DL/1 (Data Language 1) and is typically meant to include a telecommunications feature. DL/1 is a data base system in its own right, suitable for batch operations.

The most important current configurations of IMS are the following: IMS/VS under OS/VS1, SVS, or MVS operating systems; IMS-2 (IMS/360) under OS/MFT or OS/MVT; and DL/1 under DOS/VS. The most advanced features are found in IMS/VS, which was first released in February 1974.

IMS offers an integrated data communications feature, IMS/DC, which is priced separately. Interface with CICS is supported as an alternative to IMS/DC.

An application program interfaces with the IMS data base via a CALL statement, using appropriate arguments. Host languages include COBOL, PL/I, and Assembler. Under IMS/DC, a query facility IQF is supported.

Table 10: Data base management systems by vendors and numbers of users.

System	Vendor	Est. Number of Users*
DBMS Offered by Mainframe Computer Vendors		
IMS	IBM Corporation	600–900
I-D-S/II	Honeywell Information Systems, Inc. (H.I.S.)	425 for I-D-S/I
DMS 1100	Sperry UNIVAC	250
DMS/90	Sperry UNIVAC	40
DBMS-10	Digital Equipment Corp. (DEC)	75
DMS-II	Burroughs Corp.	100
DMS-170	Control Data Corp. (CDC)	(new)
Independent DBMS for Mainframe Systems		
TOTAL	Cincom Systems, Inc.	1,100
IDMS	Cullinane Corp.	200
ADABAS	Software AG	200
SYSTEM 2000	MRI Systems Corp.	200
DATACOM/DB	Insyte Corp. (formerly C.I.M. Corp.)	75
INQUIRE	Infodata Systems, Inc.	75
Model 204	Computer Corporation of America (C.C.A.)	30
DBMS Offered for Mini-Computer Systems		
IMAGE/3000	Hewlett-Packard Corp.	200
Varian TOTAL	Sperry UNIVAC (formerly Varian Data Machines)	50
DBMS-11	Digital Equipment Corp. (DEC)	50
Prime DBMS	Prime Computer, Inc.	(new)
INFOS	Data General Corp. (DG)	†
ADMINS/11	ADMINS, Inc.	†
Representative Systems from the Remote-Computing Industry		
MAGNUM	Tymshare, Inc.	225
NOMAD	National CSS, Inc.	275

* As of January 1978.
†Number of users unavailable.

The data description and manipulation languages of IMS are foreign to CODASYL specifications.

Highly attractive IMS/VS features include:

- A program isolation feature, which prevents concurrent update by multiple programs scheduled against the same data base.
- The ability to handle batch and on-line processes simultaneously.
- Various security features for monitoring and controlling data access.

Data structuring under IMS is hierarchical (represented schematically by tree structures), with data elements grouped into segments. Access paths, called logical relationships, may be established between physical tree structures, giving a networklike data configuration. A number of choices in internal pointer types and storage patterns are available; entry point access to data base roots is sequential, randomized, or indexed.

The use of VSAM as an internal access method allows support for secondary indexes and variable-length segments; these features help establish IMS's position among a small group of DBMS defining the state of the art in data structuring capability. However, IMS does not support data independence to the level of individual data items; all access is to records (that is, segments) as they physically reside in the data base. Search arguments called SSAs are supported for selective segment access; user access to IMS data bases is both controlled and enhanced by a device similar in concept to a subschema, known in IMS as a PSB.

IMS is an extremely powerful data handling system, but the overhead costs are held to be high. A great deal of administrative support is necessary on a continuing basis so that the system itself tends to consume professional resources. Some users find the calling conventions cumbersome and difficult to learn. Overall, education and training for effective use of IMS is relatively expensive.

IBM has attempted to make IMS a comprehensive data management facility, but it is not as complete as those of several other vendors. The recovery capabilities in IMS are among the best of any DBMS currently available. One significant recent enhancement to IMS is the Multiple Systems Coupling facility (MSC), announced in mid-1976 for use under IMS/DC. Aimed at distributing data base processing, MSC supports the switching of transactions between relatively independent IMS systems on distinct processors. Segregation of front-end communications support is also possible.

IMS support seems to have a firm commitment by IBM. Ratings

of user satisfaction with IMS tend to fall somewhat below those for other systems, but the number of users speaks for itself. Overall, IMS/VS is one of the most advanced DBMS on the market.

INTEGRATED DATA STORE II (I-D-S/II)

Honeywell Information Systems' (H.I.S.) I-D-S/II is the most recent version of a system that was begun in 1961, making it one of the oldest and most respected of all DBMS. Users of I-D-S/I, which was supplanted by I-D-S/II in the fourth quarter of 1975, are perhaps the most numerous for any CODASYL system.

Earlier versions of I-D-S have the additional distinction of having been the prototype for the CODASYL proposals for standardization of DBMS in the late 1960s. Originally, set concepts were discussed in terms of "master" and "detail" records, as is still the case with Cincom's TOTAL; I-D-S/I and especially I-D-S/II, however, represent efforts to stay within the evolution of CODASYL philosophy and terminology. The most noticable deficiency of I-D-S/I in this regard—which is corrected in I-D-S/II—is the lack of an independent data description language (schema DDL).

I-D-S/I, originally written for the GE-200, is now operational on the Honeywell Series 600, Series 6000, and Series 60 Level 66 computers under the GCOS operating system. I-D-S/II is available on all of these machines except the 600.

On-line processing, which operates under the GCOS Time-Sharing Executive, is extended with the I-D-S Data Query System and the Management Data Query System (MDQS).

Interaction with the I-D-S data base is accomplished using CODASYL data manipulation verbs, which under I-D-S/I must be preceded by an "Enter I-D-S" statement. Interfaces to languages other than COBOL are planned for I-D-S/II. Additional data base creation and processing capability is supported under MDQS IV.

Other enhancements included in I-D-S/II are the following:

An independent subschema description language.
A device media control language for increased control of mapping to physical devices.
Complete CODASYL privacy and security facilities.
Support for variable-length records.
Implementation of an indexed-sequential file access method.
A data dictionary facility.

Support for secondary indexing to allow partial inversion of network files.

Interactive I-D-S/II, using language largely similar to the regular DML.

A data restructuring utility.

I-D-S/II, like I-D-S/I, offers the full range of storage structuring provided by the CODASYL specifications and makes data networking available as the user requires.

With the release of I-D-S/II, H.I.S. has addressed many of the deficiencies in I-D-S/I. A centralization of data management routines and buffer pooling promise to reduce core overhead and to facilitate data access for multi-programming. A general improvement in performance is to be expected.

Also addressed by I-D-S/II is the serious compromise of data independence occasioned by lack of an independent schema DDL. In I-D-S/I, for example, data base description must appear in every application program (usually with a COPY statement); because of this, modifications in the description require extensive program re-compilation.

Restriction of user languages to COBOL and MDQS is undesirable but temporary. Given a firm commitment by H.I.S. for seeing I-D-S/II through its initial installation period in 1976 and 1977, the system has excellent potential for complete data base service.

I-D-S/I, which has users boasting the longest continuous experience with any DBMS, is a solid product. Many of these users can be expected to migrate to I-D-S/II, continuing their prosperous association with the I-D-S software line.

DATA MANAGEMENT SYSTEM DMS 1100

DMS 1100 is UNIVAC's contribution to the data base management field. To date the system itself has not been "unbundled," making its position somewhat unique among DBMS.

DMS 1100 is an overlapping subset of the CODASYL data base specifications. In some cases data handling features have been added or extended, and in others they have been omitted. Several of the most noticeable omissions are the lack of support for privacy locks—an important data security feature—and for the CODASYL subschema facility.

DMS 1100 is available for use on the UNIVAC Series 1100 hardware.

A Transaction Interface Package, TIP, is available as a communications monitor interface. Access to DMS 1100 data bases by timesharing users is supported by CTS.

Application programming under DMS 1100 is through COBOL source code. Fourteen of 16 data manipulation verbs proposed by CODASYL have been implemented, and several additional verbs have been added to enhance procedural capabilities, especially for recovery, error handling, and multi-programming. A pre-processor converts all DMS 1100 verbs to CALL statements. Future releases of special data manipulation statements for other languages, such as FORTRAN and PL/I, are projected.

Attractive DMS 1100 features include:

- A facility for restoration of "quick before" images from temporary disk storage upon system failure, plus selective or complete data base recovery.
- A facility for command roll-back, which restores the data base to its status before the start of the current command, and for run-unit roll-back, which restores the data base to its status before the start of the run-unit.
- An interface with TIMS (Total Information Management System), UNIVAC software for building large information systems.

DMS 1100 supports the three CODASYL access methods: randomized, linked, and direct. In addition, an indexed-sequential mode of physical access has been implemented. Complete network capabilities are available, comparable to any of the CODASYL-type DBMS. In addition, set implementation by pointer array is supported, as well as indexing for sets.

Two important new features are now available for DMS 1100: a high-level Query Language Processor (QLP 1100) and a report writer, Remote Processing System (RPS 1100). Both systems, announced in March 1975, are oriented toward on-line processing.

DMS 1100 has better than average data base protection features. The departures from strict CODASYL implementation may cloud the picture for future compatibility but do in fact provide several positive capabilities. Subschema and privacy lock facilities, as well as a reorganization utility, were reported to be under development in 1977. UNIVAC, which was one of the first to commence development of a CODASYL-type DBMS in 1969, continues to give the system substantial support.

Given continued development and adherence to CODASYL standards, DMS 1100 has strong potentials for future growth and dissemination. Significantly, DMS 1100 appears to have a central role in UNIVAC's marketing strategy for the coming years. A number of observers group DMS 1100 along with IMS/VS and I-D-S/II as definitive of the state of the art among currently implemented DBMS.

DMS/90

DMS/90 is UNIVAC's small computer counterpart to its major DBMS offering, DMS 1100. The system has been available since November 1974.

DMS/90, like DMS 1100, is a CODASYL-type DBMS. In spite of the fact that it is marketed by UNIVAC, DMS/90 is actually more closely related to Cullinane's IDMS than DMS 1100 since both DMS/90 and IDMS were fathered by the same development effort at B.F. Goodrich in 1970 and 1971.

DMS/90 is interesting in several respects. As with DMS 1100, the software to date has not been "unbundled" by UNIVAC. Moreover, UNIVAC's support of both large and small computer DBMS represents an attempt to provide an avenue of evolution for smaller computer users in an area not before attempted: data base systems following CODASYL standardization. However, complete compatibility between DMS 1100 and DMS/90 has not yet been achieved, a fact complicated by the distinct hardware boundary between UNIVAC's large and small computer lines.

DMS/90 is available on UNIVAC's Series 90 (90/60, 90/70, 90/80) under VS/9; the UNIVAC Series 70 (formerly RCA) under VS/9; and the UNIVAC 90/30 under OS/3. The 90/60 and 90/70 machines fall approximately into the range of IBM's 370/138 and 370/148.

Application programming is accomplished in COBOL, using a subset of the CODASYL DML verbs. A pre-processor converts DMS/90 code to CALLs.

DMS/90 fails to implement full CODASYL standards in the following areas:

- Only 12 of 16 CODASYL verbs are implemented.
- Privacy provisions, excluding that provided by the subschema facility, are not supported.

- Capability for set mode of pointer arrays and set occurrence selection is not provided.

DMS/90 supports full CODASYL data networking, including the three principal location modes. The DMS 1100 CODASYL enhancement for supporting indexed-sequential access is not implemented.

Utilities currently exist for data base initialization and recovery, backup, and storage statistics. DMS/90 has somewhat larger real core requirements than IMAGE/3000 (estimated at 131K bytes for the 90/30 and 262K bytes for the 90/60 and 90/70). Important enhancements were scheduled for 1976: re-entrant coding of DBMS modules, for multi-user support; on-line recovery features; and implementation of a device media control language (DMCL).

One especially interesting development area is the integration of IMS/90, an additional UNIVAC data management system. IMS/90 is described as a generalized on-line storage and retrieval system supporting access to direct, sequential and indexed-sequential files. A number of interesting features are supported: a high-level query/update language (UNIQUE), a communications interface, password security, and recovery functions.

The future of DMS/90 is difficult to predict. Development of the system continues at this date and has already corrected a number of early shortcomings. Interesting because it brings mainframe data base management to medium-size users, it is caught up in an intense hardware confrontation taking place in that arena. Its future is also clouded by UNIVAC's 1977 acquisition of the Varian hardware line. DMS/90 is clearly an indicator of important trends in the data base field and should be watched closely in the next several years.

DATA BASE MANAGEMENT SYSTEM-10 (DBMS-10)

DBMS-10, another of the CODASYL-type DBMS, is marketed by Digital Equipment Corporation (DEC). The system is also available on the communications network of Rapidata, which was responsible for its design and development. The system was initially available in mid-1973.

DBMS-10 is perhaps not as advanced as some of the other mainframe CODASYL systems, although development continues. One area especially criticized has been its deficiency in supporting concurrent access, a weakness that DEC has moved to correct in the past year or so. A subschema facility is supported, but its scope is relatively limited.

DBMS-10 is implemented for the DECsystem-10 and DECsystem-20.

On-line processing is available through the DECsystem-10 monitor, which is complemented by DBMS-10 reentrant modules.

Application programming against DBMS-10 data bases is accomplished in COBOL or FORTRAN host languages.

Recently released by Rapidata is X2C, a high-level nonprocedural language that has a number of positive features:

- Interface with special dictionary file(s) in which comprehensive structural information is kept on a selected basis.
- Compilation of source code rather than interpretation so that object code may be kept for later execution.
- A powerful report generation feature.
- Computational looping and input/output facilities built into the language.
- A powerful DML syntax that substantially reduces the effort required for application development.
- A data base creation and update capability.

DBMS-10 provides complete data networking, including a facility for sequential access.

Utilities are provided for initialization, print, schema update, and statistics. Recovery has been cited as somewhat lacking, and a new utility directed at this area is reported to be in the works.

Documentation, at least of the tutorial variety, is excellent, better than for most DBMS. The data dictionary facility to be featured by X2C is especially noteworthy in several respects. First, it supports all files that comprise the "data base," whether merely sequential or truly structured. Secondly, multiple dictionaries are created, which in the case of DBMS-10 files identify subschema and schema so that different logical views are presented to different sets of X2C users. Finally, data description is enhanced in several ways. X2C should be watched closely as a significant extension of DBMS-10 usability.

With the release of DBMS-10 for the DECsystem-20 and of DBMS-11, a mini-DBMS for the PDP-11, DEC has now established a complete range of data management support, from the larger user on the one hand to the medium-size and smaller user on the other. It is significant that CODASYL DBMS software is the common denominator in the various data management offerings.

DEC is rapidly moving toward a position of growing strength in the computer industry; its offerings should be watched closely for this reason. In addition, DEC is beginning to shed much of the reputation it once had for lack of interest in software products. This development is of course generally true for the mini manufacturers and is indicative of increasing confrontation with the traditional mainframers.

DATA MANAGEMENT SYSTEM-II (DMS-II)

Burroughs' DMS-II is a highly innovative system that is outstanding, by comparison, in operational performance. The system was first announced in October 1974.

DMS-II represents a significant departure from Burroughs' previous DBMS offering, DM6700, in several important ways. Perhaps the outstanding difference is the integration of various data base management routines into the operating system itself, which has noticeable effect on data retrieval speeds and helps reduce overall core requirements. DMS-II also represents a departure from CODASYL standards, although there is some overlap in philosophy.

DMS-II runs on Burroughs' B 6700 and B 7700 series computers under the MCP operating system. Newly released is support for the B 1700 Series.

For large-scale communication networks, DMS-II can be interfaced with the Network Definition Language (NDL) and Message Control System (MCS).

Application programming against DMS-II data bases is supported directly in COBOL, Algol, and PL/I through use of 17 verb commands. No pre-processing of the source code in these languages is required since DMS-II extensions to language compilers are supplied.

Performance-oriented features of DMS-II include:

- Loading of re-entrant data set access routines into main memory upon issuance of an INVOKE statement to act as MCP intrinsics.
- Implicit "frees" of data sets after selected data base operations.
- Isolation of on-line transaction error to a disk page in order to allow for continued processing with concurrent reconstruction of the page.
- Optional construction of bit vectors, representing data base

content under given selection criteria, to improve the speed of data base inquiry.

DMS-II access methods, of which bit vectors are only one, include six others: indexed-sequential, indexed-random, random (calculated), direct, ordered lists, and unordered lists. Basic file organization is supported in four modes: sequential, random, indexed-sequential, and indexed-random.

Conceptually, a DMS-II data base is organized into data sets and sets, which provide significant networking capability. Data sets, which may be either "disjointed" or "embedded," define basic storage patterns by which data are physically organized. Linkage between data sets, in any of five options, provides internal network paths. External data organization is supported by data inversion, by which "sets" of data are formed. Data access from sets may be improved by formation of "subsets" and by storage of selected data.

DMS-II includes a report-writing feature and a query language, INQUIRY. DMS-II is clearly unique among DBMS in several respects. First is the balance that Burroughs has achieved between physically linked structuring ("data sets") and inversion ("sets"); this enables the user to tailor his data base to his needs. A second unique feature, mentioned earlier, is the merging of selected DBMS routines with the operating system. Also, the capability of source language compilers to process data manipulation verbs directly is notable.

One questionable feature of DMS-II is the extent of programmer control over audit/recovery logging. Some argue that this capability is error-prone and undesirable in terms of data independence. Security, which is largely borrowed from the operating system, could be improved. One significant deficiency is the lack of a subschema facility. Overall, DMS-II is complex but nonetheless fast and relatively easy to use. Documentation has been somewhat lacking.

DMS-II users are particularly enthusiastic about Burroughs' data base system. Given its special characteristics, DMS-II is clearly a system to watch in the data base field, especially as its facilities for data structuring become more widely understood.

DMS-170

Control Data Corporation's DMS-170 is one of the more innovative systems on the market. It attempts to bring together inverted structures and CODASYL concepts under something of a relational umbrella. Components of DMS-170—for example, QUERY UPDATE—have been available for some time; others have been marketed within the last year or so. Particularly significant in this regard is the CDCS (Cyber Database Control System). Only a few users currently employ DMS-170 in full form.

DMS-170 is perhaps a prime example of an implementation of the complete data management concept. Many components are thoroughly data base in orientation; others—for example, the COBOL compiler and the SORT-MERGE processor—fall outside the traditional definition of a DBMS. Lower-level file processing is supported in DMS-170. The loose packaging of these various components into DMS-170 is designed to give a holistic concept of data management and of a machine function.

Hardware for DMS-170 includes the CDC Cyber 170 series; Cyber 70 series, Models 72, 73, 74; and the 6000 series, under SCOPE 3.4 and NOS 1.0.

DMS-170 is used directly in COBOL and via CALLs in other languages. A self-contained user-oriented language, QUERY UPDATE, may be used for DMS-170 interface. The COBOL DML is very similar to traditional COBOL I-O commands but dissimilar to CODASYL specifications.

Basic data structuring in DMS-170 is through inversion. To relate records, a JOIN operator is specified in the DDL (establishing an equivalence between a common data element), and the logical concatenation of record types is given a special relation name. A user requesting access to this relation name (via a COBOL READ) receives a physical concatenation of records that have been aggregated by the DBCS using index information.

One important feature of DMS-170 is that files involved in data base relationships are concurrently available to processing outside the data base, even for updating. This avoids a "lock-in" of the data and yields flexibility to the application environment. Users of IBM's IMS and similar systems have no such capability; in IMS, for example, a file is always an IMS file, even if internally VSAM or ISAM. Overall, DMS-170 is geared toward allowing a smoother transition to the data base environment than possible under many DBMS.

DMS-170 is not yet widely known in the market because CDC has not been particularly well known in the past for data management. Its borrowing from both the CODASYL specifications and relational theory has been called flippant by some, imaginative by others. Although DMS-170 has parallels in other systems—INQUIRE and

ADABAS in particular—it is definitely unique among the DBMS offered by mainframe companies, which have generally not tended as strongly toward inversion. DMS-170 also supports subschemas and data independence to the data item level.

The future of DMS-170—especially its performance in large data base environments—will be interesting to watch. Like Burroughs' DMS-II, it is likely to become better respected as its facilities become more widely understood.

TOTAL

In terms of the number of current users, Cincom Systems' TOTAL is IMS's most serious competitor for IBM hardware. Unlike IMS and most other DBMS, however, TOTAL has not been limited to a single hardware line but has been implemented in a number of hardware environments. TOTAL users are the most numerous for any DBMS.

TOTAL consists of several modules of phases, one of which is also called TOTAL. Compared to IMS, data handling under TOTAL is extremely streamlined and direct, with relatively little loss in efficiency, except perhaps for larger and less static data bases.

The TOTAL user is restricted to two basic types of records: a single entry "master" record and a variable number of owned "detail" records. These record types may be interrelated in such ways as to model most types of complex data structures. These data structures or "networks" borrow significantly in concept from early versions of I-D-S software.

The first version of TOTAL was made available in early 1969. Current versions of TOTAL are available for the machines listed in Table 11.

On-line processing in the IBM environment is often supported in conjunction with Cincom's ENVIRON/1 or GTE's Intercomm.

Application data handling uses CALL statements, with appropriate parameters appended. Host languages include COBOL, FORTRAN, PL/I, RPG II, and Assembler. TOTAL data handling language has little in common with the current CODASYL specifications.

Data base security features include:

- Dynamic data base logging of before- and after-images.
- With ENVIRON/1, automatic warm or cold restarts in either real-time or on-line modes.

- ◦ Utilities for periodic data base dumps.
- ◦ A task "hold" facility for the prevention of concurrent update. Under a multitask version of TOTAL, multiple application programs may share the same data base.

Data structuring under TOTAL is somewhat like that of the CODASYL model, although terminology and implementation differ significantly. The TOTAL network does not have the full range of CODASYL capabilities; for example, a record type must always be either an owner (a master record) or a member (a detail record); it cannot be an owner in one set type and a member in another. This restriction prohibits the direct relationship of master records of different types or detail records of different types. One implication of this is that a hierarchy in TOTAL can never be directly expressed with more than two levels. An additional restriction is the lack of support for variable-length records. Access to master records is strictly randomized.

TOTAL has been criticized for these and other aspects in data

Table 11: Hardware lines and operating systems for Cincom Systems' TOTAL.

Manufacturer	Hardware Line	Operating System
Burroughs	2500, 4800	MCPV
CDC	6000/Cyber 70, 170 3000L	SCOPE, KRONOS, NOS MASTER
DEC	PDP/11/34, 11/70	RSX, IAS
Harris	S100/S200 Series	VULCAN
Honeywell	200/2000 Series Level 62 Level 66/6000 Level 6	Mod 1, OS2000 GCOS GCOS GCOS
IBM	360/370 System/3 Models 8, 10, 12, 15	DOS, DOS/VS, OS, OS/VS, SVS, MVS SCP/CCP
ICL	1900 Series	GEORGE
Interdata	7, 8/32	OS 32
NCR	Century Series Criterion Series	B Series RS1, VRX
RCA/UNIVAC	Series 70	DOS
Siemens	4004	BS-1000
UNIVAC	9400/9700 90/60, 70, 80	OS/4 VS9
Varian	V70 Series	VORTEX II

structuring. Nonetheless, certain of these features have positive implications for performance and space economy—one reason why TOTAL has had initial successes in the mini environment.

Compared to IMS, TOTAL's consumption of resources is modest. Unlike IMS, TOTAL supports data independence to the level of individual items, because CALL arguments specify individual items rather than an entire record to be accessed. Subsets of the data base can be formed for a given program in subschema-like fashion.

Proponents of TOTAL are particularly vocal in their praise of the system, and for many IBM System/370 users, TOTAL represents an important alternative to IBM's IMS. Although in some respects not as advanced as other DBMS, TOTAL is nonetheless impressive in a number of ways: its cross-mainframe implementation, its early successes in the mini-computer field, and its accumulation of a sizable user base. Cincom is one of the most successful vendors of independent software and as such has contributed significantly to the evolution of DBMS software.

INTEGRATED DATA BASE MANAGEMENT SYSTEM (IDMS)

Cullinane Corporation's IDMS is one of the most attractive data base packages currently available for IBM hardware. Although only recently marketed (May 1973), the IDMS user base has expanded rapidly.

IDMS was specifically designed to comply with the CODASYL specifications and remains to date the only major DBMS of this type commercially available for IBM hardware. IDMS software, which was designed by B. F. Goodrich in 1970 and 1971, has since been adapted to several other hardware lines, including UNIVAC's Series 90 (where it is known as DMS/90) and DEC's PDP-11 (DBMS-11). In this latter environment, IDMS has the distinction of having been the first mini-DBMS of the CODASYL type.

IDMS is available for IBM System/360 and 370 under DOS, DOS/VS, OS/MFT, OS/MVT, and VS. Support is also extended to the UNIVAC Series 70, although Cullinane no longer actively markets in this area.

A Generalized Communications Interface (GCI) allows IDMS coupling to most telecommunications monitors, including CICS and Intercomm. In late 1976, marketing support was announced for a teleprocessing monitor Shadow II, allowing a more integrated DB/DC environment for IDMS users.

IDMS may be used with any host language (for example, FORTRAN, PL/I, Assembler) that supports a CALL statement. For COBOL, a special set of data manipulation statements is available for data handling functions. A special section within the Data Division allows the user to invoke a subschema (a subset of the data base data description) for use by his program. All special functions, such as the above, are supported by a pre-compiler.

IDMS features several attractive items:

- Privacy locks for greater access control.
- Data base recovery routines, including journal roll-forward and roll-back of data base files.
- A Central Access Monitor Program (CAMP) that provides for multitask processing.
- An integrated data dictionary system, including a facility for automatic data description in programmatic form (COBOL).

Data structuring under IDMS follows the CODASYL specifications for networks. Recently announced were significant extensions to previously supported storage techniques, including support for sequential structures, for primary and secondary indexing, and for a generic key retrieval capability.

Available with IDMS is an integrated version of CULPRIT, a powerful report generator. Cullinane has recently begun to emphasize the total data management concept, with the packaging of a number of system components into CDMS (Cullinane Data Management System). Components of this package include IDMS itself, teleprocessing support, an on-line query facility, a data dictionary, and various output generators under CULPRIT. Cullinane is also pursuing the back-end DBMS concept under DBMS-11, which it calls IDMS-11.

Cullinane is in a solid position of strength as the industry looks increasingly toward the CODASYL specifications and toward new concepts in data management, such as back-end DBMS. IDMS is a popular system and one whose growth continues.

ADABAS

ADABAS is a full-scale data base management system produced by the German-based corporation Software AG. At least one-half of the current users are in North America.

ADABAS, which finds its forte among medium-size to large application environments, is comparable in general data handling capabilities to any of the other major data base systems. ADABAS is unique, however, in providing an integrated data compression facility from which significant savings in disk storage, as well as *de facto* security, may accrue.

ADABAS is supported under IBM Systems 360 and 370 under DOS, OS, and VS.

Teleprocessing interfaces are available for TSO, CICS, Intercomm, Task/Master, and ENVIRON/1. Software AG recently released its own teleprocessing monitor, Com-plete, signaling a move in the integrated DB/DC direction.

Application program interface is effected through CALL statements within COBOL, FORTRAN, PL/I or Assembler source languages. A special ADABAS query language, ADASCRIPT, supports high-level retrieval requests in a stand-alone fashion. There is no overlap with CODASYL specifications. A relatively new facility receiving increasing emphasis is ADAMINT, a "macro" software facility that allows the creation of high-level, customized user views of the data base.

Attractive ADABAS features include:

- An "autorestart" capability, which allows the resumption of data base activities immediately following an interruption.
- A "restore" capability for recovery from hard read errors.
- A "restart" capability, which restores before-images following abnormal program termination.
- Special security capabilities, including support for 15 gradations of access security and for data ciphering.
- A phonetization utility for improving search results.

Under ADABAS data structuring, as with SYSTEM 2000, all logical data element relationships are given physical expression in a segregated portion of the data base. These inversion techniques result in a considerable reduction of the overhead associated with file reorganization and data base searching.

A record in an ADABAS data base is a simple physical hierarchy in which an effective limit of only one or perhaps two levels is possible. The true power of ADABAS arises from the indexing of these records and from the mapping of indexes for elements of the same type (that is, elements taken from the same domain) appearing in different record types. This process, called coupling, results in two matched lists, which represent a bidirectional "linkage" between record types.

ADABAS has been praised for its element-level independence, which is possibly as extensive as in any DBMS currently available.

Not only is access possible at the element level, but, significantly, file reorganization is not necessarily required should a field type be added to a record type. This allows a flexibility for growth far beyond many other DBMS. An additional level of independence is possible under ADAMINT.

In these and other respects, some observers feel that ADABAS approaches a measure of the separation between logical and physical concerns that is envisioned by the relational model. Development of ADABAS facilities continues in a number of areas. An integrated report generator, ADAWRITER, was released in the second quarter of 1975. Software AG is known to be active in the development of mini-computer systems.

Some critics originally questioned whether German-based ADABAS developers could give adequate support to North American installations. (ADABAS was released in 1970 and was marketed in the United States in 1972.) The question now seems moot.

ADABAS is an attractive system, which overshadows its monolithic competitor IMS/VS in a number of respects. Overall, ADABAS is one of the foremost representatives of the class of inverted DBMS.

SYSTEM 2000

MRI Systems' SYSTEM 2000 is one of the best-known DBMS in the field, with implementations for UNIVAC and CDC computer lines as well as for the IBM 360/370 environment. Estimates of the current number of users falls somewhat below 200. SYSTEM 2000 has also had notable success in the remote-computing field, where it is offered by some 15 sources and is used by as many as 350 organizations.

In terms of overall system complexity, SYSTEM 2000 falls somewhere between the extremes presented by IMS and TOTAL. Data base administration, however, is probably less difficult with SYSTEM 2000 than with either of these systems. SYSTEM 2000 emphasizes the construction of efficient indexes to data records, based on inversion of individual data fields.

SYSTEM 2000 is currently implemented on several manufacturers' mainframes: IBM System/360 and 370; UNIVAC Series 1100; and CDC 6000 series and Cyber 70 and 170 systems. SYSTEM 2000, like TOTAL, is noteworthy in this cross-mainframe implementation.

SYSTEM 2000 is interfaced with teleprocessing monitors such

as CICS or TP 2000 (the latter also marketed by MRI). The SYSTEM 2000/TP 2000 combination is highly rated by many sources. A recent enhancement provides a TCAM interface.

The Immediate Access Feature of SYSTEM 2000 allows user interface with the data base through a high-level language consisting of English-like commands. SYSTEM 2000 also has host language support for COBOL, FORTRAN, PL/I, and Assembler. In COBOL, FORTRAN, and PL/I, special verbs are used to effect data handling. These verb statements are converted to appropriate CALL statements by a SYSTEM 2000 pre-compiler. There is no significant overlap with CODASYL specifications.

Attractive features of SYSTEM 2000 include:

- A multi-thread feature, which allows multiple application access to the same data base (concurrent update is controlled).
- A facility for an audit trail, which may be used for backup.
- Field- and segment-level security, provided by password options.

SYSTEM 2000, along with ADABAS and perhaps several other DBMS, forms a class of systems distinct from others by its emphasis on data inversion. Unlike many other inverted DBMS, however, SYSTEM 2000 emphasizes hierarchical data structuring, with up to 32 levels in a given tree. Trees are "put together" by tables (called *hierarchical location tables*) that are external to the actual data but also separate from field indexes. Although powerful in a number of respects, some critics have argued that the hierarchical approach of SYSTEM 2000 does not achieve the data networking possible in other DBMS.

MRI has striven to demonstrate that SYSTEM 2000 as an inverted DBMS does not necessarily engender more overhead in update processing than physically linked counterparts and that data retrieval and data independence are notably better in the former than in the latter. SYSTEM 2000, first released in 1970, is one of the oldest independent DBMS and one of the foremost inverted systems.

MRI has recently released a data dictionary system for SYSTEM 2000, called CONTROL 2000, a step closer to the complete data management concept. Backup facilities have been improved, and a report writer has been available for some time. MRI is also active in mini-computer system development.

SYSTEM 2000 is notable in its successes in cross-mainframe implementation and in the remote-computing field. It will certainly continue in its role as a major independent DBMS.

DATACOM/DB

DATACOM/DB is an inverted DBMS marketed by the Insyte Corporation (formerly Computer Information Management Company), which also markets DATACOM/DC, a teleprocessing monitor. Taken together, these products are called DATACOM.

A major feature of the DATACOM system is its integration of data base and communications handling. The DC portion was in fact developed before the DB portion; the latter became available in 1973. Either product, however, is available separately, and a variety of successful configurations are reported by the vendor. A data base in DATACOM terminology includes a control file (containing data base definitions and other information), a single integrated index, and up to 240 indexed files.

DATACOM/DB runs on IBM hardware, from the model 360/30 through the 370/158.

Teleprocessing support is oriented primarily toward DATACOM/DC, although DATACOM/DB may be interfaced with other monitors, in particular CICS.

Application programming is effected by CALL statements, by which element-oriented parameter lists are passed to the control system. In addition, a query language is supported under DATACOM/DC.

Several important facilities in DATACOM are the following:

- A multi-DB capability, supporting access by an application program to as many as 240 DATACOM data bases.
- A multi-user facility that allows multiple users to access DATACOM data bases through a central multi-threaded copy of the control system.
- DATAQUERY, a high-level terminal-oriented query language.

Storage structuring in DATACOM/DB is based on the concept of inverted lists. Records are added to data files in load sequence; all access to the data is via index entries. Up to 15 fields per file may be inverted (a given field need not be contiguous); a total of 255 keys per DATACOM data base are supported.

Within the index for the data base, all entries from the various files are intermingled, which results in the aggregation of pointers to all like-valued records, regardless of the file which contains them. (The correspondence of inverted fields in different files is established prior to loading.) A given entry associated with an index key value thus contains both a record pointer and file identification; this information allows various combinations of retrieval options for access to related data. Non-indexed "searchable" fields may also be defined.

DATACOM/DB is oriented toward performance in on-line environments, in some cases trading optimum space management (for example, reclamation of deleted record space) for speed. Certain features are available, however, for improving space management, among them a provision for "slack" space in record files and a compression feature for eliminating certain repeating characters.

An additional capability is offered for improving performance for some sequential tasks ("native key" processing in DATACOM terminology), whereby buffering techniques speed access to records loaded in sequential order. However, reorganization is occasionally required to maintain this and other desirable features. Security in DATACOM is supported to the data-element level. Insyte has recently taken significant steps to improve DATACOM documentation.

The user base for DATACOM/DB is among the most rapidly expanding for newer DBMS, and DATACOM/DB itself is now considered, along with systems such as SYSTEM 2000 and ADABAS, to be among the top three or four inverted DBMS for IBM hardware.

INQUIRE

INQUIRE is an inverted DBMS that exhibits a number of interesting features. It is marketed by Infodata Systems, Inc.

INQUIRE has been on the market for some time (the original release appeared in 1969), but the early version could not be called a full-scale data base management facility. Although INQUIRE retains something of its original information storage and retrieval (IS&R) flavor, recent upgrades have greatly enhanced its capabilities. The most important of these are the multiple data base capability (1974), the procedural language interfaces (1975), and the CICS interface and backup/recovery facilities (1976).

INQUIRE runs on the IBM System/360 or 370 under OS and VS operating systems.

Support for INQUIRE under CICS, TSO, IMS/DC, or CMS is available.

Application programming is via CALLs in COBOL, PL/I, FORTRAN, or Assembler; a self-contained, free-format Command Language with query capability is supported in either batch or on-line modes.

INQUIRE's method of indexing is its own and does not closely resemble that found in ADABAS, SYSTEM 2000, DATACOM/DB, or other inverted DBMS. Each record in an INQUIRE data file is represented by a surrogate, which contains indexed values for that record in coded form. These surrogates, which are located in a search file, are chained together on the basis of like values for given fields. The actual value for the field resides in an index file, which points to the top of the appropriate chain in the search file and includes a count of the number of entries in the chain. This information may be used to optimize searching.

There are no actual linkages between INQUIRE data files. When a user wishes to relate records in separate files, a CONNECT statement is issued that gives the DBMS sufficient information to map together the indexes of an inverted data element common to the two record types.

Data independence to the data-item level is supported, but the lack of a subschema capability is notable. One of INQUIRE's strongest features is its text handling capability—an area largely ignored by most current DBMS. One enhancement in this area was recently developed: a proximity-searching capability for string analysis and document retrieval.

Infodata is pursuing development toward interfaces with word processing systems. At the same time, INQUIRE has developed in more or less the opposite direction, toward more traditional data base applications, such as payroll and inventory. Although the system is proven viable in these areas, some critics have argued that INQUIRE is not as stringent about data integration as other DBMS.

INQUIRE brings together notable features in a somewhat unique approach to the data management problem.

MODEL 204

Model 204, marketed by the Computer Corporation of America, is a flexible DBMS, although somewhat less well known than various of its counterparts. Data access under Model 204 is primarily by data inversion, placing it in a class with SYSTEM 2000, ADABAS, and others.

Model 204 is supported on IBM System/360 or 370 under OS and VS operating systems.

Full-scale teleprocessing may be supported under CICS and Intercomm. For smaller-scale user-oriented functions, Model 204 has a set of built-in teleprocessing modules.

Host languages for the batch environment include COBOL, BAL,

PL/I, and FORTRAN, using CALL statements. Especially for on-line users, Model 204 offers a completely self-contained language, oriented to easy interactive inquiry, although it may also be used for updating and for batch processing.

Attractive features of Model 204 include the following:

- A multi-thread option for improvement of throughput.
- Data security to four levels: records, record sets, files, and devices.
- Checkpoint/restart facilities using an audit trail.
- Data compaction and free-space chaining, both of which improve storage.
- A field-level option for data encoding.

Storage structuring under Model 204 is accomplished primarily by the inversion of multiple fields so that run-time requests can be satisfied by comparison of index values rather than by search of actual data. Several options, however, are supported for controlling the physical storage of records so that batch processing—including sequential report tasks—can be improved.

Model 204 exhibits flexibility in system configuration, allowing the user to tailor operational support to his needs for on-line and batch processing. The user language is rated highly and is relatively easy to learn.

Model 204 is notable in its attention to search capabilities; it provides a set of powerful relational operators and numeric "range" retrieval. Another unusual feature is the provision of integrated math options. System overhead is reported not to be excessive, given cautious inversion. One useful performance-oriented option is the capability to defer index updating, although this may degrade data value in some cases.

Model 204 has not yet been proven, in terms of the number of users, to the same extent as other DBMS. Overall, the system is noted for flexibility and careful design.

IMAGE/3000

Hewlett-Packard's IMAGE/3000 is a remarkable system that brings full DBMS services within reach of the users of smaller, less expensive computer systems. At the time of its release in mid-1974, the system was the first mini-DBMS to be offered by a major mini-computer manufacturer.

IMAGE/3000 follows the network model and closely resembles TOTAL in a number of respects. The system itself runs on a machine with a minimum 128K bytes of real core. Formerly, a single data base data set (file) could not exceed 47M bytes—the capacity of the Hewlett-Packard disks—but this restriction has since been removed. IMAGE/3000 is capable of handling most medium-size applications, at a software cost of about 20 percent to 40 percent of larger DBMS.

IMAGE/3000 runs on HP/3000 computers under the MPE/3000 operating systems. Two smaller versions of IMAGE software are available: IMAGE/2000 for the HP/2100 under DOS-III and IMAGE/1000 for the HP 21MX series under RTE-11 and RTE-111.

Telecommunications are supported by operating system software and are complemented by IMAGE software.

Application programming is accomplished by CALL statements within host languages COBOL, FORTRAN, BASIC, RPG, or SPL (HP's high-level system programming language). A high-level interactive user language, QUERY, is available at a modest additional cost.

Attractive QUERY/3000 features are the following:

- Complete update capability, including immediate availability of data for retrieval.
- Support for multi-level IMAGE/3000 security features.
- Tutorial aids, such as syntax assistance, and data base structural mapping.
- Extensive search, edit, sort, and report capability.
- Ability to store frequently used procedures to be invoked as needed.

IMAGE/3000 uses a method of storage structuring that features master and detail data sets. Each data set is a collection of records, or "data entries," which consist of individual data items. For detail data sets, one or more data items are defined as "search items"; all data entries having identical values for the search items are chained together (using forward and backward pointers). For master data sets, a single search item is defined, whose values are unique. A given master data entry is then linked with similarly valued chains in the detail data set(s). Access to master data entries is normally calculated (randomized), although serial and direct access is possible.

Storage structuring under IMAGE/3000 has the simplicity and directness of TOTAL and provides generally streamlined access. Some limitations exist—for example, no support is provided for variable-length data entries, and there are no direct means of indexed-sequential access—but these do not prevent full data networking.

Utilities are generally good; security, which is multi-classed and extended to the data item level, appears excellent. Support for a query language is noteworthy. Although many doubts were raised about IMAGE software upon its release in 1974, the system has since proven itself in a variety of applications and has received a number of favorable appraisals. By pioneering mini-DBMS technology and marketing, Hewlett-Packard has now achieved a position of strength in the mini data management field.

Hewlett-Packard offers IMAGE/3000 as a central feature of a highly attractive line of mini-computer hardware and software that is designed for an opening market of smaller data processing applications. On the whole, the system has potential for significant contributions to DBMS evolution.

VARIAN TOTAL

Varian TOTAL, first released in November 1975, represents the first of a closely timed set of releases of Cincom's successful TOTAL software for the hardware lines of popular mini manufacturers. These manufacturers presently include Harris, DEC, and Interdata, with others likely to follow. Varian itself has since been acquired by Sperry UNIVAC—a development of potential significance to mainframe users.

The data base environment envisioned by Varian TOTAL differs little in concept from that in mainframe offerings. The TOTAL network is substantially the same, as are administrative steps in implementing it. Despite the evident difference in size, there are no theoretical limits on the extent of a Varian TOTAL data base. Over 2,500 master and detail data sets can be defined; practical size limits depend largely on usage and system configurations.

A processor with a minimum of 128K bytes of main memory is required; actual/memory sizes in the Varian line have been pushing upward steadily. One hardware innovation is particularly noteworthy: the use of microcoded firmware to implement the randomization algorithm. An important recent enhancement allows locking for update at the record level.

Varian TOTAL runs on the V70 series under VORTEX II.

Host languages include any supporting a CALL: FORTRAN, RPG II, COBOL, and Assembler. No query language is yet available, a deficiency in comparison with IMAGE.

The emergence of a class of systems such as Varian TOTAL is significant in a number of respects. First of all, mini-DBMS bring the benefits of data base organization and data independence within the reach of smaller users. While the cost/performance ratio of mini hardware steadily improves, the availability of software is increasingly a factor. Secondly, the existence of mini-DBMS with mainframe counterparts raises the possibility of back-end configurations, from which numerous benefits to larger users can accrue. Such systems bring the day of distributed data bases one step closer.

DBMS-11

With the release of DBMS-11 in mid-1976, Digital Equipment Corporation (DEC) extended its CODASYL compliance to its mini-computer line, the popular PDP-11. Although DBMS-11 is actually an adaptation of Cullinane's IDMS software, it nonetheless complements DEC's mainframe CODASYL offering, DBMS-10.

The DBMS-11 implementation is relatively extensive, especially for a system in its initial releases. Support for concurrent usage, subschema definition, recovery, and other features is evident. The DDL and DML syntaxes are in close compliance with CODASYL specifications; network implementation is by physical linkage.

Initial hardware support is for the PDP-11/70 mini-computer under IAS. This machine, like the top of the Hewlett-Packard, Varian (UNIVAC), Data General, and other mini-computer lines, is perhaps more accurately described as a midi-computer.

Data base interface is via the CODASYL DML in COBOL and by CALLs in FORTRAN, BASIC, and MACRO-11 programs. No query facility is initially available.

DEC, not known in the past for software development, was not the first mini manufacturer to arrive at the DBMS market. Since it is the largest, however, and one of the most respected, its move into the data base field is certain to have significant impact. DBMS-11 is the first CODASYL mini-DBMS (another has since been released by Prime Computers) and thus represents an important test of the CODASYL specifications in the mini environment. The CODASYL specifications envision a broader interpretation of network data structures than do either IMAGE or TOTAL.

Finally, DBMS-11 opens significant possibilities in the areas of back-end DBMS and distributed data base systems. The former is already well under development for DBMS-11; the latter represents a long-standing DEC goal.

PRIME DBMS

Prime Computer entered the mini-DBMS field in early 1977 with the release of CODASYL-compliant Prime DBMS.

Prime DBMS is described as consisting of five major components:

1. A DDL translator for data base description.
2. Subschema facilities for ANSI 74 COBOL and FORTRAN IV.
3. DML support by pre-processors in COBOL and FORTRAN.
4. A re-entrant DML command processor.
5. An on-line, interactive facility for data base administration, including a DMCL capability.

Concurrent access and recovery capabilities are supported. Size limitations are practically nonexistent; actual limitations are determined by the amount of disk storage available. Among other features, the subschema capability allows omission and redefinition of data items.

Prime DBMS runs on the Prime 400 and 500 machines, with 768K and 1024K bytes respectively.

On-line transaction processing is basically supported by Prime's Forms Management System (FORMS), which is compatible with the DBMS.

Data base access is via CODASYL DML, supported by a precompiler in FORTRAN and COBOL.

An important feature of Prime DBMS is that conventional files, created by Prime's Multiple Index Data Access System (MIDAS), may be used directly by the DBMS. This implies the extensive use of inversion in the Prime DBMS network, although other features are also evident.

Prime Computer has brought together significant concepts in CODASYL compatibility, inverted data structures, and new hardware capability in its Prime DBMS. The future of the fledgling system will be interesting to watch.

INFOS

Data General Corporation, the third largest mini manufacturer after DEC and Hewlett-Packard, offers INFOS, a data management facility for its Eclipse line of machines.

INFOS supports three lower-level access methods—sequential, random, and ISAM—in addition to the higher-level Data Base Access Method (DBAM). Variable-length records are supported in both ISAM and DBAM. DBAM is essentially a compatible extension of ISAM, in which indexing on multiple keys is supported. A DBAM index is structured by levels, which correspond to keyed levels in the indexed record. A number of structural and processing options are supported, making DBAM a powerful tool for file access.

INFOS, which was released in early 1975, is supported on the Eclipse C/300 under RDOS, with a maximum 256K byte core. A new commercial processor has since been released: the C/330 with 512K bytes.

Interface to INFOS is through an extended syntax in COBOL, supported directly by the ANSI-74 DG compiler or by CALLs in FORTRAN or Assembler.

While INFOS satisfies a traditional need in mini-machines for efficient record-level filing systems, it does not achieve the data independence that has come to be identified as definitive of data base systems. This deficiency is seen most clearly in the lack of separation between INFOS data base creation and application program logic (that is, there is no independent DDL). Other data base characteristics, such as data integration and subschema support, are also notably lacking.

INFOS is certain to evolve (the recent release of an interfacing IDEA data entry/access software package is one example) and may at some point give rise to a significant inverted DBMS capability.

ADMINS/11

The development of independent software has traditionally been relatively more important in the mini environment than on mainframe counterparts. One of the foremost examples of an independent software package is ADMINS/11, a data management facility for the DEC PDP-11.

ADMINS/11 and INFOS represent opposite extremes in the data management spectrum. Whereas INFOS is essentially a powerful file access method, ADMINS/11 may be considered a complete data management facility. The former is oriented to the user who is capable in the technology; the latter is oriented toward the non-programming user, who cares little about the internal workings of the machine. Some observers have called ADMINS/11 a data management "black box"; others have termed it "relational" because of its divorce of the logical from the physical.

ADMINS/11 runs on the DEC PDP-11, under the RSX-11D operating system.

Interface with ADMINS/11 is through a self-contained high-level user language; a FORTRAN interface is also supported.

The interrelation of data in ADMINS/11 is largely an execution-time activity. Three basic types of data relation are featured:

1. *Composite screens.* Preestablished definitions may be invoked for the on-line juxtaposition of related records, based on data values contained in the records.
2. *Virtual records.* A record type may be defined that consists of data elements from separate files; the elements are aggregated when the record is accessed.
3. *Relational products.* Entire files may be related on the basis of common keys (a JOIN-like operation) in order to update one or both or to create an output file.

Inversion is used extensively in support of these operations.

ADMINS/11, commercially released in January 1975, had its origin in an NSF-funded research project at M.I.T. By virtually eliminating the need for application programming and by featuring powerful "relational" operators, ADMINS/11 approaches new ground in data independence.

MAGNUM

Tymshare's MAGNUM is one of the best examples of powerful new systems emerging from the remote-computing industry, which as a whole is increasingly emphasizing data management applications.

MAGNUM's approach to data handling is largely relational in nature. A MAGNUM data base, called a schema, consists of two basic types of declarations: field definitions and relation definitions.

A relation definition includes a list of previously defined field items, some of which may be keyed. Besides the stored relations, relations can also be defined "locally" within user-written MAGNUM procedures. A local relation is thus one defined in terms of other relations through the operations of the MAGNUM language.

There are actually two MAGNUM languages: a command language for simpler reporting and maintenance, and a data management language for more complex tasks. The syntax of the latter, which is very much like ALGOL, emphasizes nested logic for successive operations on local or stored relations.

MAGNUM, first released in mid-1975, is supported in the DECsystem-10 environment. Host language interfaces for special processing tasks are reportedly being developed. Tymshare, which also offers a communications network TYMNET, reports no plans for making MAGNUM available for in-house purchase.

Tymshare's offering of MAGNUM is especially oriented toward medium-size to large organizations that require on-line transaction-type systems supporting access to a central data base from multiple locations (that is, geographically dispersed organizations). Tymshare reports current support for one two-billion character data base.

MAGNUM is also attractive to smaller companies (less than $50 million of sales) and to individual divisions of large organizations receiving inadequate processing support from an in-house computing facility. Potential competition with mini-DBMS in these areas is evident. MAGNUM has been recently enhanced to support simultaneous updating; other enhancements are being made to improve security.

MAGNUM is perhaps one of the best examples of the type of large-scale user-oriented data management systems now within reach of current hardware technology. It demonstrates that the commercial impact of the relational model is beginning and that the elimination of COBOL programming is feasible—even desirable—in many types of applications.

Tymshare is pursuing other areas of development as well: portions of MAGNUM are being integrated into a proprietary intelligent terminal, using micro-processor technology.

Tymshare's emphasis on MAGNUM development (Tymshare also offers SYSTEM 2000 and FOCUS for use on its IBM hardware) is an indication of the growing importance of data management to the remote-computing industry. MAGNUM is an interesting product in its own right and innovative in a number of respects.

NOMAD

NOMAD, a data management facility offered by National CSS, Inc., is comparable to MAGNUM in a number of respects. It was released in September 1975.

In a NOMAD data base, items are grouped into segments, which can be hierarchically positioned into a tree structure, much as in IMS. Unlike in IMS, however, segments or trees are not logically related using physical linkage; rather, a run-time relational capability is supported, in some ways similar to MAGNUM.

Also like MAGNUM, NOMAD emphasizes user-oriented interaction with the data base by either of two means: a high-level command language or a self-contained procedural capability for more complex processing tasks. Unlike MAGNUM, however, NOMAD features a substantial subschema facility. Data independence to the element level is supported.

NOMAD runs within the IBM 360/370 environment. National CSS, which also offers a communications network VP/CSS, plans to market an in-house OS/VS version in 1978. Support is being developed for simultaneous updating and for host language interfaces. Also available from National CSS is Mathematica's RAMIS.

Both NOMAD and MAGNUM have been criticized in some quarters as dead-end systems, in which the user faces undesirable lock-in to a particular system. The counterargument is that by emphasizing high-level user-oriented languages, advances in hardware technology can be accommodated without impact on existing applications. In addition, the relational approach envisioned by these systems eliminates much of the need for application programming and any consequent investment of resources.

Overall, MAGNUM and NOMAD are significant first experiments in large-scale commercial systems under the relational model. Although they are by no means "pure" relational systems, to many observers they are steps in the right direction.

National CSS, second in size only to Tymshare among independent remote-computing companies, rates NOMAD as one of its most successful products. The future of both MAGNUM and NOMAD—and other systems of their class—is by no means assured, but these systems nonetheless constitute one of the most active sources of innovation in the data base field.

DATA MANAGEMENT SOFTWARE: VENDOR ADDRESSES

Vendor	System
ADMINS, Inc. P.O. Box 254 Wethersfield, Connecticut 06109	ADMINS/11
Applications Software, Inc. 21515 Hawthorne Blvd. Torrance, California 90503	ASI-ST
A.R.A.P. 50 Washington Rd. Princeton, New Jersey 08540	DRS/370 DRS/2
Arthur Andersen & Co. 69 West Washington Street Chicago, Illinois 60602	LEXICON
Burroughs Corporation Burroughs Place Detroit, Michigan 48232	DMS-II
Cincom Systems, Inc. 2300 Montana Ave. Cincinnati, Ohio 45211	TOTAL Cincom Data Dictionary
Computer Corporation of America 575 Technology Square Cambridge, Massachusetts 02139	Model 204
Control Data Corp. 8100 34th Ave. S. Minneapolis, Minn. 55440	DMS-170
Cullinane Corporation 20 William Street Wellesley, Massachusetts 02181	IDMS CULPRIT IDD

Vendor	System
Data Base Management Systems, Inc. 12100 N.E. 16 Ave. North Miami, Florida 33161	BIS/3000
Data General Corporation Route 9 Southboro, Massachusetts 01772	INFOS
Digital Equipment Corporation 146 Main Street Maynard, Massachusetts 01754	DBMS-10 DBMS-11
Eastern Air Lines, Inc. International Airport Miami, Florida 33148	Data Base Directory
ELS Systems Engineering P.O. Box 2415 East Cleveland, Ohio 44112	Product 3
Florida Computer, Inc. 99 N.W. 183rd St. Suite 122 Miami, Florida 33169	Data Boss/2
Harris Corporation 1200 Gateway Drive Fort Lauderdale, Florida 33309	Harris TOTAL
Hewlett-Packard 1501 Page Mill Rd. Palo Alto, California 94304	IMAGE/3000 IMAGE/2000 IMAGE/1000
Honeywell Information Systems, Inc. 200 Smith Street Waltham, Massachusetts 02154	I-D-S/I I-D-S/II EDMS
IBM Corporation Data Processing Division 1133 Westchester Ave. White Plains, New York 10604	IMS/VS (DL/I) DB/DC Data Dictionary
Infodata Systems, Inc. 5205 Leesburg Pike Falls Church, Virginia 22041	INQUIRE
Informatics, Inc. 21050 Vanowen St. Canoga Pk., California 91303	MARK IV

Vendor	System
Insyte Corporation 3707 Rawlins, Suite 325 Dallas, Texas 75219	DATACOM/DB Data Dictionary
Interactive Information Systems 10 Knollcrest Dr. Cincinnati, Ohio 45237	IIS DBMS
Management Systems and Programming 133 Mount Auburn Street Cambridge, Massachusetts 02138	DATAMANAGER
Mathematica, Inc. Box 2392 Princeton, New Jersey 08540	RAMIS
Microdata, Inc. 17481 Red Hill Ave. Irvine, California 92705	Reality Royale
MRI Systems Corporation 12675 Research Blvd. Austin, Texas 78766	SYSTEM 2000 CONTROL-2000
National CSS, Inc. 300 Westport Ave. Norwalk, Connecticut 06851	NOMAD
Panasophic Systems, Inc. 709 Enterprise Dr. Oak Brook, Illinois 60521	Easytrieve
Prime Computer, Inc. 40 Walnut Street Wellesley Hills, Massachusetts 02181	Prime DBMS
Program Products, Inc. 95 Chestnut Ridge Rd. Montvale, New Jersey 07645	Data Analyzer
Rapidata 20 New Dutch Lane Fairfield, New Jersey 07006	X2C (DBMS-10)
Software AG 11800 Sunrise Valley Dr. Reston, Virginia 22091	ADABAS Data Dictionary

Vendor	System
Sperry Univac Division Sperry Rand Corporation P.O. Box 500 Blue Bell, Pennsylvania 19422	DMS 1100 DMS/90 (Varian TOTAL)
Synergetics Corporation 1 DeAngelo Drive Bedford, Massachusetts 01730	Data Catalogue
Tandem Computers, Inc. 20605 Valley Green Dr. Cupertino, California 95014	Enscribe
Tymshare, Inc. 20705 Valley Green Dr. Cupertino, California 95014	MAGNUM
University Computing Co. 7200 Stemmons Freeway Dallas, Texas 75247	dbIV UCC TEN
Varian Data Machines Sperry UNIVAC 2722 Michelson Dr. P.O. Box C-19504 Irvine, California 92713	Varian TOTAL

GLOSSARY

access—the retrieval, insertion, modification, and/or deletion of data in a storage structure.

access method—any algorithm (for example, randomization or inversion) used with respect to a given storage structure to retrieve records or to place them into storage.

after-image—data logged in a journal subsequent to the application of a change.

alias—the name given to an area, set type, or record type in a subschema, by which it is subsequently known to the subschema and user program (CODASYL).

alternate key—a key field that is not the primary key of a file; keys in indexed-random structures are sometimes designated "alternate."

area—a named collection of records, usually corresponding to a file (CODASYL).

associative memory—computer memory wherein access is effected by data content rather than by location. In an associative memory, an operation is performed simultaneously on all items satisfying a given criteria.

attributes—data items that describe an entity; in the relational model, the values for a given data item type in a relation.

Bachman diagram—graphic notation for network data structures (developed by Charles Bachman).

back-end DBMS—the support of all or most DBMS functions by a dedicated processor, typically a mini-computer, which is interconnected with a mainframe system. All requests for data base access by user programs are passed to the back-end DBMS for servicing.

back-out—see *roll-back.*

before-image—data logged in a journal prior to the application of a change.

binding—the tying together (fixing) of specific data types required by an application program with data as it physically resides in the data base.

bit array—a set implementation technique whereby each record in a data base or file is represented by a single bit, which may be on or off to signify membership or non-membership, respectively.

block—a physical grouping of records in some storage structures; usually the primary unit of transfer between the storage device and main memory.

Boolean array—see *bit array.*

CALC—randomized access to records (CODASYL).

candidate key—one or more data item types in a relation such that the values of the items uniquely identify tuples in the relation (relational model).

cardinality—the number of tuples in a relation (relation model).

centralization—an orientation of data usage and control in a given data processing environment, wherein systems are directed toward central management rather than individual user groups. An MIS is heavily centralized; data base structures and systems can also be centralized. Also, centralization refers to the sharing of a central computer resource in order to minimize costs.

chain—a linked list in which the last record contains a pointer to the first record in the list.

checkpoint—a logging of the entire machine state at a given point in time so that recovery is possible from that point.

CODASYL—Conference on Data Systems Languages; an organization composed of representatives from computer manufacturers and various users, which has as its goal the creation of specifications for standardizing data management languages.

component—a data item in a given tuple (relational model).

compression—the shortening of data for storage (for example, by eliminating repeating characters).

concatenation—the aggregation of separately stored data entities into a physically contiguous area of memory.

concurrent access—access to a data base by two or more application programs (run-units) being executed simultaneously in a machine. The prevention of harmful interactions between the run-units is a major concern of DBCS.

content-addressable store—a storage device supporting access to data on the basis of data value rather than strictly by location.

control system—see *data base control system.*

coordinate file—in a DMS, a related file (usually indexed-sequential) to which access may be effected automatically during the pass of a master file.

corporate data base—a data base characterized by a high degree of integration in data structuring and a high degree of centralization in usage and administration.

currency—data base position. Currency indicators are maintained by a DBCS, using data base keys (CODASYL).

cycle (cyclic structure)—a data structure resulting from the definition of a series of set types such that the owner record type of every set type is a member of the previous set type (CODASYL).

data administrator—see *data base administrator* (CODASYL).

data aggregate—a named collection of data items within a record; for example, a repeating group (CODASYL).

data base—a collection of interrelated, largely unique data items or records, in one or more computer files, which may be processed by multiple application programs. A data base is created and maintained by a DBMS. In CODASYL, a data base is those data under the control of one schema.

data base administrator—a person or team assigned to coordinate and direct DBMS-related activity in the organization, from physical support of data bases on the one hand to the coordination and analysis of information requirements on the others.

data base control system (DBCS)—that portion of the DBMS which actively supports user access to data base files (CODASYL).

data base description—also *data base definition;* see *schema.*

data base dump—a copy on tape of all or a portion of the contents of a data base at a given point in time. A data base dump is a primary means of backup.

data base key—a unique identifier for a record occurrence, corresponding to a storage location (CODASYL).

data base machine—a processor responsible for all or most DBMS functions, which are implemented within the hardware rather than by software.

data base management system—see DBMS.

data base procedure—special computation required for a specific data base; for example, for checking privacy keys (CODASYL).

data description language (DDL)—the symbolic entries used to define a data base under a given DBMS; the DDL delineates a data structure.

data dictionary—a software facility that maintains data on the informational content of a data base and often provides utility services, such as record description, to the user. A data dictionary capability is sometimes integrated within the DBMS; it is especially useful for the control and development of an operational data base environment.

data dictionary system—a program or group of programs for implementing a computerized data dictionary.

data directory—a term sometimes used to refer to that part of the data dictionary (if any) used directly by the DBMS.

data element—a conceptual unit or item of data, stored as a field within a record.

data independence—a characteristic of data base systems arising from the segregation of data structure definition (that is, the DDL) from data access (that is, the DML).

data item—a named data element (CODASYL).

data management system—see DMS.

data manipulation language (DML)—the set of instructions supported by the DBMS for access to the data base.

data model—a conceptual representation of data, how they are used, and how they are interrelated. A data model is converted into a data structure using a DDL. In the relational model, a data model is the set of all relations—that is, of all data stored in the data base.

data redundancy—a characteristic of traditional master file systems, in which duplicate data are often carried by two or more files.

data structure—the implementation of a data model for purposes of computer storage; the data structure is created using the DDL of a DBMS.

data sublanguage—a language for interrogating and updating a relational data base; it usually lacks computational capability (relational model).

data submodel—those relations available to a given user (relational model).

data usage matrix—see *frequency matrix.*

DBA—see *data base administrator.*

DBCS—see *data base control system.*

DBD—*data base description* or *data base definition;* see *schema.*

DB/DC—data base and data communications, often with the implication of integrated support.

DBMS—a computerized system consisting of numerous components, which have as their collective purposes the implementation, management, and protection of large-scale data bases.

DDL—see *data description language.*

deadlock—a situation that occurs in concurrent access environments, in which two or more run-units each have records "locked" that are needed by the other(s). Since no run-unit controls all the records it needs, none can proceed. In general, deadlock can occur for virtually any resources in a shared environment.

decentralization—systems oriented toward (and largely controlled by) actual user groups; with respect to hardware systems, distributed processing represents decentralized usage.

degree—the number of data items in a tuple (relational model).

descriptor—a term often used in inverted DBMS to denote an inverted field.

determinant—an attribute or set of attributes on which the values of one or more other attributes depend (relational model).

device independence—support for hardware devices apart from application programs (for instance, within the DBMS). In data base systems, device independence implies that the data base can be moved between storage devices without impact on application systems.

device media control language (DMCL)—the symbolic entries used to map a data structure onto physical devices. The DMCL may also control buffering, paging, overflow, and so forth (CODASYL).

direct access method—an access method wherein record keys correspond one-to-one to physical locations in storage. The location of a given record may be uniquely derived from its key.

distributed data base—a data base organization wherein usage is largely decentralized and portions of the overall data base are supported at individual user locations, presumably by intercommunicating (distributed) processors.

distributed processing—a hardware configuration in which a large centralized computer is augmented or replaced by two or more smaller machines, presumably intercommunicating and typically located near actual data usage.

DMCL—see *device media control language.*

DML—see *data manipulation language.*

DMS—a system designed as a facility for the reporting of data from a master file in multiple sequences, usually in a single pass. A DMS exhibits some, but not all, of the features of a DBMS and is, by comparison, more highly oriented toward retrieval and reporting capabilities. Certain varieties of inverted systems are also classified as DMS.

domain—the set of all possible values for a data item type from which attributes are chosen (relational model).

dump-restore—roll-forward of a data base dump.

empty set—a set that has an owner occurrence but no member occurrences (CODASYL).

encoding—the scrambling of data for storage.

encryptation—see *encoding.*

end user—a person in an organization who uses data in meeting organizational responsibilities. An end user is typically without data processing skills.

end user facility—a system that facilitates use of computerized systems, such as a DBMS. A query language is an end user facility.

entity—something within an organization or its environment that is relatively stable and about which information can be collected (for example, employees, customers, or orders).

entity class—a grouping of all like entities (for example, employees as personnel).

entry—see *record;* also used to refer to a DDL statement.

entry point—any record or segment available to the first access of the data base.

entry point access method—an access method for entry point records.

extended monitored mode—a means of keeping more than one record in a monitored mode (CODASYL).

field—a data element as defined in a given record.

file—that physical portion of the data base managed as a single entity by the operating system of the computer.

flat file—a single-level record array with only one record type; a relation in normal form.

foreign key—in a relation, one or more data item types whose values correspond to those of a candidate key in another relation (relational model).

frequency matrix—a mapping of data elements by usage requirements, often as a means of spotting associations and potential keys; a tool in data base design.

front-end processor—hardware, often in the form of mini-computer, dedicated to the communications function in a large processing environment.

full inversion—a method of inversion in which all record fields are inverted so that the record as such does not necessarily need to be stored.

hashing algorithm—see *randomizing algorithm.*

hierarchical DBMS—a DBMS under which data structuring is characterized by the organization of data into repeating groups under a single root—that is, by a treelike data structure.

hierarchical structure—a data structure in which there may be multiple repeating segments under a given root. A typical COBOL record with one or more OCCURS is hierarchical (see *tree structure*).

host language—a computer language (for example, COBOL) in which the DML for data base access is embedded.

host processor—the processor in which data base application programs are executed.

index—under access by inversion, the separate area of storage containing organized pointers to the original storage area.

indexed access method—a storage structuring of an index whereby key values are paired on a one-to-one basis with record pointers.

indexed-random access method—indexed access in which the order of entries in the index is different from the order (if any) of records in the source area; that is, the index is organized on a key value that is not used to order the source area.

indexed-sequential access method—indexed access in which the order of entries in the index matches the order of records in the source area; that is, both index and source area are sequentially organized on the basis of the same (primary) key.

information storage and retrieval (IS&R)—a traditional type of application (not necessarily computerized) in which access to individual records is characterized by retrieval for information value rather than for production tasks of various types. IS&R applications are often archival in nature, with low update activity relative to retrieval activity. IS&R applications are often associated with DMS, although DBMS are also capable in this area.

integration—the elimination of partially overlapping data management schemes and substitution of a central data structure in their place (for example, the integration of master files into a data base).

integrity—data accuracy and consistency.

intersection data—those data describing the relationship between two data base records.

inversion—an access technique in which data values from individual records are segregated into a separate area of storage, which points back to the original area.

inverted access method—a storage structuring of an index whereby a given key value is associated with a pointer array to all similarly valued records.

inverted DBMS—a DBMS under which storage structuring is characterized by a predominance of data inversion.

inverted structure—a storage structure supporting inversion.

IS&R—see *information storage and retrieval.*

journal—a system file, usually on magnetic tape, wherein an audit trail of changes to the data base is kept, largely for the purpose of recovery.

Journal of Development (JOD)—the official publication for CODASYL proposals of language standardization.

key—any field upon which access to records may be effected without searching records themselves for a match on data value; also, a field used to facilitate the physical access of "related" records or to physically order records in a set. In the relational model, *key* is short for *candidate key.*

linkage path—a series of one or more records or segments with pointers to other records or segments. Any given set of pointers defines a linkage path.

linked list—a set of records in which every record contains a pointer to the next record in the list.

list—a collection of records, often with the same connotations as "set." The term list has fallen into disuse.

list processing—operations on record lists.

locking—a means to prevent harmful interactions between run-units being concurrently executed. Under locking, a record is made unavailable to all run-units except one, which has requested that updates by other run-units be prevented. The record itself is said to be locked.

lock-out—a condition in which run-units are unable to proceed because of deadlock or other circumstances making required resources unavailable.

log tape—see *journal.*

machine independence—the ability of application systems to migrate between hardware lines.

management information system (MIS)—a computer system oriented toward producing decision data, that is, data useful to centralized management for administration, planning, policy formulation, and so forth. An MIS usually implies summarization and interpretation of large amounts of "raw" data. Corporate-style data bases often have potential for MIS.

master file—in the traditional processing environment, that file containing all data required by a given application. A master file is usually not shared between applications.

member—a record type, other than the owner record type, participating in a set type. A set has zero, one, or more occurrences of member record types (CODASYL).

midi-computer—a term sometimes used to describe the top of the line of machines offered by mini-computer manufacturers. Midi-computers increasingly support data base applications.

mini-DBMS—a DBMS implemented on a small to medium-size hardware configuration, typically one offered by a mini-computer manufacturer rather than a mainframe manufacturer.

MIS—see *management information system.*

monitored mode—a method of handling concurrent access; in monitored mode, the current record of a run-unit is kept under surveillance by the DBCS. If another run-unit updates the record, the first run-unit is notified when it attempts an update (CODASYL).

multiple-level record array—a record array in which each contained record can be followed by its own record array (for example, a COBOL record description with multiple levels of OCCURS).

multi-processing—support for application systems by two or more processors;

the processors themselves are treated as resources for improving overall throughput.

multi-programming—support by an operating system for two or more programs to occupy main memory at the same time and to share the resources of a single processor.

multitask system—a system able to support multiple tasks at once, largely by overlapping I-O. (The term is often used to describe the data communications environment of a data base system.)

multi-thread—code in a program so designed as to be available for servicing multiple tasks at once, in particular by overlapping I-O. Multi-thread code must be re-entrant.

navigational access—a characteristic of networklike data bases and physically linked DBMS in particular, in which the programmer must choose between alternative linkage paths provided within the (network) data structure.

network DBMS—a DBMS under which data structuring is characterized by the membership of records in sets, as either owners or members.

network (processing)—a system of intercommunicating processors through which "distributed" processing is supported; also, a configuration of distributed processing in which every processor communicates directly with all other processors.

network (structure)—a data structure characterized by the membership of records in sets, as owners and members (CODASYL).

normalization—a process of altering the format of relations in order to improve their performance in user operations, especially updating. A flat file is in "normal" form; the third normal form is deemed best for relational operations (relational model).

owner—the record type declared to own a set type; every set has one and only one owner record (CODASYL).

page—a physical division of data in the data base; often the actual unit transferred to and from storage.

partial inversion—a method of inversion in which a subset of record fields is inverted; the record is normally stored in its entirety.

physical pointer—an address of an area in storage, either absolute or relative.

physically linked DBMS—a DBMS under which storage structuring is characterized by a predominance of physical pointers for establishing relationships between data.

physically serial access method—an access method wherein records exist or are accessed one after the other without reference to keys.

pointer—a link to a data area in storage, by a physical or symbolic pointer.

pointer array—a collection of addresses that point to all members of a set or group of records.

portability—support for a language on more than one hardware line. Portability yields machine independence.

position—the current record within the navigational access of a data base.

pre-compiler—a program that interrogates an application program and replaces DML statements with CALLs to DBMS routines.

primary key—a key field, usually unique, used to physically order records in some file organizations (for example, ISAM) or to provide primary access in randomized storage structures; in the relational model, one candidate key in a relation.

privacy key—a password (or other appropriate data) given by a run-unit to be applied to a privacy lock (CODASYL).

privacy lock—a value or a procedure which, as specified in the DDL, is used to check user passwords for specified operations (CODASYL).

program—a set or group of computer instructions.

quality assurance—see *quality auditing.*

quality auditing—any technique used in the administration of a data base to check the continuing integrity of contained data.

query language—a high-level user-oriented language, often interactive, that supports data base access without a host language.

randomized access—an access method whereby potential record keys correspond on a many-to-one basis to available physical locations in storage. A mapping function (randomizing algorithm) determines the actual location for any given record.

randomizing algorithm—a transformation or mapping function used in the randomized access method.

realm—a named logical subdivision of a data base as specified in subschema. A realm corresponds to an area (CODASYL).

record—a group of data items and data aggregates stored as a named collection in a data base (CODASYL). A record is called a segment or an entry in some DBMS.

record array—a table in which records of a set are physically juxtaposed.

record type—the definition or description of a record within a DDL. A data structure is composed of various record types; in an actual data base, many records of a given type are stored.

recovery—any procedure, invoked in an operational data base system, whose purpose is the correction of the detrimental effects of a machine or software failure or of a processing impasse (for example, deadlock). Roll-forward and back-out are types of recovery.

recursive structure—a data structure characterized by the relating of records of the same type, typically in the sense of components (substructure) and where-used (superstructure); often used in bill-of-materials applications.

re-entrancy—a characteristic of code wherein the state of the process is kept external to the process itself so that execution may be interrupted at any point in order to service another task. Multi-thread code must be re-entrant.

relation—the set of all tuples of a given type (relational model).

relational DBMS—a DBMS supporting a relational view of data—that is, flat files and data sublanguages.

relational model—a theoretical approach to data management based on tables and their manipulation; proposed by E. F. Codd and others.

relational operator—a named operation (for example, JOIN) on one or more tables (relations) in the relational model.

remote computing—the purchase of processing time on a system supported by an independent time-sharing company.

reorganization—an operation required periodically for data bases, the purpose of which is to reinitiate storage structures after updating has filled existing space, distorted physical locations, distended chains, and so forth. In reorganization, data are typically unloaded and then reloaded after space has been reallocated.

report writer—a facility oriented toward the batch generation of reports.

restart—reinitiation of run-units, often from a prior checkpoint, after a software or machine failure.

retrieval—access to data in a storage structure without update.

ring—see *chain.*

roll-back—the application of before-images from a journal to a data base in order to reverse the changes effected by one or more run-units.

roll-forward—the application of after-images from a journal to a data base in order to bring a copy of the data base up to date.

root—in a hierarchical data structure, the record or segment to which all other records or segments are subordinate (the top of a tree).

run-unit—an execution of one or more programs. A run-unit is typically under the control of a DBMS or other control system and may be batch or a task in an on-line environment.

schema—the DDL for a given data base definition (CODASYL).

search field—any field known to the DBMS so that conditional access based on data value can be effected.

search key—a field known to the DBMS through which access to records may be effected without searching record content (for example, via an index); also, the data value supplied for a search field.

secondary indexing—see *indexed-random access method.*

secondary key—see *alternate key.*

segment—see *record.*

segmentation—the division of data into relatively small groups or collections of fields that exhibit a correspondence in meaning and/or usage. Segmentation is an important feature of physical space management and data access in many DBMS.

selective roll-back—the roll-back of those changes made by a particular run-unit.

sequential access—physically serial access performed on records ordered by key value; any access to records ordered by key value.

set—a collection of records in a data base, with one occurrence of an owner record type and zero, one, or more occurrences of member record types. A set of records bears a conceptual relationship, sometimes with a commonly valued data item (CODASYL).

set type—the definition of a set in the DDL.

single-level record array—a record array, normally consisting of records in the same format, containing no internal record arrays; a flat file (see *multiple-level record array*).

single-thread—code that must service a task to completion before servicing other tasks (see *multi-thread*).

singular set—a set whose owner is specified to be the system so that only one set occurrence is possible (CODASYL).

star—a hierarchical configuration of distributed processors.

storage structure—the configuration of data as they reside in computer storage, including the physical means for access. A data structure is supported by one or more storage structures.

subschema—a control device, specified by using an independent language, that defines a view of the data base appropriate to a given user program (CODASYL).

symbolic pointer—a data value, segregated from a record or segment, by which access to the record or segment may be effected.

synonym record—a record whose randomized key value points to a storage location already occupied by a previously randomized record.

teleprocessing monitor—a software facility, often interfaced with DBMS, that provides support for multiple on-line users via terminals in a highly transaction-oriented environment.

tree structure—a data structure in which each record type is related to exactly one record type above it, except for one "root" record type, for which no higher record types exist. At each lower level in the tree there may be zero, one, or more record types related to a record type at the next higher level.

tree traversal access—navigational access in a hierarchical data structure.

tuple—an ordered group of several data items, corresponding to a simple record (relational model).

unbundling—the separation of pricing by hardware manufacturers for machines and software.

VIA—storage of records of a given type in such a way as to optimize access through a given set type; for example, storage "near" an owner (CODASYL).

SELECTED READINGS

General Reference

Berg, John L., ed. *Data Base Directions: The Next Steps.* NBS Special Publication #451. Washington, D.C.: National Bureau of Standards, 1976.

Cohen, Leo J. *Data Base Management Systems: A Critical and Comparative Analysis.* Wellesley, Mass.: Q.E.D. Information Sciences, 1975.

Date, Chris J. *An Introduction to Database Systems.* Reading, Mass.: Addison-Wesley, 1975.

Fong, Elizabeth, Joseph Collica, and Beatrice Marron. *Six Data Base Management Systems: Feature Analysis and User Experiences.* NBS Technical Note #887. Washington, D.C.: National Bureau of Standards, 1975.

House, William C., ed. *Data Base Management.* New York: Petrocelli Books, 1974.

Jardine, Donald E., ed. *Data Base Management Systems.* New York: American Elsevier Publishing Co., 1974.

Katzan, Harry. *Computer Data Management and Data Base Technology.* New York: Van Nostrand Reinhold Company, 1975.

Martin, James. *Computer Data-Base Organization.* Englewood Cliffs, N.J.: Prentice-Hall, 1975.

———. *Principles of Data-Base Management.* Englewood Cliffs, N.J.: Prentice-Hall, 1976.

Palmer, Ian R. *Data Base Systems: A Practical Reference.* Wellesley, Mass.: Q.E.D. Information Sciences, 1975.

Ross, Ronald G. *An Assessment of Current Data Base Trends.* Wellesley, Mass.: Q.E.D. Information Sciences, 1977.

Sundgren, Bo. *Theory of Data Base.* New York: Petrocelli/Charter, 1975.

The Nature of Computerized Data Base Systems

Bachman, Charles W. "The Programmer as a Navigator." *Communications of the ACM,* November 1973, pp. 653–658.

"The Cautious Path to a Data Base." *EDP Analyzer,* edited by Richard G. Canning, June 1973.

Cohen, Leo J. "Four Data Management Packages: Some Qualitative Issues." *Proceedings of the 38th GUIDE International Conference,* May 1974, pp. 420–427.

———. "The Performance Management Problem for Data Base." *Proceeding of the 40th GUIDE International Conference,* May 1975, pp. 751–762.

"The Current Status of Data Management." *EDP Analyzer,* edited by Richard G. Canning, February 1974.

Curtice, Robert M. *Access Mechanisms and Data Structure Support in Data Base Management Systems.* Wellesley, Mass.: Q.E.D. Information Sciences, 1975.

———. "Data Independence in Data Base Systems." *Datamation,* April 1975, pp. 65–71.

———. "Integrity in Data Base Systems." *Datamation,* May 1977, pp. 64–68.

Michaels, Ann S., Benjamin Mittman, and C. Robert Carlson. "A Comparison of the Relational and CODASYL Approaches to Data-Base Management." *Computing Surveys,* March 1976, pp. 126–151.

Nolan, Richard L. "Computer Data Bases: The Future Is Now." *Harvard Business Review, September–October 1973, pp. 98–114.*

"Problem Areas in Data Management." *EDP Analyzer,* edited by Richard G. Canning, March 1974.

Selection and Acquisition of Data Base Management Systems: A Report of the CODASYL Systems Committee. New York: Association for Computing Machinery, March 1976.

Tsichritzis, D. C., and F. H. Lochovsky. "Hierarchical Data-Base Management: A Survey." *Computing Surveys,* March 1976, pp. 105–123.

Administration of Data Base Systems

"The Data Base Administrator: Parts I & II." *EDP In-Depth Reports,* edited by Richard J. Clark, August and September 1974.

"The Data Base Administrator." Report of the Data Base Administration Project, GUIDE International Corp., November 1972.

"The Data Dictionary/Directory Function." *EDP Analyzer,* edited by Richard G. Canning, November 1974.

Jones, Paul E. *Data Base Design Methodology.* Wellesley, Mass.: Q.E.D. Information Sciences, 1976.

Lefkovits, Henry C. *Data Dictionary Systems.* Wellesley, Mass.: Q.E.D. Information Sciences, 1976.

Lyon, John K. *The Database Administrator.* New York: John Wiley & Sons, 1976.

———. *An Introduction to Data Base Design.* New York: John Wiley & Sons, 1974.

"Recovery in Data Base Systems." *EDP Analyzer,* edited by Richard G. Canning, November 1976.

Ross, Ronald G. "Data Base Management Systems: An Overview of Data Base Technology." *Government Data Systems,* December 1975/January 1976, pp. 22–27.

Yasaki, Edward K. "The Many Faces of the DBA." *Datamation,* May 1977, pp. 75–79.

CODASYL Systems

Bachman, Charles W. "The Evolution of Storage Structures." *Communications of the ACM,* July 1972, pp. 628–634.

———. "Implementation Techniques for Data Structure Sets." *Data Base Management Systems,* edited by Donald A. Jardine. New York: American Elsevier Publishing Co., 1974.

Blasius, Richard E. "Countering CODASYL Critics." *Datamation,* June 1975, pp. 169–170.

CODASYL COBOL, Journal of Development, 1976. Canadian Government Specifications Board, 1976.

CODASYL Data Base Task Group October 1969 Report. New York: Association for Computing Machinery, 1969.

CODASYL Data Base Task Group April 1971 Report. New York: Association for Computing Machinery, 1971.

CODASYL Data Description Language, Journal of Development, June 1973. NBS Hand book #113. Washington, D.C.: National Bureau of Standards, 1974.

Taylor, Robert W., and Randall L. Frank. "CODASYL Data-Base Management Systems." *Computing Surveys,* March 1976, pp. 67–103.

Triance, John M. "COBOL Is Too Big." *Datamation,* July 1976, pp. 156–160.

"What's Happening with CODASYL-Type DBMS?" *EDP Analyzer,* edited by Richard G. Canning, October 1974.

Relational Systems

Chamberlin, Donald D. "Relational Data-Base Management Systems." *Computing Surveys,* March 1976, pp. 43–66.

Codd, E. F. "A Relational Model of Data for Large Shared Data Banks." *Communications of the ACM,* June 1970, pp. 377–387.

Date, Chris J. "Relational Data Base Concepts." *Datamation,* April 1976, pp. 50–53.

Renaud, Dominique. "ADABAS and the Relational Model." *Communications of the Third International ADABAS Users Conference,* July 1976.

Mini-Computers and DBMS

Boylan, David T. "DBMS for Minis." *Computer Decisions,* January 1976, pp. 66–69.

Burnett, Gerald J., and Richard L. Nolan. "At Last, Major Roles for Minicomputers." *Harvard Business Review,* May–June 1975, pp. 148–156.

Floam, Gary. "Putting a Data Base on a Mini." *Datamation,* June 1976, pp. 97–98.

"Hewlett-Packard Takes On the Computer Giants." *Business Week,* June 7, 1976, pp. 91–92.

Marienthal, Louis B. "Small Computers for Small Businesses." *Datamation,* June 1975, pp. 62–78.

"Minicomputers Challenge the Big Machines." *Business Week,* April 26, 1976, pp. 58–63.

Theis, Douglas J. "The Midicomputer." *Datamation,* February 1977, pp. 73–82.

Yasaki, Edward K. "The Mini: A Growing Alternative." *Datamation,* May 1976, pp. 139–142.

Distributed Systems

Champine, G. A. "Six Approaches to Distributed Data Bases." *Datamation,* May 1977, pp. 69–72.

"Distributed Systems and the End User." *EDP Analyzer,* edited by Richard G. Canning, October 1976.

Hunter, John J. "Distributing a Database." *Computer Decisions,* June 1976, pp. 36–40.

"Network Structures for Distributed Systems." *EDP Analyzer,* edited by Richard G. Canning, July 1976.

Patrick, Robert L. "Decentralizing Hardware and Dispersing Responsibility." *Datamation,* May 1976, pp. 79–84.

Russell, Richard M. "Approaches to Network Design." *Computer Decisions,* June 1976, pp. 20–22.

"What Is Network Architecture?" *Computer Decisions,* June 1976, pp. 24–33.

Data Base Systems: Past, Present, and Future

Bachman, Charles W. "A General Purpose Programming System for Random Access Memories." *Proceedings of the Fall Joint Computer Conference,* 1964.

Curtice, Robert M. "The Outlook for Data Base Management." *Datamation,* April 1976, pp. 46–49.

"The Debate on Data Base Management." *EDP Analyzer,* edited by Richard G. Canning, March 1972.

Fry, James P., and Edgar H. Sibley. "Evolution of Data-Base Management Systems." *Computing Surveys,* March 1976, pp. 7–42.

Pullen, Edward W., and Robert G. Simko. "Our Changing Industry." *Datamation,* January 1977, pp. 49–55.

Withington, Frederick G. "Beyond 1984: A Technology Forecast." *Datamation,* January 1975, pp. 54–73.

INDEX